MY SCOTLAND, OUR BRITAIN

A Future Worth Sharing

GORDON BROWN

**SIMON &
SCHUSTER**

London · New York · Sydney · Toronto · New Delhi

A CBS COMPANY

First published in Great Britain by Simon & Schuster UK Ltd, 2014
This paperback edition published in Great Britain by Simon & Schuster UK Ltd, 2015
A CBS COMPANY

1 3 5 7 9 10 8 6 4 2

Simon & Schuster UK Ltd
1st Floor
222 Gray's Inn Road
London WC1X 8HB

www.simonandschuster.co.uk

Simon & Schuster Australia,
Sydney

Simon & Schuster India,
New Delhi

A CIP catalogue record for this book is available from the British Library

Paperback ISBN: 978-1-4711-3750-1
eBook ISBN: 978-1-4711-3751-8

Typeset in the UK by Hewer Text UK Ltd, Edinburgh
Printed in the UK by CPI Group UK Ltd, Croydon CR0 4YY

To John and Fraser and in memory of Jennifer

Gordon Brown served as Prime Minister and leader of the Labour Party from 2007 to 2010, Member of Parliament for Kirkcaldy and Cowdenbeath from 1983 to 2015 and as Chancellor of the Exchequer from 1997 to 2010, making him the longest-serving Chancellor in modern history. Brown's time as Chancellor began with the granting of independence to the Bank of England and was marked by sustained investment in health and education, the reduction of poverty and increasing overseas aid. As Prime Minister, Brown's tenure coincided with the global financial crisis, and he was one of the first to initiate calls for coordinated global action and chaired the London Summit of 2009. Since 2012, he has been the United Nations Special Envoy for Global Education. Brown has a First Class Honours degree and a Doctorate in History from the University of Edinburgh and spent his early career working as a lecturer. He is married to Sarah Brown, Chair of the Global Business Coalition for Education, and they live in Fife and London with their two sons, John and Fraser. Brown is the author of several books and the founder, with his wife, of Theirworld, a charity to which the profits of this book will be donated.

CONTENTS

Our Scotland

GORDON BROWN'S SPEECH TO THE
MARYHILL COMMUNITY CENTRAL HALL

Glasgow, 17 September 2014

At last, the world is hearing the voices of the real people of Scotland.

The silent majority will be silent no more. And our patriotic vision, proud of our Scottish identity, proud of our distinctive Scottish institutions, proud of the Scottish Parliament that we, not the nationalist party, created.

And proud that, with the powers of that parliament, we can guarantee that the National Health Service will be in public hands, universal, free at the point of need as long and as ever as the people of Scotland want it.

And proud, also, that we are increasing the powers of that parliament – faster, safer, better, friendlier change than ever the nationalists could propose. And proud, too, that we cooperate and share; indeed we Scots led the way in cooperating and sharing across the United Kingdom – common defence, common currency, common and shared rights from the UK pension to the UK minimum wage, from each according to his ability to contribute, to each according to his needs, and that is the best principle that can govern the life of our country today.

And our patriotic vision is up against a nationalist vision that has only one aim in mind: to break every single constitutional and political link with our friends and neighbours in the United Kingdom, and we will not have this.

The vote tomorrow is not about whether Scotland is a nation; we are, yesterday, today and tomorrow. It's not about whether there is a Scottish Parliament; we have it, after a referendum ten years ago. It's not about whether there are increased powers; we are all agreed to increase the powers.

The vote tomorrow is whether you want to break and sever every link, and I say let's keep our UK pension, let's keep our UK pound, let's keep our UK passport, let's keep our UK welfare state.

And let us tell the undecided, the waverers, those not sure how to vote, let us tell them what we have achieved together.

We fought two world wars together. And there is not a cemetery in Europe that does not have Scots, English, Welsh and Irish lying side by side. And when young men were injured in these wars, they didn't look to each other and ask whether you were Scots or English, they came to each other's aid because we were part of a common cause.

And we not only won these wars together, we built the peace together, we built the health service together, we built the welfare state together, we will build the future together.

And what we have built together by sacrificing and sharing, let no narrow nationalism split asunder ever.

And let us tell also those people who have been told unfairly by the nationalists that, if you vote No, you're a less than patriotic Scot. Tell them this is our Scotland. Tell them that Scotland does not belong to the SNP. Scotland does not belong to the Yes campaign.

Scotland does not belong to any politician – Mr Salmond, Mr Swinney, me or any other politician – Scotland belongs to all of us.

And let us tell the nationalists this is not their flag, their country, their culture, their streets. This is everyone's flag, everyone's country, everyone's culture and everyone's streets.

And let us tell the people of Scotland that we who vote No love Scotland and love our country. The Scotland of the Enlightenment and the Scottish inventors. The Scotland that was the author of the right to work, here in Glasgow, and the right to free healthcare. The Scotland that helped build the economic laws of this country, the welfare state of this country and contributed to the development of international aid.

And do you know, all these achievements and all the more achievements I could mention, these happened not outside the Union, but inside the Union. They happen not in spite of the Union, but because of the Union.

And none of us is any less a Scot as a result of it.

And let us tell those people who have still got doubts and are wavering, people who were thinking of voting Yes yesterday but could be persuaded today. Let us tell them about the real risks.

This is not the fear of the unknown; this is now the risks of the known. An economic minefield where problems could implode at any time. An economic trapdoor down which we go, from which we might never escape.

Real risk one: the uncertainty about the currency, unaddressed by the SNP. Real risk two: the default from debt that they threaten, unaddressed by the SNP. Real risk three: having to build £30 billion of reserves at the cost of the NHS and the welfare state, unaddressed by the SNP. Real risk four: prices rising in the shops, unaddressed by the SNP. Real risk five: interest rates and mortgage rates going up, unaddressed by the SNP. Real risk six: a million jobs dependent on our trade and our membership of the UK – shipbuilding, finance – all the problems unaddressed by the SNP. And real risk seven: a massive financial hole that cannot be made up – even a fraction of it – by oil revenues. A massive financial hole that means the risk to the National Health Service does not come from us – it comes from the policies of the Scottish National Party.

But let us tell people, who are aware now of the risk but think Scotland would be somehow more progressive under the nationalists. Let us tell them of our vision of the future of Scotland, not the Scotland of insults and abuse and threats and recriminations.

The Scotland of Adam Smith and John Smith, the Scotland of civility and compassion, the Scotland of comradeship and community is bigger and better than what we have seen.

Tell them, the people, of our vision of the future of Scotland. Yes, a strong Scottish Parliament for fairness, battling for equality across the United Kingdom, but our vision is bigger than that. At every point, in every place, at every time – particularly through our membership of the United Kingdom – to fight for what is our instinct, what is our dream, what is our demand: a world not of a separate state but a world of social justice that people can believe in.

And do you know what sort of message would we in Scotland send out to the rest of the world, we the people who found a way of cooperation across borders, we who pioneered a partnership between nations, we who have stood as a beacon for solidarity and sharing: what kind of message does Scotland send to the world if tomorrow we said we're going to give up on sharing, we're going to smash our partnership, we're going to abandon cooperation and conflict and we're going to throw the idea of solidarity into the dust? This is not the Scotland I know and recognise, and we must make sure it is not the Scotland we become.

Now, tomorrow the vote I will cast is not for me. It is for my children. It is for all of Scotland's children. It is for our children's future. And you know, when the SNP says 'now is the time' and 'now is the moment', and yet the decision is irreversible? Are they not forgetting one thing? That this is not a decision just for this time – this is a decision for all time. This is a decision that cannot be reversed or undone. This is a decision from which there is no going back. This is a decision when, once it's done, it's done. And so I say I have to vote and take account of the needs of my children and future generations and the future of our country in centuries to come.

And if you have any doubts about unanswered questions, if you have any doubts that have been unrecognised by the SNP, if you still have problems with what they're saying, then if you're thinking of the future of Scotland and if you don't know, the answer has to be No.

And if you're like me, and a million more people who are convinced that the case for cooperation is greater than any case put for separation, then I say to you: hold your heads high. Show dignity and pride. Be confident. Let us have confidence that our values are indeed the values of the majority of the people of Scotland. That our principles of sharing and cooperation are far better and mean more to them than separation and splitting apart. Have confidence that people know that our Scottish Parliament and its new powers give people the powers they need and meet the aspirations of the Scottish people. Have confidence, stand up and be counted tomorrow.

Have confidence, have confidence tomorrow and have confidence enough to say with all our friends: we've had no answers. They do not know what they are doing. They are leading us into a trap. Have confidence, and say to our friends: for reasons of solidarity, sharing, justice, pride in Scotland, the only answer for Scotland's sake and for Scotland's future is vote *No*.

FOREWORD

Christmas Eve 2013. After an evening wrapping presents for my children, seven and ten years old, and finally depositing them under the Christmas tree, I was sitting staring out across the rough, grey waters of the River Forth and contemplating how to complete a chapter for a new book about how the world might shape up in the year 2025.

I was speculating about the prospects of the generation I call 'globalisation's children': young people brought up in a world in which Asia is now challenging America, where the global middle class – one billion in 1990 – is quadrupling in size, where the abolition of poverty is no longer an 'impossible dream', but where dislocation and disruption are making people everywhere feel vulnerable and insecure.

What interests – and worries – me is the growing gap between the limitless opportunities that young people are crying out for – African and Asian girls desperate for the chance of education, unemployed youth in the Middle East and throughout the world demanding jobs and a better quality of life – and, despite the opening up of the global economy, the limited opportunities actually open to them. I had just visited China and Africa and was about to travel again to Pakistan and then Nigeria as part of the campaign my wife Sarah and I started to secure the right to educational opportunity for every child.

But after spending a few days at home in Fife I had time to reflect and began to ask what kind of opportunities beckoned for *my* children as they grew up in our own country.

My boys had started to be aware that Scotland might leave Britain as a result of a referendum. Only one or two questions so far and the parcels under the Christmas tree were, unsurprisingly, still more of a discussion point for them.

But, as my thoughts turned to events in Scotland, I kept asking myself the same question. What *were* the prospects for my children – and millions of children in Scotland and Britain – in 2025 and the years beyond? If we went for independence we were making an irreversible decision that, for good or ill, my children and their children would have to live with all their lives and, as I thought more about their futures, I sensed that in the referendum debate we were actually being asked the wrong questions.

The rapid advance of new technology – in genetics, IT, biotech and even artificial intelligence – the opening up of trade, the global spread of communications and the increased understanding of the power of education to change and improve lives gives us an unprecedented opportunity. Advances in both what we know and what we can teach mean we have never been better placed to build stronger and fairer societies in this ever more interdependent world.

And while I know that the big driver of that interdependence – globalisation – can make it feel like we are being buffeted by forces we cannot control, it is my belief that there is no country better placed to take advantage of it than Scotland.

History shows that Scots are pioneers. From the steam engine to the television, Scots have been responsible for so many of the technological advances that have shaped the modern industrial economy.

Scots have been pathbreakers for medical breakthroughs that

have saved millions of lives, explorers of places no one had ever thought existed, traders adventuring to the ends of the earth, missionaries braving some of the most dangerous outposts in the world and with the English, Welsh and Irish, creators of the first industrial revolution and the largest empire built by mankind.

In these great enterprises the people of our small country – less than 0.1 per cent of the world's seven billion population – have had an enormous global influence on the world's imagination and development, far beyond our numbers, making Scotland a vanguard nation.

Today there is a new challenge that our history makes us uniquely placed to meet and master: capitalising on the opening up of travel and communications and the global flows of people, ideas and goods. I see Scotland uniquely placed to embrace the immense possibilities offered by globalisation and to champion new ways of mastering it while retaining pride in our distinctive identity as Scots.

That is where I think Scotland's national destiny lies, in leading the world in coming to terms with the idea that interdependence doesn't need to mean a smothering of national pride. In fact I think interdependence can mean something greater, giving those countries with a contribution to make an even larger canvas on which to paint their ideas for the future and a patriotic satisfaction in doing so. And so it is part of my argument in this book that not only do advocates of independence supply the wrong answer, they are actually starting by asking the wrong question.

Because the question cannot be whether we can rise up and 'be the nation again'. There is no 'again' about it: Scotland is one of the oldest-established nations in the world. We are a proud nation and always have been.

Likewise the question cannot be whether we can have our own national institutions and the freedom to run them. From our churches, to our system of justice, right through to our schools, colleges and universities, our hospitals and social-work services, we already have our own distinctive Scottish national institutions which we run without outside interference.

When it comes to the 'levers of power', most of them are already in our hands. We are about to implement what is, in effect, a new power-sharing agreement between Scotland and the UK. And it has now become clear that one power that the nationalists have always demanded – full control over the economy – is now one the Scottish government says it doesn't want, preferring a British currency and British control over our interest rates.

So it seems to me that the real question is not whether Scots can be proud patriots and put Scotland first: of course we can, and we do. Nor is it whether Scotland has independent institutions which reflect our unique values and interests: we do, and we always have. Nor is it whether Scotland has powers to do that which we want to do in policy terms: we already have the powers of a parliament, with more on the way. The real question, then, is whether, as we chart a global future for our children, it makes sense to abandon all political connections with our neighbours in the rest of the United Kingdom at a time when cooperation between nations, rather than separation, seems a better way forward.

When we are trying to make globalisation work for us, is it to our advantage to break all constitutional connections with a neighbour that takes 70 per cent of our exports and end the collaboration with the rest of the United Kingdom which finances the vast majority of our scientific and technological research and innovation – the vital pathway to new products, new businesses and future employment here in Scotland? Severing the link with the rest of the UK seems particularly out of sync with Scotland's needs when economies are becoming more integrated, when there is increasing public recognition of nations' interdependence and when a fixation on the power of the state runs counter to the haemorrhaging of state power to citizens' networks and non-governmental institutions.

Captivated by old-fashioned notions of statehood, the clean break that nationalists propose is a nineteenth-century answer to a twenty-first-century problem.

For their argument to be compelling they have to believe that our nationhood is suppressed – when it is not; that we have no independent national institutions – when we do; and that there is no power-sharing worth its name in the UK today – when clearly there is.

If we already have the right to our cultural freedom, have long-established independent national institutions and have a form of power-sharing that already gives us a government in Scotland, whose powers we plan to extend in the next few years, there is in reality but one thing missing: the elimination of all political links with our neighbours, friends and families down south.

And then I started to look at the case we were putting for a No (to leaving the Union) vote. Opponents of independence have two responses that are important: one prosaic, the other somewhat more abstract. But while there is solid evidence behind both, they seem so different from each other that often people cannot see the connection between the two.

Independence is a mistake, some say, because, on the one hand, we will be materially worse off as a result of declining oil revenues, the fiscal deficit, the growing social-security bill and of course the risk to our trade links with England.

Independence is a mistake, some say, because, on the other hand, it runs counter to the increased interdependence of all countries everywhere: it is not just our neighbours but all the family of nations whose actions impact on what happens here at home. In this worldview, the most important thing is for all countries to find new ways of working together rather than splitting apart, and independence runs profoundly against the tide.

In fact the best answer is the one that brings these two arguments together.

We are better off when we make the most of our interdependence.

We are better off when, in recognition of our close connections with each other, we pool and share our resources equitably across the United Kingdom.

And we are better off when we use the strength of our own relationships in the UK to project our collective power on the world stage.

And it is these insights that are at the heart of this book and, indeed, Scotland's story. Because our history tells us that Scots have succeeded in fashioning the future again and again by resisting the temptation to be isolationist or exclusionary.

To take one example, just think of the great Scottish inventors we grew up hearing about at school. We all know how many of the great human breakthroughs in science, medicine, technology and engineering have a Scottish source, but many also had a cross-border component, or achieved their greatest impact thanks to collaboration across the UK.

The steam engine prospered with a partnership between the inventor Watt in Scotland and the developer Boulton in England; Alexander Fleming was a Scot who discovered penicillin in London and only saw it mass produced because of Florey and Chain in Oxford; John Logie Baird developed the TV not from his home in Helensburgh, Scotland, but from Hastings in Sussex, England.

Although born in Scotland, Robert Watson-Watt developed radar in the south-east of England as part of a team working with the RAF; Peter Higgs is an English-born Nobel Prize-winning physicist who trained in Bristol and London before his breakthroughs at Edinburgh University; the inventor of Dolly the Sheep, Ian Wilmut, works at Roslin, near Edinburgh, but was born in Warwickshire and educated in England; and James Black, born in Lanarkshire and brought up in Fife in a house next to where my grandfather was born, had to leave Scotland for his first job in Malaysia and developed his two major scientific inventions, one a cure for ulcers and one for heart disease, working down south.

Scots did not lose out but gained through cooperation and often succeeded not in spite of an English link-up but because of it. Being part of the UK did not diminish these inventors' Scottishness and nobody feels less pride in breakthroughs which happened in Scotland because the people working on them weren't always born here. On the contrary, more often than not the UK provided a platform for us to maximise our impact and to reach out to the world. And it is difficult to sustain the allegation that this wider association destroyed or even diminished our Scottishness, which is clearly as strongly felt as ever. More importantly, cooperation between nations – whether through collaboration in research, the cross-fertilisation of ideas or working together for common purposes – is how the future will be fashioned. This book suggests that sharing and solidarity, built on our interdependence, is a bigger idea than independence.

And there is an even greater achievement that Scotland's partnership with Britain has to its name.

We take it for granted that whether you are Scots, English, Welsh or Northern Irish, you have equal social and economic rights as citizens of the UK: an equal right to a UK-guaranteed pension, an equal right to help when unemployed, an equal right to fully funded healthcare free at the point of need and an equal right to minimum standards of protection at work, including a UK-wide minimum wage, no matter who you are and where you reside.

It seems so natural now, but just stop and think about it. No other multinational association anywhere in the world achieves this – neither the European Union, nor the United States of America, nor any other combination of neighbouring countries comes anywhere near offering the social and economic rights of citizenship that we have created.

For all its limitations and for all we need to do to make it better and fairer, it has been – at least for half a century – one of the best insurance policies in the world.

And my proposed UK constitutional reforms – outlined later in this book – will permanently entrench equality between our nations.

So, if I am being asked if Scotland is a nation, the answer is 'yes'. Scotland already is and will always be a nation.

If I am been asked if Scotland must have its own national institutions, the answer is 'yes'. For centuries of Union, Scotland has preserved its own national institutions.

If I am asked to support political, decision-making power being in the hands of the Scottish people, again: 'yes'. Scotland has its own parliament and government.

If I am being asked to support the constitutional recognition of equality between the nations: again, 'yes'. Ensuring equality between the nations is at the heart of my proposals for the future.

But that is not what this referendum is about. The issue at stake is whether we want to end all constitutional connections with the rest of the UK. My answer? *No*. A strong Scottish Parliament within the United Kingdom can lead the world in facing the new challenges of globalisation.

This book is an explanation of how, as a proud Scot, I have come to this conclusion.

It is a personal account of my Scotland, the nation I was born into, and our Britain, the multinational state we have created together.

I lay bare my family's ancestry over 300 years of the Union and how it shaped my background. I chart what it was like for me growing up in Scotland in the 1950s and 1960s.

I try to explain, through my own upbringing, the influence of religion, education and our unique industrial structure in shaping my identity and our nation's identity. And I then try to set out all the dramatic changes of the past fifty years that make the prospects of my children and this new generation so different from mine.

This is the reason I have entered the debate. Having lost the UK general election in 2010 and having as Labour leader accepted responsibility for our defeat, I never thought it right to return to frontline politics. While I wanted to do my best to help Kirkcaldy and Fife and repay some of the loyalty the people I represent had shown me, I took the view that once you have lost it is time to write yourself out of the script – and let others take centre stage. But as a patriotic Scot I cannot opt out of a debate and decision that affects children whom I love and people whom I respect and represent, all the more so since we are being asked to make an irreversible decision that will have consequences for generations.

This is not a political tract: it is a story of my affection for Scotland. In writing it I have been influenced and assisted by the people I have met and worked with and who have befriended me along the way – my family and in particular my wife Sarah, my brothers John and Andrew, and Fife neighbours and friends whom I have talked to and whose views I respect greatly – Peter and Marilyn Livingstone, Alex Rowley MSP, Jayne Baxter MSP, Lindsay Roy MP, Bill Taylor, Murray Elder, Henry McLeish, and local historians and writers George Proudfoot, John Hunter, Bill Livingston, Bob Eadie, Allan Crow and Chris Sparling, who have taught me a great deal I did not know about Fife.

I have been grateful for conversations with some of our greatest historians, including Tom Devine, Colin Kidd, Ian Levitt, Lindsay Paterson, T. C. Smout, Paul Addison, Linda Colley, David Cannadine, Nick Phillipson, Fonna Forman, Iain McLean and, before he sadly died, my old history tutor John Brown and his wife Geraldine. I have drawn on the work of two great experts on the constitution, Michael Wills and Jim Gallagher. I have benefited from conversations with Carol Craig, Alistair Moffat,

Wilf Stevenson, and my parliamentary colleagues, including friends in, and leaders of, Better Together and the United with Labour campaign. Gregg McClymont MP and Neil Davidson QC have advised on pensions and I have been fortunate in being able to talk directly to acknowledged experts in their own fields – John Curtice, Brian Ashcroft, Craig Calhoun, Peter Jones and David Bell, David Eiser, David Comerford and David Muir, whom I thank for giving their time. I have been fortunate to draw on the expert advice of a former editor of the Scottish *Daily Record*, Bruce Waddell, and I have benefited from conversations with Allan Rennie, now Chief Executive of the Record Group. None of them are to blame for any factual or other mistakes which are my responsibility.

I am very grateful to Fife police and the security team who make it possible for me to work and conduct my parliamentary duties in Kirkcaldy and London and manage the travel I do.

I have been given expert research help led by Andrew Hilland with Ross Fulton, helped by Jyoti Bhojani, Cormac Hollingsworth, Callum Munro, Susanna Pettigrew, Rachael Thomas and Kate Wilsea. Kirsty McNeill has read the whole work and I am grateful for her comments, which have informed the final text. Gil McNeil has once again generously managed the project and Mike Jones has patiently overseen this process from beginning to end, taking only a few days off for the birth of his beautiful baby girl. The House of Commons Library has, as usual, given the best of specialist research support.

But this book has been written with my two sons John and Fraser – and their future – in mind. They and millions of Scots will have to reap in future years what we sow in September 2014. It is dedicated to them.

INTRODUCTION

I love my country. Simple as that. I am passionately and proudly Scottish. I love what my country stands for and what our people have achieved in the world.

Some people have a love–hate relationship with their country. Mine is a love–love relationship.

I have cheered, and despaired, as Scotland played at Wembley, roared and groaned during rugby internationals at Murrayfield and revelled in Andy Murray's and Chris Hoy's successes. The glories of Robert Burns, the triumphs of the Scottish Enlightenment and the greatness of Scottish literature, music and films have nourished me. My membership of the Church of Scotland, the Church in which my father was a minister for sixty years, has always sustained me.

I was born in Scotland; brought up in Scotland; educated at a Scottish state primary school, the West School in Kirkcaldy; at a state secondary school, Kirkcaldy High School; and all my time as a student was spent at Edinburgh University, where I took both undergraduate and postgraduate degrees.

As children, we were firmly rooted in Scotland. I didn't visit London until I was twelve; or, like most of my generation growing up in the fifties and sixties, travel abroad until I was sixteen.

Until then all my holidays were spent in Scotland, staying with relatives, either on a farm in Perthshire or in my mother's home village in Aberdeenshire.

Very occasionally we would have a weekend stay in Crieff at one of Scotland's Hydro hotels. That was chosen by my father because ministers' families were invited there at reduced rates thanks to a bequest and, perhaps more importantly for him, because it was then one of the few alcohol-free hotels in the country.

And so when I became a Member of Parliament in 1983 I had spent little time in London and had rarely visited it. Over the past thirty years, I have spent much more time in London as an MP, Chancellor and Prime Minister, and I've always been impressed by its concentration of arts and heritage, by the wonderful museums, world-class theatres, magnificent libraries, great art galleries and by its diversity. But the civil servants I worked with were always bemused by my instinctively Scottish way of describing my two homes: London is where I stay; Fife is where I live.

So I yield to no one in my pride in being Scottish. I feel no awkwardness in saying this for my sense of myself has always been Scottish. Some have tried to play down their origin but, with me, feeling Scottish has always seemed like a reflex. And although we were living and working in London, Sarah and I insisted that all our children were born in Scotland. It is here, at home, that my sons are enjoying their schooling and forming lifelong friendships. And in addition to my duties as the MP for Kirkcaldy and Cowdenbeath, it is from here too that Sarah and I now work on organising our global campaigning projects to win every child an education, and join our efforts with hundreds of thousands of other Scots who support international justice campaigns and charities around the world.

Being a Scot in British politics has not always been easy. Jeremy Clarkson described me as 'a one-eyed Scottish idiot', and the commentator Kelvin MacKenzie, the possessor of a very Scottish name but a very un-Scottish set of prejudices, said that I represented all that was worst about the Scottish people – anti-entrepreneurial, on the make and spendthrift. In my last days at 10 Downing Street, the *Sun* attacked me as 'the Scottish squatter', encouraging the implication that, as a Scot, I had no business being there.

But I am British too. And, in common with at least 50 per cent of Scots today, I have close relatives living in England, including my younger brother and his family. Sarah, my wife, has a Scottish father and an English mother. Many of my relatives before me have worked in England, my mother spending much of her wartime army service working in central London. Her experience reminds us of the continuing influence on us of the Second World War and its history of shared sacrifice not just on the battlefield but across the whole of Britain on the home front.

So, born into the Scottish nation, I was also born into the British state – and I have tried to understand why being British is a different kind of identity. It is not as simple as saying 'I feel Scottish but I am British', because the loyalty, especially when representing Britain abroad, can be no less keenly felt. The Scottish actor Ewan McGregor put it eloquently when he said that he loved Scotland but he liked the idea of being part of Britain.[1] And Britishness has always seemed to me, at its best, to advance an inclusive idea about a plural, multiple, multinational identity that is able to accommodate difference: we can be Scots, English, Irish, Welsh *and* British. Indeed it is easily and comfortably hyphenated, explaining why many people now say they are black British or Muslim-British in a way I've not often heard someone say they are black-Scottish or Muslim-English.

And yet now that there is to be a referendum to decide whether the Scots should remain in Britain or break away, one of its saddening features is how the debate appears to narrow the options available to the Scottish people. Too often the referendum choice is presented as a simplistic one – are you for Scotland or for Britain? – as if we are in a zero-sum game, where one identity can only gain at the expense of diminishing another. You are to feel Scottish or you are to feel British, as if it is impossible to be both.

It is as if we were for ever caught atop an emotional roller coaster at a never-ending football or rugby international where, with feelings running at a heightened, even frenzied level of emotion, everything becomes stark – black versus white, wrong versus right, even David versus Goliath or, as some would have it, overlord versus victim, coloniser versus colonised. When the debate takes this turn, Scots are being forced into an exclusionary Scottishness, as if to think any other way would mean we were trying, as the writer Jonathan Freedland has eloquently put it, to simultaneously hold contradictory thoughts.[2]

As we shall see, the black-and-white version of national identity is crude and incomplete. Even our identity – the very sense we have of ourselves – is itself subject to challenge and change. National identities may seem enduring, even eternal, but in fact they evolve. The solid certainty we have at 3 p.m. on a football or rugby-international afternoon can easily soften because loyalties, in the real world, are complex and over-lapping. Plenty of people feel like I do – loyal to a home town like Kirkcaldy, proud to be part of a wider county like Fife, but also fiercely Scottish, comfortably British and enthusiastically European and global in outlook too. I am also a citizen of the United Kingdom but, of course, no one talks of themselves as UKanian in the way that people think of themselves as American, German, Russian and Italian. Even when our Olympic team was, technically, the UK team, it was called Team GB. While recognising that the United Kingdom is our state including Scotland, England, Wales and Northern Ireland, and Great Britain is Scotland, England and Wales only, I will for ease, as most people do and with no disrespect to the Northern Irish, use the terms United Kingdom and Britain almost interchangeably throughout this book.

NATIONALISM ON THE RISE

The speed at which Scottish political nationalism has moved from the fringes to the mainstream, then to an electoral majority in the Scottish Parliament and now to threaten the very existence of Britain is extraordinary.

The rise of political nationalism in Scotland is remarkable because there is no vexatious dispute over borders, no great religious issue now at stake, nor any major language or ethnic issues that bitterly divide us.

There have been, thankfully, no bombs or bullets, no violence, no hunger strikes, and there have been no massive demonstrations, no big marches, no popular protests at anything like the level we saw from the 1970s to the 1990s over things such as the poll tax, spending cuts and the creation of the parliament itself.

If there is a constitutional revolution under way, then it is a quiet one. The nationalist movement to rid Scotland of the British state is quite unlike anything that happened when America broke away in the 1770s; when most of Ireland seceded in the 1920s; or when the Indian subcontinent and the African colonies liberated themselves in the 1940s and 1960s respectively. Then, and later across other continents, there were struggles fuelled by tension between different nationalities, protests at discrimination against ethnic groups, violent attempts to prevent the free flow of citizens from one nation to another, and even civil wars.

Of course today nationalism is never far from the front pages of our newspapers – and we should not doubt the power of nationalism when we see, as I write, reports of an assertion of nationhood in Ukraine, a rebellion by groups of non-Han Chinese, breakaway movements in Central Africa, unrest in the now-divided Sudan; and, in the Western world, a new statement of cultural separation in Canada's Quebec, strong breakaway movements in Spain and Belgium, and even a privately called referendum on separation from Italy in Venice. Every major empire or hegemony – the British, the Soviet, the Chinese and the American – has underestimated nationalism.

But while other states in Europe, Asia and Africa have fought internecine wars over borders, argued violently over religion, language, ethnicity and the rights of minorities, the island of Great Britain had been immune from political nationalism – until now.

For most of my life, we Scots have accepted uncritically – and to a large extent unthinkingly – the benefits of being part of Britain, with the advantages gained from Britain rarely, until recently, challenged or even doubted. Ireland has always been seen as an exception because it is viewed as an island apart with a different history and, what mattered more for most of the time, a different set of religious traditions. But within Britain we haven't had violent struggles between the Scottish and the English for centuries and this book is partly an attempt to explain why.

Normally secession movements gain traction through allegations that their country has been colonised and their people oppressed. But, far from there being a hardening of Scots resentment against Britain, recent opinion polls suggest that support for political nationalism has risen even as the majority of Scots now feel that, at least in the past ten years, they have been getting a better deal out of the UK. Even now the majority of Scots feel some attachment to Britain and only a minority think of themselves as exclusively Scottish and not in any way British at all.[3]

And yet the Union today seems more at risk than at any time in its history.

So it is important to ask why a relationship that has lasted for more than 300 years, that has survived economic disasters, forced emigrations and generations of abject poverty – and during which time Scots, English and Welsh have served together in the eight continental wars of the eighteenth and nineteenth centuries, and the two world wars of the twentieth century – has gone so sour.

We have to ask why in 2014 – when in certain respects Scotland is faring better economically in comparison with England than ever before – Scots are contemplating ending what detached commentators would accept is one of the most successful multi-national alliances the world has ever known.[4]

My starting point is that any credible analysis of Scotland's position should start from a thorough understanding of how we got here, not least because if September's vote might undo 300 years of Scottish history, it is important to understand where it fits into the stories of Scotland and Britain.

For the supporter of independence, the answer is simple: nationalism is on the rise because Scotland is a nation and a nation should have a state.

But that contention doesn't explain *why* political nationalism has exploded into life *now*, nor *why* it has done so *now* without all the other conditions in place that normally accompany and legitimise political-independence movements, from disputed borders to racial discrimination.

Indeed, nationalists may not be asking the right question. For the real question is why, after three centuries when Scots could express our identity through our own national institutions *inside* Britain, many now feel the need to be *outside*.

Why, when Scotland is already a nation that has maintained the autonomy of its own national institutions within the Union, and has a parliament whose writ is uncontested in areas from education and health to transport, the environment and much of industry, do we want to break all our political links with Britain?

And why do we want to sever all these political ties at the very point when Scotland is being offered an enhanced form of power-sharing with the United Kingdom? Moreover, why sever all constitutional ties when there is a wide consensus that we actually want to be part of the United Kingdom's common monetary policy?[5]

Why now? And why not before? For if, as political nationalists believe, the desire for independence is an irresistible consequence of national consciousness, why then was their kind of political nationalism of such little consequence in the Scotland of the eighteenth and nineteenth centuries, when agitation for independent states was at its height elsewhere in Europe and when Scotland's Church, legal profession and education system were doing so much to maintain the continuity of Scotland's distinctive national story and a strong national consciousness? And if, as nationalists also argue, the British state acts as a permanent structural brake on Scotland's economic growth, why did political nationalism gain so little support when Scotland was being devastated by unemployment rates as high as 25 per cent in the inter-war years or in the 1980s when Scotland was suffering under a deindustrialisation that was more brutal than even that experienced by the North and Midlands of England?[6]

We also have to ask cultural as well as economic questions. Why did Scottish nationalism make little or no inroads when throughout three centuries we were fighting what some nationalists might have imagined to be other people's wars; when we were suffering some of the worst haemorrhaging of our population through higher emigration rates than just about any country in the world; and when, at various points in our history, there were intense theological differences that could have renewed the religious wars between Scotland and England?

We have to ask why a breakaway movement is demanding a separate state at a time when more Scots have English relatives than at any time in history, perhaps 50 per cent today as against, at a guess, only 2–3 per cent in 1707; at a time when, around the world, ideas of interdependence seem more relevant than ideas of independence; and at a time when the power of people across global social networks seems to be challenging and even eclipsing the power of states, making the old political nationalism, which was fixated with taking over the trappings of state power, seem also less relevant.

I do not ask these questions rhetorically but to try to understand why the trajectory of Scottish nationalism is so unlike the other forms it claims to parallel. Can we explain why there was no significant Scottish-led rebellion in 1832 or 1848, when Britain was convulsed by riots over political reform; and why no significant Scottish nationalist uprising in 1919, when there was a huge sense of injustice as British promises that there would be 'Homes fit for Heroes' were swept aside and workers left to the mercy of a post-war depression? If repression is the trigger for an assertion of national identity, why not in the period from 1746 when Highlanders were brutally suppressed in the aftermath of Culloden? If religious differences are a potential starting pistol for a secessionist movement, why not in 1712 when the British Parliament usurped the authority of the Scottish Church? If resentment against unfair treatment is a likely cause, then why not in the 1980s when, at the time of Mrs Thatcher's government, the sense of grievance at an inequitable relationship was probably at its height?

It is small wonder that commentators struggle to explain what has happened: neither the political nationalists who have driven the change, nor the Unionists who have resisted it, offer a clear sense of what really lies behind the recent rise of a hitherto unsuccessful party, the SNP, and what appears to be an upsurge in support for independence or at least for fundamental constitutional change.

For we have to explain why political nationalism is on the rise *at this time*, when *at all times* there has been a strong Scottish consciousness of our distinctive national identity; when *at all times* we have – as Scots – not been passive but assertive about protecting and preserving our identity; when *at all times* we have sought to build, nurture and cherish distinctively Scottish institutions that reflect and advance our identity; and when *at all times* we have insisted that the British state does not interfere with the rights of our institutions to operate in an autonomous way.

So for me the central Scottish mystery of modern history is not that people feel they want to assert their Scottishness (we have *always* felt Scottish), not that there is a demand for Scottish institutions to express that identity (our institutions have *always* done so), but that while for 300 years we have expressed our identity, run our own institutions and latterly shared political power as part of Britain, now many want to do so without being part of Britain.

Why did we go for 300 years without feeling the need to convert nationhood into statehood thus giving the impression that our aspirations could be guaranteed within the British state? Why did our sense of being a nation not convert itself into a demand to be a fully fledged state even in the wake of the American and French revolutions, when political institutions could no longer justify their existence on the basis of divine or dynastic rights but had to do so on the basis of popular consent and thus on the basis of the right of individuals to determine the government?

And why did most of Scotland stand silent and unmoved as a series of international treaties appeared to promote and popularise what was presented as akin to a basic principle of politics: that nation and state were interchangeable and that members of a nation should expect to be citizens of a nation-state?

Did the demand for a fully fledged Scottish statehood remain weak for three centuries because our national identity was *already* expressed through our own separate religious, educational, legal and civic institutions? Did the demand remain weak because these institutions *already* enjoyed autonomy and freedom from interference? Or did the demand remain weak for purely instrumental reasons because we could itemise the practical, concrete benefits many millions of Scots felt they gained from the Union's economic successes and imperial strength?

When nationalists argue that what's new is the 'desire to be the nation again', they are wrong. Through thick and thin, we have always thought of ourselves as a nation.

When people say that what's new is the demand of the Scots to have our own institutions, they are wrong too. We maintained distinctive, and generally separate, national institutions for 300 years. In fact, it is difficult to sustain an argument that Scotland's cultural freedom and religious and civic institutions were suppressed. Direct rule was not attempted through most of the three centuries of the Union. So, if there has been a fundamental shift of Scottish opinion in recent years, it is that more people than ever before want to break all constitutional links with Britain.

As we will see in later chapters, the Union has changed and changed again to respond, in part at least, to Scottish sentiments and demands. In the first phase of the Union, who controlled the institutions of the state mattered little to people anyway, as they were much more interested in who controlled the Church. Keeping the state at arm's length from the Church was the hottest political issue of the time.

In the second phase, you could itemise practical benefits to Scotland from being part of the British state – from access to the markets of the Empire, security against France, the protection of our religious freedom, and the building of a Britain-wide economic infrastructure from roads to postal services. But crucially, if there was little pressure from the members of the Scottish nation to establish a separate state, there was also little pressure from the members of the British elite to swallow Scottish national identity or subsume the institutions that expressed and shaped it. The 'independence' of key Scottish institutions appeared to be guaranteed not just by the formalities of the Act of Union but also by a kind of informal 'non-aggression pact' that prevented interference by British institutions in areas the Scottish people felt were properly theirs alone to manage.

For reasons we explore, Scots did not do what many other

people experiencing rapid industrialisation and bewildering waves of social change that seemed alien did. Other nations organised themselves around ethnic loyalties and recalled traditional national identities in popular movements to create new states that would promise to shelter people from industrial upheaval. Being among the first to industrialise and perhaps more aware of the benefits that our first-mover status gave us as Scots in common with Britain, we instead entered the second phase of the Union's development: determined to maintain the independence of our own national institutions like our Church and also with a clear sense of how we could benefit from empire and shape the Union to serve our interests.

The third phase of the Union, the twentieth-century phase, was shaped by the shared sacrifices of UK armed forces and civilians in two world wars and by the shared achievement of the aftermath of war, a welfare state and National Health Service that made us see our Britishness as more egalitarian than in the days of empire.

Now, in a fundamental shift in the dynamics of Scotland's relationship with Britain, a considerable section of Scottish opinion feels no connection with Britain and wants to break all political links with it. This movement has grown as all nations grapple with the 'levelling' forces of worldwide economic and social change, known as 'globalisation'. As industries, companies and workforces feel at the mercy of what seem uncontrollable, runaway global trends and forces, there is a sense that in turn we feel less secure and our traditional ways of life feel challenged and under threat. At the same time, long-established Scottish institutions, notably the Churches, have seemed unable to rise to the challenge of articulating or answering people's anxieties or offering them the sense of stability and protection they seek. But no post-war history of Britain can be written without acknowledging the third force for change: the weakening of that strong post-1945 sense of belonging to Britain which we will discuss in our chapter on British identity but which most commentators attribute to the end of empire and our changing economic, military and political status in the world.

There is, of course, one alternative worldview: the suggestion that globalisation will make us feel more cosmopolitan in our outlook and less attracted to the separatist tendencies that were so common in the nineteenth-century response to industrialisation. The argument is that we will be more willing to contemplate multiple or plural identities and less inclined to cling to traditional loyalties. That theory is being challenged not just in Scotland but at the heart of Europe: in Belgium, Catalonia, Lombardy and parts of Eastern Europe where political nationalism is on the rise. But history tells us that nationalist sentiment does not always lead to a demand for nation states. One recent study on Europe by the eminent historian Norman Davies, *Vanished Kingdoms*, itemises 600 national identities that have virtually disappeared. Some groups who considered themselves nations never became states. Indeed, Scotland was one of 500 independent European polities in the 1500s that were reduced in number to 350 by the 1800s. In his classic *Nations and Nationalism*, the social anthropologist Ernest Gellner tells us that, although no one will ever know exactly, there could be somewhere between 6,000 and 8,000 identifiable ethno-linguistic populations scattered round the globe. Yet today there are less than 200 states. Gellner, of course, explains that the demand for separate states is more prevalent when economic development is uneven and inequitable and when people feel threatened by rapid disruptive changes in their lives. Both in response to the waves of industrialisation in the nineteenth century and globalisation now, populist secessionist movements seem more adept than traditional political parties at responding to popular grievances and then channelling people's anxieties into the demand for a separate state.[7]

1951 – A HALF-CENTURY OF CHANGE

Growing up in Scotland in the 1950s, going to university in the late 1960s, and working in and from Scotland from the 1970s, I have had a front-row seat from which to witness the dramatic transformation of the Scottish economy and Scottish society over fifty years, and from which to witness the disruption, dislocation and turbulence in which movements for change can grow and thrive.

In retrospect, 1951, the year in which I came into the world, now looks more like the end of an old era than the beginning of a new one.

When I was delivered in Glasgow, I was one of the newborn Scots who pushed our country's population beyond five million for the first time.[8] My father's work as a minister had taken him to St Mary's Church, Govan, which was literally next door to and overlooked the Clyde and the famous Govan shipyards. I spent my first three years at the beating heart of industrial Scotland before moving back to my father's native Fife to go to school in an industrial town about to come under pressure from pit and factory closures.

If the early 1950s into which I was born could not be described as a time of confidence – the country had just lived through years of austerity – it was nonetheless a time of stability and what seemed to be certainties. The soul-searching over empire, Europe and economic decline had not yet come to dominate our politics. Instead there was a belief that the same fixed Scottish pattern of work, religion and family life that had built up over a century since the Industrial Revolution would prove lasting.

It was not to be. From the 1960s onwards, the pattern of Scottish industrial life – the nature of the work, the skills required for the work and, most important of all, the amount of available work – changed just as dramatically as old patterns of rural life had been transformed by the Industrial Revolution more than a century before.

It is hard to overstate the impact this transformation has had on who we believe ourselves to be. Scotland, and Clydeside in particular, had been a world leader in coal, steel, shipbuilding, engineering and textiles for a whole century from the 1840s. In the chapters to come, I will chart the impact of deindustrialisation. I will sketch out the economic changes caused by globalisation and, side by side, the social changes, in particular changes in our workplaces and changes in our religious life, that have led to the weakening of traditional Scottish and British institutions that were sources of both identity and authority. While their decline repeats a trend and phenomenon across the Western world, it has been particularly traumatic for a Scotland that was once defined by the strength of its industrial economy and its traditional institutions. And I will suggest that we cannot fully understand the demand to renegotiate the relationship between Scotland and Britain without first appreciating the impact on the collective Scottish mind of the collapse of our traditional industry, the decline of the Churches and the weakening of many of the shared institutions of our civic life.

By 1951, despite the ravages of the inter-war recession and then war, little in our industrial structure had changed. The Clydeside of 1914 had produced one-third of the world's ships, one-third of the world's railway locomotives and rolling stock, and as much as one-fifth of the world's steel.[9] In the late forties and early fifties, with just a tiny fraction of 1 per cent of the world's population, Scotland was still producing anything between 12 and 15 per cent of the world's ships – punching, you might say, nearly 100 times our weight.[10]

For 100 years the heavy industries of Scotland had provided employment for 40 per cent of our workforce.[11] No other industrial country had such a concentration of its workers in heavy industries.[12] In 1951, 350,000 of the country's 900,000 manufacturing and mining workers were employed in one sector, the metal trades.[13] And the deep mines and many open-cast mines that between them employed nearly 100,000 men had just been nationalised amid plans to expand the industry and build super-pits.[14] The once pre-eminent Scottish textiles industry was now overshadowed by engineering but, still, the linen, jute and linoleum industries employed 175,000 workers across Scotland.[15] It was agriculture and fishing had that had seen a spectacular fall over the previous century, down from 27 per cent of the workforce to just 7 per cent.[16]

During the inter-war years, Scotland's deficiencies in the rapidly expanding light industries had become apparent but the threat had been ignored. While England developed modern consumer-based products, the Scotland of 1951 manufactured no aircraft, no cars, nor even any tinplate.[17] Ten years later, a landmark survey of the Scottish economic scene, the Toothill Report, was to lay bare our weakness in science, electronics and consumer-based industries. Only 6 per cent of the 1951 workforce were professional workers.[18] No one living near the Clyde in the 1950s, however, could doubt the continuing and entrenched power of the male-dominated, heavily organised engine room of the world's first Industrial Revolution, a Glasgow that still revelled in its status as the second city of the Empire and in its powerful role in Britain and the world.

Matching this long-established concentration of industrial power was another distinctively Scottish social phenomenon: that of people of all classes living together in social housing. From 1920 to 1960 over 600,000 new Scottish homes were built by the state; and in the Scotland of fifty years ago, more people lived in state-owned, council-rented properties than in any other democracy in the world.[19] It meant that at both work and at home, the Scottish national imagination had a distinctly cooperative tinge to run alongside the focus on individual reason the Enlightenment had given us.

And the collective power of the trade unions and of the state – both local and national government – was matched only, in Scotland's eyes, by the even greater collective power held by the

Churches. It will be hard for younger readers to imagine, but during the 1950s the great theologian Reinhold Niebuhr came to Scotland to tell us that America had the most church-minded population in the world, with one exception: Scotland.[20]

In the Scotland of 1951, two million men and women out of an adult population of 3.5 million were members of a Church. There was no parallel for such high levels of religious affiliation in Europe, and certainly not in England and Wales. In contrast to Scotland's 57.8 per cent membership, the figure for England and Wales was just 22.9 per cent. Despite being the established Church, the Anglicans had only 10 per cent of English and Welsh adults in their ranks, compared with the 35 per cent of adults in Scotland who were members of just one denomination, the Church of Scotland. The Catholic Church was booming in Scotland, too – one estimate puts the number of Catholics in Scotland in 1951 at 750,000.[21]

These were not just token affiliations either. Around the churches, Sunday schools, youth clubs, sports teams and extra-mural associations flourished. And religious conventions kept levels of divorce and unmarried parenting low. The overwhelming majority of Scots who got married in the 1950s did so in a religious ceremony in church. Only 5 per cent of Scottish babies were born outside wedlock, down from 9 per cent less than a century before.[22] The power of the Churches in an already macho culture made for difficult times for Scottish women, and gay people too. Indeed, the march of feminism was much slower in Scotland than elsewhere. Despite the long history of strong Scots women – from Jenny Geddes to Mary Barbour's rent-strike army of 1915 – women like my mother were still expected to tend to hearth and home.[23]

Indeed, when we look at the jobs people did and their religious commitments, the Scotland of 1950 looked much more like the Scotland of 1850 than the Scotland we know today.

And thus by the middle of the last century Scots were more

likely than their English counterparts to work in an industry and observe a faith which had remained broadly unchanged for much of the Industrial Revolution.

But that is not to say that the people of Scotland and England lived completely separate lives. In the post-war years a quarter of a million Scots spent time in the armed forces before conscription ended in 1959.[24] So most Scots families had a direct association with the British military, whose Scottish regiments were among its best and most valued.[25]

That built upon our shared experiences in the Second World War – a common trauma that bound Scotland, England and Wales to Britain in a profound way. There can be no doubt from the accounts of both wars that when someone was wounded or at risk no one asked which nationality they were before rushing to help: they thought of themselves as British soldiers fighting together, as one, for a common cause.

After the Second World War, having signed up for war together, served together, fought, mourned and won together, the Scots of 1951 felt very much part of a united country that was now also sharing the benefits of a British welfare state. A collectivist Britain – the post-war Labour government that created the National Health Service was still in power when I was born – felt a not uncomfortable place for Scots to be.

So this was the Scotland I was born into, a Scotland where your class, your religion and the role of the state were all taken as a given. It was a Scotland where, as David McCrone writes, even those Scots who had graduated from manual to white-collar occupations still described themselves as working class.[26]

Fast forward to 1967 and everything was in flux. I had just turned sixteen and was leaving school. Mark Twain had said of his move as a teenager from the highly religious, heavily moralistic small town in which he had been brought up to the chaotic and alcohol-fuelled frontier town of Virginia City, Nevada that 'this was no place for a puritan . . . and I did not long remain one'.[27] In making the jump from Kirkcaldy High to Edinburgh University I had something of a sense of what he meant.

Kirkcaldy and Edinburgh are separated only by the narrow Firth of Forth, but might as well have been separated by an entire ocean given how different they were in that first year of my university life. Although my fresher experience was not all that I had hoped – I spent much of that year confined to hospital trying to rescue my eyesight after a rugby accident I had suffered at the bottom of a loose scrum – I could tell enough about what was going on around me to know that 1967 was a turning point for me personally, and for Scotland.

The swinging sixties might have been a little less swinging in the Canongate than Carnaby Street but, despite being the home of Scottish Protestantism, Edinburgh was changing. In January 1968, just before I returned to hospital for yet another eye operation, I was in St Giles' Cathedral to hear Malcolm Muggeridge deliver what now seems a comically self-indulgent pulpit denunciation of three Edinburgh students (Anna Coote, Yvonne Baginsky and Steve Morrison) who had used the columns of the *Student* newspaper to challenge the university student health service to offer free contraception. A social revolution was under way and students were at the heart of challenging old forms of Scottish authority. What had previously been a prohibition-minded society was fast earning the title of the 'permissive society'.

At the same time, it was impossible to miss what was happening at home in Fife. Every working day, as I grew up, a mass of men had left their houses at the same time to get to the linoleum factory or to go down the pits. You felt as if a whole town was going to work. We had experienced conditions as close to full employment as an industrial town is probably ever going to get. But then, a bombshell. The factory a few hundred yards from my home – Barry, Ostlere and Shepherd, one of around forty textiles firms in Fife that had survived war, inter-war recession and war yet again – announced that it would close, with 450 Kirkcaldy workers thrown out of work.[28] Friends of our family left for England, some went abroad and many older men never worked again. Bigger textile closures followed in Kirkcaldy and then even more extensive mining job losses as the pits of Fife fell one by one in a devastating domino crash lasting right through to the late eighties.

We weren't alone. The years that followed – particularly the late 1970s and 1980s – were terrible times for Scottish industry as long-established world-renowned household names like Singer of Clydebank, Hillman Imp at Linwood, Leyland at Bathgate, British Aluminium at Invergordon and, later, Gartcosh, Massey Ferguson, Ravenscraig and every coalmine became memories. Scotland's industry was destroyed in a form of social vandalism for which the then government has never been forgiven. But the implications of Scotland's industrial decline spread far beyond the electoral fortunes of the Conservative Party.

Stung by the trauma of this deindustrialisation, Scottish society changed, creating a vacuum which political nationalism has been able to fill. While many of the trends deindustrialisation brought in its wake – the rise of a new middle class, a consumer revolution, the growth in higher education, the break-up of the nuclear family – were part of a pattern of post-industrial change happening all round the Western world, what stands out is the speed and scale of the reversal of Scotland's fortunes. Suddenly Scotland was lurching from one extreme, an overdependence on heavy industry, to another extreme, in which the clear-out from manufacturing was greater and seemed more brutal than almost anywhere else. In 1951, Glasgow was the second city of the Empire; by the 1990s the standard view was that it wasn't even the second city of the UK. 'We have lived through an economic revolution of substantial proportions, essentially as significant as earlier transformational times in Scottish history' the world-renowned Scottish historian Professor Tom Devine has concluded.[29] 'Although change in human history is obviously a constant, the last quarter of a century in the history of Scotland has been a period of pronounced structural change which has not been experienced in Scotland, or by the Scottish people, on any scale since the classic industrial and agricultural revolutions of the late 18th and early 19th centuries.'[30] The great novelist William McIlvanney described what happened as the shallowing of Scotland and saw himself 'surviving the shipwreck'.[31]

As the underlying economic reality of Scotland has changed, so too has the social structure built upon it. From a post-war peak of 1.2 million, Scottish trade-union membership is now 635,000. It is a different kind of industrial movement too: whereas the soul of the union movement used to be the working-class men of private-sector heavy industry, today's typical Scottish trade-union member is more likely to be a female graduate.[32] 'In a relatively short space of time, the Scottish working class went from being one of the most highly organised working classes in the history of industrial capitalism,' concludes William Knox in his study of 200 years of work and industry in Scotland, 'to a fragmented one . . . barely able to defend its economic and political interests.'[33]

So one of the great foundations of Scottish collectivism – the factory-yard mass meeting and the pithead gathering – has simply died a death. So too has the kind of mass religious participation which bound so many communities from the Highlands and Islands right down to the Borders. Since 1999, most respondents to the annual Scottish Social Attitudes survey have not identified with any religion. Church of Scotland membership has fallen rapidly in recent years. It stood at 770,217 in 1991 but fell to 464,355 in 2009. And according to the 2011 census, the number of people identifying as Christian has fallen by nearly half a million since 2001.[34]

As church attendance has waned, so too has religious influence. Once 80 per cent of marriages were religious ceremonies in church:

now the figure is less than half. Just fifty years ago, 5 per cent of births were to unmarried parents. Now the figure is 50 per cent. Divorce has more than quadrupled since the 1950s. And of course marriage is less common: fifty years ago about half of women in their early twenties were married; now just 8 per cent are.[35] I am not passing any judgement on the families in question – simply noting that our collective institutions no longer determine, as they once did, how people organise their private affairs.

At the same time, another part of Scottish collectivism is weakening. Where once council-built homes met the housing needs of the majority of Scots, now they house just 15 per cent. Other ties to the state are coming loose, too. Once conscription linked every Scottish family to the fate of the armed forces, but now as few as one in every 100 Scottish households is a forces family.[36] Change is all around. Looked at in this way, the question is not how could the politics of Scotland change from 1951 to now – but, rather, how could they not? With such rapid social and economic transformation, it is not at all surprising that the people of Scotland are looking for new certainties to replace the old. And with a strong sense that the scale of transformation is a uniquely Scottish experience, is it not unsurprising that the claims would grow that our specifically Scottish problems need a specifically Scottish solution too?

If I am right that the story of Scottish society over the last fifty years has been one of two great declines – changes in the way we organise our industrial life and in the way we organise our religious life, which took place against a backdrop of globalisation – then an appeal for a different politics becomes much easier to understand.

Bear in mind too that throughout this whole period another old comfortable certainty was being challenged: people now openly talked of 'the managed decline' of a Britain that had once been the greatest economic and military power on earth. Indeed, almost every political debate that has raged during my political life, whether it is about Europe, immigration, nationalism or the state of the economy, has come back to one question: how to cope with Britain's change from its past status as the world's number-one power.

In Chapters 1 and 2, I will try to show where Scotland is now, compared to the 1950s, and assess what the changes in our fortunes mean for our sense of who we are. But for now it is just as important to note that these forces for change – the intense pressures from the opening-up of the global economy, the inability of traditional Scottish institutions to respond, and the weakening of the old ties to Britain – have hit Scotland and caused us to question whether Scotland's national identity can ever again be expressed, and our aspirations met, within the confines of the British state.

INDEPENDENCE AND INTERDEPENDENCE

Yet for three centuries until this sudden surge of political nationalism you could make simple, easily understood, and well received arguments in defence and even in praise of the Union that most people thought were unanswerable. In the eighteenth century, the Union between Scotland and England was acclaimed and admired because it guaranteed our defence and security. Set up, in part, to defend all parts of Britain against an invasion by the French, it was a Union to repel people seen as foreigners and to wage war where necessary.

By the nineteenth century, the Union was widely praised as a unique and successful trade association that made us wealthier – a common market that enabled Britons to trade together and allowed commerce to flourish, jobs to be created and prosperity to be spread across the whole country. And for many years we were able to show the benefits in cash, jobs, and prestige that flowed from it, and laud them as indisputable.

The twentieth century gave new strength to the Union as we all made the same sacrifices in pursuit of the same cause: a world free from fascism.

More recently, we have become more aware of a twenty-first-century argument for Union, that we are all inescapably part of the same fragile, vulnerable island, with each of us unable to buy ourselves out of ecological decline. Recognising that pollution is no respecter of artificial borders, people have started to see the environmental case for the Union that our quality of life on an island we share is best built around common UK-wide policies.

There is also a case for the Union that comes from the shared institutions that we have built up over 300 years and which we admire as not Scottish or English but British. The NHS, our armed forces, the monarchy and the BBC have longevity and popularity, and we share them equally across four nations. More recently there have emerged a range of what might be called new British institutions – not just the UK National Lottery but unifying Britain-wide organisations like Pride of Britain, Comic Relief and Children in Need. More important are the shared commemorations of Armistice Day, the shared celebrations of royal events, the support across the whole country for Team GB at the Olympics and the widespread applause for Danny Boyle's opening ceremony which portrayed the shared values that bind us all together.

These arguments – about defence, trade, family ties, the environment and our shared institutions – are important and, for me, compelling, but they are, for most people, no longer decisive. Today none of these individual arguments – at least taken in isolation – clinch the Unionist case for the majority of Scots. In fact opinion polls show that they command less popular support in Scotland than the assertions that we are more Scottish than British, that distinctive Scottish values are being ignored or neglected in Westminster and Whitehall, and that we do not get the government we choose. I will explore later why there has been a weakening in people's identification with being British just at the time when the incomes of the peoples of Scotland and England have converged, and ask whether and in what way this may be due to Britain's changed status in the world.

But beyond these historic arguments for Union – about defence, trade, and our shared institutions – there is a second set of arguments for being part of Britain. It is founded on a big idea, the growing interdependence of peoples. In the 1960s and 1970s a fellow Fifer, Ian Rankin, followed a similar path to the one I followed in the 1950s and 1960s – primary and secondary schooling in Fife, university in Edinburgh. Summing up his experience and parodying the first page of James Joyce's famous collection of short stories, *A Portrait of the Artist as a Young Man*, Rankin wrote:

> As a child I was given a new diary every Christmas and I would open it and mark the inside front cover with my details.
>
> Ian Rankin
> 17 Craigmead Terrace
> Bowhill
> Cardenden
> Fife
> Scotland
> Great Britain
> United Kingdom
> Europe
> The World
> The Universe
>
> To me they seemed concentric circles with my house at the very centre. I was a child of the world and of Europe but more locally (and more meaningfully) belonged to the village of Bowhill, which was in the process of being swallowed up by the postal designation of Cardenden . . . When the national team played I would cheer for Scotland. If Great Britain were in competition at

the Olympics I would be rooting for them. At the Ryder Cup, I'd be keeping my fingers crossed for Europe against the USA . . . If asked I always explained that I was Scottish rather than English. 'British' didn't bother me but 'English' did mainly because it was just plain wrong.[37]

That strikes me as a fair reflection of where most of us were coming from – feeling more Scottish than British, but more British than not. And, like Ian Rankin, I always want to add an extra thing to the list: I am British – but I'm from Europe, the world and 'the universe' too. It seems to me that we are tying ourselves in knots trying to understand something which Rankin grasped instinctively as a boy, and which today's students and young people can process in the blink of an eye. When I was younger a faraway place was Newcastle or Cardiff or London: now young people think nothing of taking cheap flights to Eastern Europe, America, Africa or even Asia. Today they are also connected to the wider world permanently through social media, making it far easier for them to interact with and understand strangers as well as friends and family on the other side of the world.

For the generation who can be accurately called 'globalisation's children', the interdependence of nations isn't an option or even an argument – it's a fact of life like time, tides and the weather. And yet the demands of this age of interdependence – so obvious when we are faced with epidemics, nuclear proliferation, international terror networks, financial contagion and climate change – are not being met or even heard in the current debate on the national question as they are considered by many to be too abstract or distant up against more localised polemical claims about how independence can secure 'Scotland's' oil, end Scotland's bedroom tax, or finally free Scotland from Tory misrule for ever.

Yet our interdependence – inside countries and between them – is the defining fact of our age and it is right that we consider what it means for us and our future, both in how we approach the world and how we relate to England, Wales and Northern Ireland. But fifteen years after Scotland changed with the creation of our parliament we have yet to put the best modern case for how a strong Scottish Parliament that is part of the UK can help us meet the challenges of a far more interdependent world. We need a conversation that shows how with both a foundation in common social and economic rights, and a willingness to share power across four nations, a modern UK constitution offers the world a model for how a more integrated globe that respects cultural diversity can work best. We do need a debate about the SNP's unanswered questions in their programme for independence – of course we do – but, even more than that, we need a discussion that starts from first principles about how Scotland and Britain can lead the way in making sense of globalisation, balancing the pressing need to work together for common goals with the respect that must be accorded to people's desires to belong.

Indeed it was Scottish notions of solidarity that combined with English ideas of toleration and liberty to create a union that remains greater than the sum of its parts. What makes the United Kingdom unique, and potentially a beacon for a more connected world, is the idea – inspired and realised by Scots – that we all benefit when we pool and share both risks and resources across nations. It is a cooperative principle that has been demonstrated to work in practice. Now that we have both a Scottish Parliament and a UK Parliament we can think of our association less in terms of a Union – a term that suggests a top–down arrangement with one boss in one capital – and more in terms of a partnership. Now that there is devolution to Wales and Northern Ireland alongside a London Assembly too, the Union is starting to look so much more flexible than its critics have traditionally allowed.

Later in the book I will ask that we consider for a moment what we have achieved together by building upon our interdependence: we are four nations but whether you are Scots, English, Welsh or Irish you have an equal right to the same basic pension, the same minimum wage, the same right to free health-care and the same basic level of social security. No other group of four nations achieves this in any part of the world.

It is the 'sharing' we do that makes the difference between a Scotland that might have historically been poorer than England and one where Scots have just about the same average income as their English neighbours, and makes equality between the nations a concrete possibility.

And it is the 'sharing' that converts the abstract idea of interde-pendence into the everyday reality of individuals and communi-ties benefiting from our partnership. These benefits – equal rights to healthcare, to help when unemployed, to minimum standards across the whole of the country, and to the same pensions no matter where you are – are interdependence in action, solidarity in practice, partnership and compassion at work. If this is right then it suggests that the Union has become much more than a contract entered into over 300 years ago for mutual advantage and self-interest. In fact we have now built not just what might be called an instrumental unionism, from which we benefit in a self-inter-ested way, but an intrinsic unionism in which we are prepared to cooperate and share and which now demands a recognition of the equality between the nations of the UK.

In that sense, the Union is closer to a covenant than a contract, because it asserts the existence of one moral community. Despite all the inequalities that remain and the anomalies, deficiencies and injustices still to be addressed, we have created the world's first and most progressive system of pooling and sharing resources between distinct nations.

The European Union's single market is an extraordinary achievement, but even its supporters (myself among them) could not equate the free movement of goods and labour that it enables with the complete equality of economic, social and political rights which citizens of the United Kingdom enjoy. In Britain we have created something more than a single market: we now have a social market, perhaps the best insurance policy in the world.

The significance of that idea cannot be overstated. Australia and New Zealand are neighbouring countries but they do not pool and share risks and resources; nor do Brazil and Argentina. The links between Mexico, America and Canada are built on trade and commerce and on cooperation on security but not on pooling and sharing their resources. Nor are those of the adjacent states of Malaysia and Singapore. In some cases the conflicts between neighbours – Israel and Palestine – are so great that they cannot find anything they can do in common. Even inside federations – America, Australia and Canada and, of course, the old Soviet Union, Czechoslovakia and Yugoslavia – there have been limits to the willingness to share and equalise. The USA, which guarantees equal political and civil rights across its states, has failed to create shared economic and social rights and as a result the citizens of poor states and provinces have far less access to welfare than those in richer states. And the European Union struggles precisely because, despite its great ambitions for social cohesion across the whole continent, a country like Germany will never yield to Greece similar rights to pensions, minimum wages or social security that the nations of the UK have agreed amongst ourselves in a process that has lasted 100 years.

In Europe income inequalities remain so great that the typical citizen of the poorest state in the European Union – indeed in the eurozone – has just 20 per cent of the income of the citizen of the richest state.[38] Even in the USA the typical citizen of the poorest state is 50 per cent poorer than the typical citizen of the richest state.[39] There are, of course, still massive inequalities inside the nations of the UK, but no longer between them. So in this book I show that there is no obvious way that either in the short term or in the long term we are better off by undoing the agreement to pool and share our resources and that, far from reducing inequality, an independent state which broke the arrangements to pool and share would be likely to see inequality rise.

MY SCOTLAND

This book tells the story of my Scotland.

Chapters 1 and 2 are about our Scottish national identity. I suggest that for three centuries of the Union our Scottishness was expressed through our separate law and education systems, our distinctive cultural and civic institutions, our sport and perhaps most of all through our distinctive religious beliefs and practices. But as the influence of religion has declined, what makes us feel Scottish and what we identify with most has changed and is changing.

Chapter 3 questions whether a distinctive Scottish view of the world is myth or reality and suggests that, even if there is much fiction among the facts, the stories we tell ourselves still reveal a lot about who we think we are. I was brought up on an egalitarian set of beliefs – not an ideology that said we had to create the same outcomes for everyone, but a belief we had to build our society around equal opportunities and fair outcomes. I have always found that this idea is best expressed by the commitment to 'equal opportunities for all, unfair privileges for no one'. Of course Scotland does not stand alone in holding these views, but early on in modern history we had unique ways of expressing them – ideas like 'the lad o' pairts' and 'the demo-cratic intellect' are distinctly Scottish in both motivation and expression and we will hear more about them in coming chapters.

I was also brought up to believe in a Scots tradition of civic responsibility, that we owe obligations to others that go beyond family ties or the dictates of the state. Again no one is suggesting Scots are uniquely communitarian. But because of our different historical experience we had to think our way through the challenges and pitfalls of the unique situation in which we found ourselves: members of a proud nation in a society without a state. It may be that it was this which led the thinkers of the Scottish Enlightenment – Smith, Hume, Hutcheson, Robertson and others – to pioneer, at least for the modern world, the idea that there was a space between the market and the state in which should sit a web of churches, schools, voluntary associations, charities and clubs. So out of the Scottish Enlightenment came a view of what a modern society could look like: one in which, by building and deploying what is now called 'social capital', citizens could flourish in a shared space beyond the state, the marketplace and the family home.

I am prepared to accept that there are limits to the popularity and prevalence of these ideas, and I do not claim that we are any more communitarian or egalitarian in reality than our counterparts in, say, the north of England or in Scandinavia. But national stories with even a grain of truth in them are important to the tale nations tell about themselves. Every Burns night we like to remind ourselves that 'A Man's a Man for A' That' and every Hogmanay we sing 'Auld Lang Syne', two rituals which locate for us the importance of both equality and community to the Scottish psyche.

Chapter 4 evaluates our life as part of the Union, a union that changed, changed again and is now changing yet again. The Union was said to be one that 'incorporated' Scotland: it did not, however, assimilate us, just as it did not conquer or subjugate us. When we came together in 1707 it was not because we decided we were now to be all of one nation – we remained distinctively Scottish, English and Welsh before later adding the Irish. But we came together for two reasons: to defend ourselves and to stop being poor. Because we had been at risk of invasion from France, and because there was always a 'danger', as shown in 1715 and 1745, that a Catholic would seek to take the throne, there was both a widespread anti-French sentiment and a majority view to prevent a Catholic succession that spanned both sides of the border. And it was agreed that, if we were to escape poverty, then we should secure the advantages in commerce from our empire and thus there developed a pro-empire sentiment right across the three nations who comprised the post-1707 Union. But while many Scots benefited from the growth of Britain as a commercial and then imperial power, and from the uninterrupted trade with England that Union brought, it may be that the Union did not spark the dissatisfaction that brought secessionist movements into being elsewhere because Scottish institutions were left alone.

In fact we can discern a number of different phases in the relationship between Scotland and Britain in the Union, as alluded to above. We could talk of the initial period of partial union or 'semi-independence', characterised by non-intervention by Westminster in Scottish social affairs but energetic Scottish participation in the continental wars and imperial ventures led by the British state. Then, as the state centralised economic and social power in London, Scots first sought measures of administrative decentralisation that gave them some control of their own affairs and then, in recent years, political devolution. Understanding these phases in the relationship between Scotland and Britain is not only of academic interest. It helps explain that the 1707 Union has not been fixed or immutable, but has had to adapt to change.

But what is left of the Scottish connection with Britain today? Chapter 5 looks at what we mean by British identity and how the post-1945 reappraisal of Britain's status in the world altered Scotland's' view of what it is to be British.

Of course no one today argues that the original forces behind Britishness – a shared empire, a common Protestant religion and a common anti-French sentiment are now the glue that holds the Union together, and we know what brought people together in a pre-democratic age – shared support for war and empire – is less important when the issue is what can hold people together in a democratic age.

I will show that an essential part of being British in the post-war years was a common NHS and a common welfare state and the pooling and sharing of risks and resources across four nations that made them possible.

But there is no doubt that Britain's changing status in the world has led many Scots to doubt the benefits of the Union and ask what is the value of our continued partnership. When the renowned European philosopher Jürgen Habermas writes of 'constitutional patriotism' – how people of different ethnic roots can develop a common loyalty to one state – and when others write, like David Miller on liberal nationalism, and the Canadian writer Charles Taylor on unity amidst 'deep diversity' – it may seem their words are directed at the USA or even the European Union, but they may have relevance too for the four nations of the UK.

Their starting point is that the unity of a multinational entity or a country like the USA – that includes within it people with roots in many nations – cannot depend on race or ethnicity, but has to depend on something equally powerful that is capable of binding people together. Habermas does not dispute that there is a tendency for liberal democracies to lurch into nationalism and to summon up myths of a common descent that appeal 'more strongly to their hearts and minds than the dry ideas of popular sovereignty and human rights' and thus have more traction in building unity among people. But he writes also of a patriotism that can unite people of different ethnic backgrounds around values that they share, in America's case agreement on a constitution, Bill of Rights and a belief in liberty and opportunities. Meeting the test to become an American citizen does not require a particular national, linguistic, religious or ethnic background but a willingness to commit to ideals of liberty, equality of opportunity and republicanism.

Charles Taylor has written of the difficulties of achieving unity when as in Canada – where Quebec has different religious and linguistic traditions from the rest of the country – there is a 'deep diversity'. He argues that in these circumstances multiculturalism has to give way to what he calls 'interculturalism', the official recognition of different political communities, and that only when people of different cultures are prepared to enter into a deliberative dialogue with each other is it possible to build unity from a shared commitment to liberty, equality, opportunity and republicanism.

But if I can rewrite the aphorism about patriotism attributed to the famous British nurse Edith Cavell, 'constitutional patriotism may not be enough'.[40] David Miller is sceptical about constitutional patriotism as a substitute for nationality, because it does not provide the kind of political identity that nationality provides – in particular, it does not explain why the boundaries of a political community should fall here rather than there, nor give you any sense of the historical identity of the community. Here the work of the head of the London School of Economics, Professor Craig Calhoun, is instructive. He reminds us that we are wrong to think of our cultural distinctiveness as Scots or English or Welsh as a hangover from the past. 'We must reject the notion . . . that the cultural conditions of public life including individual and collective identities,' he writes, 'are established prior to properly public discourse.' Indeed what some think of 'as a relic of an earlier order, a sort of an irrational expression, or a kind of moral mistake' is, he says, 'an essential part of people's lived reality.' And he shows us that a Habermas or Miller-style consensus on 'the rules of the game', even one that all can subscribe to, may not be compelling enough to hold diverse groups together in one state. More decisive, he suggests, is the solidarity people feel from their interaction in social networks, from functional integration – drawing on the same public services for example – and from participation in common institutions. The key question is whether solidarity – which he defines as 'the creation of concrete social relationships, of bonds of mutual commitment forged in shared action, of institutions and of shared modalities of practical action' – is sufficiently strong to be truly motivating for its members. Finally he raises doubt as to whether 'solidarity' can 'stand alone as an adequate source of belonging and mutual commitment.'[41]

Britain has of course a shared inheritance, a shared set of cultural experiences and recollections – most recently the two world wars that involved all-round sacrifice across the four nations. But when we explore what relevance the ideas of 'constitutional patriotism' or 'liberal nationalism' or 'interculturalism' have to the future of Britain, we will find, as Calhoun suggests, that Britain needs not just a shared set of values but a common contemporary culture *and* shared values *and* the solidarity that comes from sharing resources across four nations.

By charting the history of the pooling and sharing of risks and resources across the United Kingdom in Chapter 6 we find that since 1918 we have built a UK-wide welfare state and health service that has created common social and economic rights for citizens of all four nations – to a level that no other multinational grouping of nations has ever achieved – based on solidarity and sharing. There was indeed a sharp break between our pre-twentieth-century history – the minimal state – and the last hundred years with the creation and then build-up of our welfare state, making the Union of 2014 radically different from the Union of 1914.

As I will show, it was Scots, driven on by the importance they attached to Scottish values of justice and community, who argued most vehemently for the principle that resources be allocated across the United Kingdom on the basis of need and for these twentieth-century innovations – a UK-wide pension, UK-wide unemployment benefit, UK-wide healthcare rights and UK-wide minimum wages. Indeed we can trace the pressure for these rights from a Scotland whose leaders chose to abandon Scotland's own separate centuries-old social-policy institutions in favour of a British welfare state.

The act of sharing which we see in the welfare state can start from a sense of belonging but the converse may also be true – the act of sharing can contribute to a sense of belonging. While I recognise that to have mutual interests – which can easily come and go and thus be transient and temporary – is not the same as feeling a sense of solidarity, I ask whether there is evidence that the act of sharing risks and resources across the whole country now encourages a sense of belonging that can bind our four nations closer together in future years.

Chapter 7, Chapter 8 and Chapter 9 look at a possible constitutional settlement that respects the diversity of our country but is built around the sharing of risks and resources. My plan is for a constitutional expression of our idea of equality between the nations of the United Kingdom. I then look at two possible options for the economic and social future of Scotland – independence under a Scottish National Party administration as against a strong Scottish Parliament working within the United Kingdom. I ask whether it is possible to maintain both a system of pooling and sharing risks and resources while devolving power to where it is best employed. The question is whether we can combine the benefits of liberty (with a stronger democracy including a strengthened Scottish Parliament) with those of equality (continuing to share risks and resources across the United Kingdom). I believe that within Britain we can work together to guarantee the maximum devolution of power while ensuring that those in greatest need receive the greatest help, and thus retain the benefits of cultural self-determination while enjoying the advantages that flow from an interdependent partnership.

So let us recap: nationalists want to believe that political nationalism has been on the rise because people feel Scotland has to 'be the nation again'. Then they argue that political nationalism has been on the rise because Scotland wants its own national institutions. Then they say it is about self-government and the right to make our own decisions.

But Scotland has always been a nation, always had control of her own institutions, and is today more empowered in national decision-making than at any point since the Wars of Independence. Indeed the nationalists have decided that they do not want the levers of power that include managing their own currency, interest rates, inflation targets and money supply, and are even prepared to say they would accept a fiscal pact with the rest of the United Kingdom.

In other words, the secessionists are asking for what we already have – with one exception: the real change they want is to break all political links with people in the rest of Britain

In the following chapters I want to explore why that would be a mistake and would represent a fundamental misreading of this moment in history. Advocates of a Yes vote are right to say that Scotland faces a defining choice, but it is not the one they think it is. Scotland is at a moment of destiny and I think the way forward is not to break all political links with friends and family in England, but to fashion a way of rising to the unique social, cultural and economic challenges of this new global era. This is no time to think small at a time when Scotland should be thinking very big.

Scotland has shaped the world we know today, with an impact on human history far beyond that which you'd expect from a country our size. The question facing us in September is whether we will meet the profound challenges of our time by drawing on the values and talents of Scots – and our ability to combine a just and honest patriotism with a commitment to international co-operation – to once again shape not just Scotland, but Britain and the world. Globalisation is the challenge of our age: there is nowhere better placed to answer it than the nation that has always looked outwards, Scotland.

As I will show, political nationalism has been able to exploit the tensions and anxieties that have arisen from a period of dislocation and disruptive social and economic change as Scotland has moved from an industrial society to a post-industrial society, from a deeply religious nation to a secular one, and from a people who identified with an outward-looking imperial Britain to one that struggles to come to terms with Britain's new status in the world. It is unlikely to be an accident that the rise of political nationalism has coincided with the decline of our traditional industries, our traditional civic institutions and our traditional view of Britain in the world and that political nationalism was not on the rise in the eighteenth, nineteenth or for most of the twentieth century, when none of these forces were present.

So can we really say in all seriousness that the Scottish question – and the real complaint that is fuelling the demand for secession – is an absence of cultural freedom? Can we really say in all seriousness that the Scottish question is the suppression, or even the assimilation, of once-great Scottish national institutions? And can we really say that the Scottish question is Britain's unwillingness to share power with Scotland? Or is the actual Scottish question – and perhaps the biggest complaint – not alienating, dislocating industrial, economic and social change, for which the demand for a separate state has become a proxy for a larger set of social, economic and cultural questions which nationalism is seeking to answer not with genuine society-wide change, but with constitutional reform?

Like most advanced industrial countries Scotland today faces huge global challenges – industrial, economic, social and cultural – as globalisation directly impacts on our lives. What we produce and consume, how we enjoy our leisure and interact with each other not least through social media, and where we travel are all intimately affected by our increased interdependence – by the global flows of capital, the global sourcing of goods and services and our ability to communicate instantaneously with people across the world. Not surprisingly what we believe and think important – our norms, values, ideologies and traditions – are constantly being challenged. Traditional social structures, especially those based on class and religion, are under pressure. There is a strong sense too that our identity is not what others ascribe to us but what we choose for ourselves.

For people who feel threatened by the precariousness of their employment and by the increased cultural diversity in their country, it has meant an escalating sense of insecurity and vulnerability, even a sense of powerlessness and cultural dislocation.

All of these factors, taken together, mean the nationalists are right to identify this moment as a critical moment of decision for the people of Scotland. It is what we might call a 'hinge of history'. But the enormity of the challenges we face calls us to meet this moment with the same creativity and courage with which Scotland has faced her previous decisive moments.

Scotland's destiny has never been to take the easy answer. When we have needed to fight, we fought. When we have needed to debate, we debated. And when we have needed to devise completely new ways of doing things in the interests of our people, that is the challenge to which Scots have risen.

I have said we have always been an exceptional nation as one of the first countries to industrialise and a driver of the British Empire. We were also explorers, inventors and missionaries who travelled to the ends of the earth. And we became, as I will show, later the leading advocates of a twentieth-century innovation, the British welfare state. We are one of the first countries to feel the pressure of being buffeted by global forces and we are now at the very sharp end of debates about the shape and the richness of identities in the post-imperial, globalised world. But that also gives us a special responsibility to pioneer new ways of dealing with the fallout from globalisation, and we will best do so not by abandoning but by drawing on our experience of how interdependent nations can work together.

The vast changes in Scottish society may lead some in response to contemplate breaking up Britain, but I believe the bigger and more defining question is how Scotland can secure the benefits of global change. For when we talk of seeking equality between the nations of the UK do we not also mean receiving a fair share of the gains from globalisation? Independence may be a big idea. But for nations to share risks and resources in an interdependent world while also securing and developing what we cherish about our national identity is an even bigger idea – and is the shape of the world to come.

CHAPTER 1

Who Are the Scots?

Every family has a story to tell about the way their lives and their views and values were shaped. This is mine.

I can trace my ancestors back to the time of the Union and the time when Scottish records started to be kept. Before he died at the age of eighty-four in 1998, my father – drawing on a note that had been handed to him by his own father – traced our family's story. Mine is one of hundreds of thousands of Scottish families who have benefited from the brilliant and conscientious way that Scottish parish registrars recorded births, marriages and deaths over centuries. My father was able to track, generation by generation, the local connections our family has had, not just to Fife but to specific villages and towns: Lochore, Ballingry, Lochgelly, Cowdenbeath, and Auchterderran.

Today my constituency of Kirkcaldy and Cowdenbeath includes not only all the towns and villages where my grandfather, grandmother, and their families grew up but also Kirkcaldy, where my father was a minister in the 1950s and 1960s and where I grew up and attended school.

There are plenty of MPs doing amazing work for the people that they represent, whether that is their 'home' seat or not. But I can't deny that it gives me special pride to represent my school friends in parliament and to speak on behalf of the community that made and raised me.

I can track my family's history through all the 300 years of the Union, starting with the civil wars and the violent religious struggles of the first years of the Union and then through the dramatic and explosive sequence of changes which transformed a subsistence rural economy into commercial agriculture, forced a high proportion of Scots off the land, created the turbulence and often chaos of the world's first Industrial Revolution and then saw the rise and fall of world-beating iron, steel, coal and textile industries.

This economic revolution – and, alongside it, the all-pervasive influence of religion – were the two great forces at work in the first two centuries of Union. The transformation of Scotland from a rural backwater to an industrial powerhouse represented perhaps a bigger change than that undergone by any country during that period. Rapid industrialisation and urbanisation was combined with one of the greatest haemorrhages of people through emigration on earth. It is said that, person for person, more Scots emigrated than the Irish, the Poles and the Italians and that there are now forty million people of Scots descent round the world. But as other Scots scattered – to North America, Australia and of course England – the Browns of Fife dug in.[1]

Like so many other families, they played their small part in assisting the transition from a nation of small plots of land that were part of big landed estates through to the era of land 'improvement' and new farming techniques. We were here still as Fife made the next transition – from farming to mining – and throughout the rise and fall of Fife's industry. For each of the decades and centuries the Browns have been Fifers, the biggest issue facing Fife has always been the search for work. While my ancestors were, in the early to mid-nineteenth century, labourers in this agricultural revolution that reclaimed, improved and intensified the cultivation of the land, Fife's most successful crops being wheat and barley, much of the land they worked was, like most Scottish land, unproductive, difficult to improve and missed out on mechanisation. Even now, as our national historian T. C. Smout tells us, two-thirds of Scottish land is 'rough grazing' and arable farming 'a minority pursuit'. Today around two-thirds of farm income is from livestock.[2] But while Fife was a successful outlier bucking these trends, a lot of Fife's land was eventually eaten up as coal mining took over. The land dominated by the farm became the land dominated by the pit. Fife coal – along with that of Lanarkshire and Ayrshire – fuelled the factories, the shipyards and the textile mills of Scotland's industrial belt and in Fife's case an even bigger export trade from local ports.

During the pre- and post-Union decades, lowland Scotland had no peasant class endowed with any legal rights of ownership of land. Instead there was a hierarchy of status – the landowners at the top, followed by the tenant farmers, then the 'cottars' (who by 1850 had been pushed out in the rush to modernise), then the servants and the labourers who often had six-month contracts but who, if able-bodied but out of work, were badly treated by the Poor Law.

The Browns started as farm labourers, rising to become tenant farmers who rented 200 acres or so from the aristocratic land-owner. A tenancy was not as secure as it might have looked: land-owners had the right to remove tenants after what was normally a ten-year lease and that gave them the power to impose, in Tom Devine's words, 'the firm hand of proprietorial authority'.[3]

In the 1700s the Browns were poor in a Scotland where very few were wealthy. They lived at Inchgall Mill in Lochore, on a farmstead which is a ruin today. It was a farm built around the old Lochore Castle, which dates back to the time of the Picts and the Romans. Inchgall's characteristics were briefly recorded in the history books when the famous Scottish writer Sir Walter Scott paid a visit.

Like most families of the time, the Browns had to move to

where the work was. So around 1800 my branch of the Brown family moved from Inchgall Mill to land just outside the town of Lochgelly. My great-great-grandfather, Alexander Brown, took over the tenancy of the East Lochhead farm and later, as the family expanded and needed more land to farm, his brother John moved to take over the tenancy of Wester Lochhead.

While at Lochhead, much of the land that had previously been written off as swamp was intensively drained and reclaimed. The improvement of farms happened faster in Fife than almost anywhere else in Scotland. As it proceeded apace, land ownership became more concentrated: by the 1870s, just 1,500 people owned 90 per cent of the land of Scotland. It also meant fewer tenants and labourers were needed, so times got even tougher for the Browns.

My great-grandfather John Brown made the next move, to the neighbouring farm at Brigghills, a transfer forced upon the family by a change in their circumstances. In the midst of all this uncertainty, my great-grandfather's father-in-law had persuaded him to lend him money to take on a run-down tenancy at Brigghills. As my grandfather recorded in a written note, the Brigghills farm was 'in such a state that it could not grow crops of any kind'. He was unable to make it profitable and so my great-grandfather was faced with a choice: either lose all the savings they had poured into it, or give up his own tenancy and take over the running of Brigghills. He chose the latter and it was there that my paternal grandfather was born in 1878.

Just as John Brown was trying to work out how to repair Brigghills after many years of neglect, there was the fall-out from a big spike in the cost of renewing long-term leases and then a national farming crisis caused by the collapse in potato prices. The family was about to be caught between their inheritance – the poor state of their new farm – and the future, the pressure to cede much of the land to coal mining.

The mines had already taken over as a larger employer than

farming before 1914. Pit employment reached a peak of 30,000 just after the First World War, with three or four times as many people working there as on the land.[4]

LEAVING THE LAND

The fate of my grandfather, born in 1878, and that of his brothers and sisters, is a fair illustration of what happened to many farming communities as the twentieth century got under way. All went to school in Auchterderran from the time they moved to Brigghills in 1878 to the early 1890s. They left school as early as they could – at fourteen – to help work the land. My great-grandparents' first child, Janet, stayed on the farm and died unmarried in 1939. Next were John and Alexander. When they were old enough, both left for Edinburgh. Alexander became a writer and his book of poems on Fife was published before he died tragically in a tram accident in Edinburgh in 1920. The last born, James, was to die an infant. The second sister, Lizzie, married another farmer nearby, whose family had been on the Wester Coluhally farm for centuries. And that left the three youngest sons – my grandfather and his two younger brothers, David and George – struggling to find enough work to keep them on a farm already diminished in size and output by mine workings.

The start of the twentieth century brought perhaps the biggest change – one that was to decide Brigghills' future – with the announcement that the Lochgelly Iron & Coal Company intended to sink a new larger pit to the east of the town. Such was the scale of the project that the nearby Eliza Pit would now be utilised as an emergency shaft. The new colliery was located at the entrance to my grandfather's farm, at the foot of the Eliza Brae, close to the River Ore and the railway line, and less than a mile from its large neighbour to the east, the Bowhill Colliery. By 1909 that Brigghills pit alone employed 1,400 men, working two shifts, growing to 1,700 in 1912. The collection of nearby pits together employed over 5,000 men.[5]

Villages expanded and new towns like Cowdenbeath – named by some 'the Chicago of Fife' – sprang up to house hundreds of immigrant workers. Fife pits employed 30,000 miners out of Scotland's 140,000 and Britain's 1.5 million. By the outbreak of war, Fife produced 10 million of Scotland's 40 million and Britain's 300 million annual tonnage. Some of Fife's coal stayed in Scotland, but much was exported to Germany, Russia, France and Scandinavia.[6]

The oldest relatives I remember meeting – my father's father, and my two great-uncles – were all born at Brigghills Farm, but my grandfather was not to remain there. For a brief moment he thought he was in luck: in his early thirties, he was promised by his uncle that the lease of the nearby Little Raith Farm would be transferred to him when it was renewed with the Wemyss estate in November 1911. At that time most Fife men didn't marry until thirty or so. They waited because they had little security in their work and because they did not want to fall victim to a Poor Law that offered, at best, only limited and temporary payments to unemployed men. So, on the basis of the promised tenancy, my grandfather felt he could safely marry Rachel Mavor at Easter Lochhead in September 1910, but sadly the estate owner passed the tenancy to someone else when it came up for review.

My grandfather, newly married, went in search of work. He spent the next twenty years moving around Fife. First he went to Lochhead to work as a shepherd and then he went to New Gilston, arriving there only days before my father was born in October 1914. This was just a few months after the outbreak of the First World War and my grandfather had to decide whether to enlist. His cousin, who had trained to be a carpenter, joined up and became one of thousands of men from the east of Scotland who tragically lost their lives in battle. But my grandfather's work was listed as essential for the war effort and so he stayed behind on the farms. He had gone to New Gilston on the promise that the land – which, at that point, was not enclosed – would be fenced off for sheep: without fencing it was impossible to make sheep farming profitable. When the landowner reneged on the promise, my grandfather was forced to move again, this time to act as shepherd to Thomas Webster at a nearby farm called Nisbetfield.

But no labourer's job was ever secure for long. In the fast-changing circumstances of the immediate post-war months, Thomas Webster gave up the tenancy and the family had to move to yet another farm, near Pitlessie. My grandfather's work now was as a shepherd on the Rankeillor estate. It was owned by the second Sir Michael Nairn, the son of the successful chairman of the famous Kirkcaldy linoleum company who had been knighted in 1905. As we shall see, this was a family that was known for its philanthropy as well as the paternalistic way it ran both their famous linoleum factories and their recently acquired estates.

The post-war years were difficult for everyone. Unemployment rose dramatically. Poverty levels were so high in Fife that parish councils petitioned the government to take responsibility for unemployment relief. Work was highly insecure then, and my grandfather had already lost both work and the tied accommodation that went with it many times. So in 1928 he used the small savings he had built up to buy his own house for the first time and the family of three moved into the village of Kingskettle.

It was in the same decade that an uncle of my father's left the Brigghills tenancy the family had occupied for more than fifty years for good. By 1936 all members of the family had moved out of farming in the Lochgelly area, after more than 200 years there. For my family, as for so many, the only connection to the land we once farmed is handed-down memories.

With my grandfather without full-time work for much of his later life and with most of the family pushed off the land, the inter-war years that caused so many to emigrate were difficult for the Browns. Scotland, unlike England, did not experience a new Industrial Revolution in the first half of the twentieth century. England generated 500,000 jobs by 1933 in cars, electronics, aircraft, and even bicycles. Not least because we had no domestic market for these new goods, Scotland had only 16,500 new jobs spread across all these new industries.[7]

The next fifty years saw the collapse of all Fife's biggest industries – mining, linen and linoleum. Some people were lucky to get on through education. My father was the first in our extended family to go to university, to St Andrews, where he matriculated during the Great Depression to study Divinity. Back then a fraction of young Scots got the chance of university. My father's opportunity, as he acknowledged, was only made possible by a string of teachers who invested in him as his family moved around Fife and by a repayable loan from Fife County Council.

My paternal grandmother's family came from Dysart near Kirkcaldy. My grandmother's father, who ran a successful building firm, not only helped rebuild Dysart Tolbooth in the 1880s but the Dysart harbour itself. When her mother died and her father remarried, my grandmother took work as a housekeeper in England before she married my grandfather in 1910. Dysart's port thrived as one of those exporting coal from Fife but when it was challenged by a new Methil port, created by the Wemyss estate, Dysart Council went bankrupt trying to rebuild a harbour able to compete with Wemyss and other harbours like nearby Burntisland. In the end the near bankrupt council was forced to amalgamate with Kirkcaldy.

My mother was raised in a village near Aberdeen, the youngest of three children. Like so many others, her life was transformed by the Second World War. Sent to London to play a very minor part in the code-breaking operations, she became an army sergeant who missed her chance to go to university. After she met my father through her closest friend, she married in 1947 and soon I was the second of three children born in 1948, 1951 and

1956. My father's work as a minister took him first to Glasgow before the war, then to wartime Dunoon, then back to the same industrial parish in Glasgow before coming to Kirkcaldy, near where his father lived. And so the childhood I remember was in Kirkcaldy, where I lived from the age of three.

THE CHARACTER OF KIRKCALDY

The Kirkcaldy of the 1950s was a manufacturing and coal-mining town with a rural hinterland. It was by then a town of 50,000 people, but it was still a close-knit community. It was famous as the home of linoleum, but also as the birthplace of the economist Adam Smith. He would not, in my view, have written *The Wealth of Nations* – the argument that trade unlocks growth and prosperity – if he had not spent his youth looking out from the High Street where he lived onto a two-mile promenade and a port full of ships taking Kirkcaldy produce around the world.

I grew up alongside school friends who were the sons and daughters of a workforce that still relied on those same Scottish connections to the wider world to shift their coal, their textiles, their linoleum, their iron, their steel and their ships. And it was a community in which the ties of solidarity were bound tightly – ties created during the struggle of the General Strike and later by the resistance to pit closures in the 1980s. Perhaps the writer who gets closest to the heart of what it is like growing up in an industrial community – this time in Ayrshire – is William McIlvanney. In *Docherty*, McIlvanney does not ignore the tensions, the tragedies and the violence of life, but he also writes of the bonds between miners who work deep underground, sharing risks from which no one could opt out. Amidst what he calls a 'decaying industrialism', he says that 'so little was owned, sharing became a precautionary reflex'.[8]

The history of Fife, like that of most mining communities, is also the story of dignity in response to regular industrial disasters. I recall how in Kirkcaldy in 1973 five men died underground at Seafield Pit despite massive, indeed weeks-long, efforts in which fellow miners put themselves at risk in a vain attempt to find and rescue them. McIlvanney writes movingly of people whose 'grim struggle to survive' did not lead to everyone for himself, but to communities closing ranks to meet the needs of the weakest of their number.[9]

Kirkcaldy in those days was not just a mining town but also a textiles town. The main factory, Nairns, was led by a paternalistic employer who, unusually for the times, employed a large proportion of women and provided his workers with housing and company-led entertainment and leisure. When the founder of the firm, Sir Michael Nairn, obtained his knighthood in 1905, he invited all employees to a celebration at his Fife country estate – one where my grandfather was later employed as a shepherd – and there is a note of his thank-you letter, written in a patrician and almost condescending tone, saying that while he had expected them to be rowdy and cause damage to his property he had been pleasantly surprised by their good behaviour.[10]

So when I was at school I felt myself to be part of one settled community where the adults worked and worshipped together, while kids played football on what was called Volunteers' Green (where First World War would-be army recruits had assembled to sign up for service) and at the magnificent Beveridge Park. Private schools were a world apart for us: you could count the kids in Kirkcaldy who went to private school on a few hands. It is perhaps too much to say that we were not aware of the differences in income and circumstances between us but we – more or less – joined the same youth clubs and sports teams whether our parents were on the factory floor or in the manager's office (or, in my case, the manse).

So I grew up shaped by my family's background, by the work my ancestors did, by the aspirations they had for their children, by the friendships I made and by the culture we were all born into. And for me the politics of place has never presented the agonising identity crisis that seems to consume Scottish politics today. The farms of Fife sustained my family for generations and the community of Kirkcaldy made me the person I am today. But my abiding attachment to this place and its people does not preclude other identities or loyalties. In fact, I believe it is precisely what enables them, because strong roots give you confidence to grow.

TELLING SCOTLAND'S STORY

But, strangely enough, I missed out on a formal education in the Scottish history I am discussing. In most accounts, Scottish history stopped at 1707 anyway, but for me it was never really taught at all. It was not on the curriculum at my school or in many others at the time. Indeed, as recorded by the writer Kenneth Roy, the Scottish High Court judge Lord Cooper delivered one of his magisterial rebukes when he said of Scottish education that 'it was calculated to condition the Scottish mind to turn instinctively towards London . . . The exclusion from the curriculum of all but a tokenistic smattering of Scottish history, a policy pursued by governments of both political persuasions, could not have been other than wilful . . . in denying children an adequate knowledge of their own culture and identity, it asserted the relative insignificance . . . of Scotland.'[11]

I was part of what one writer, Marinell Ash, called 'the strange death of Scottish history' – a knowledge of history that used to be the mark of the broadly educated Scotsman had come instead, she argued, to be seen as a mark of a narrow parochialism most wanted to abandon. I was an unwitting victim of what the prominent philosopher George Davie called Scotland's loss of 'intellectual nerve' and thus one of those thousands of history students whom another historian, Bruce Lenman, was thinking of when he said that the teaching of Scottish history had been ignored by the whole education system since 1850. In the decade after the Second World War, my history department at Edinburgh University had insisted on teaching British history students an additional course on Scottish history, but that had died out long before I arrived in 1967. Because we were viewed as a stateless nation that did not fit the traditional way of teaching history – through kings and governments – the study of Scotland's past had been marginalised into what some called 'a backwater' and what others called a dead end. One history professor, quoted by Tom Devine, remarked that we learned more about the history of Yorkshire than of Scotland.[12] The seminal works which broke the century of neglect – R. H. Campbell's *Scotland since 1707*, published in 1965, William Ferguson's *Scotland: 1689 to the Present Day*, published in 1968, and T. C. Smout's *A History of the Scottish People 1560–1830*, published in 1969, were just starting to have an impact during my undergraduate years but not quickly enough to inform the general teaching of history. So my entry into an understanding of Scottish history was not through formal courses, but through a general interest in the history of social and economic conditions in the nineteenth and twentieth centuries, which eventually draw me into a study of what had been happening in Scotland.

Thus for the most part I learned about Scotland outside the classroom. And while I missed out on much of the romantic phase of Scottish history writing – the Nigel Tranter-esque period – I and others have been fortunate that recently, thanks to the brilliance of historians like Tom Devine, T. C. Smout and Colin Kidd, a school of Scottish history has emerged that is serious, highly regarded and profound. It is because of their work that Scotland has moved on from myth-making about past glories to being more honest about our historical successes and failures. Their scholarship has put much talked-about events in our history in their proper context, showing, for example, that there is no unbroken line of Scottish aggression against England and explaining how important moments – like victory at Bannockburn in 1314 and defeat at Flodden in 1513 – relate to the stages of our historical development. One of my teachers was the brilliant Scottish history professor T. C. Smout, whose work on Scottish economic history revolutionised its study. And he and Devine (whom I was fortunate to consult for advice as a student more than forty years ago) and more recently Colin Kidd, Linda Colley and a school of labour historians led by Ian MacDougall have given Scotland our own history, the story of a nation that is much more than the 'adjunct' of Britain that in too many historical overviews it had become.

I cite these authors liberally in the chapters to follow because I believe their school of research has truly profound implications for our sense of ourselves as we approach the referendum and the next stage of our history. As perceptive critic Marc Lambert suggests, 'if Scotland is really to construct a healthy 21st century identity, honest history is required wherein the general public discourse of and in Scotland is the acknowledgement that Scots have spilt far more blood in internecine conflict than (in fighting) with the English'. For him an honest accounting must involve 'the Scot who fought against Scot at Culloden; the Scot who cleared the land; the Glasgow merchants of the Industrial Revolution and empire who regarded the workers, often Gaels who peopled their factories, as less than human; as beasts'.[13]

I am also sympathetic to his claim 'that the dictates of class have played a far greater role in Scottish sorrow than invaders'.[14] That is not, of course, to say that class identity and interest are the only animating forces of history. Other forms of communal identity – including religion, culture and nationhood itself – are of profound importance. But I am pleased that the teaching of Scottish history has now evolved beyond either exclusively unionist or exclusively nationalist world-views to allow us to reach a more rounded sense of ourselves.

THE CALEDONIAN CANON

If I lost out at school on an understanding of Scottish history, my sense of identity was enhanced by my own reading of Scottish literature. Scotland has great painters like the Colourists, many of whose works are in my local Kirkcaldy Library, Art Gallery and Museum a few hundred yards from where I grew up. There is a wonderful set of Charles Rennie Mackintosh murals only recently discovered in the nearby Dysart church. I have watched the growth and then the crises of Scottish Opera and watched the renaissance of the Scottish Ballet, the Royal Scottish National Orchestra, the Scottish Chamber Orchestra, the National Theatre of Scotland and the National Galleries of Scotland.

Throughout my life I have been interested in Scottish film from the early films of John Grierson to the pioneering work led by Lynda Myles at the Edinburgh Film Festival where, briefly, I was a member of its board. But it is the written word – more than all the other forms of culture – that I believe marks Scotland out most of all for its distinctiveness.

The Reformation, of course, encouraged ordinary people to learn to read the Bible and so literacy mattered more in Scotland than elsewhere. But I knew little of our pre-Reformation culture and art until recently when I read Andrea Thomas's *Glory and Honour: The Renaissance in Scotland*. Her account tells us about the poetry of Dunbar and Lindsay in the Renaissance courts of James IV and V but also about the 'jewellery, tapestries, panel paintings, buildings, gardens, courtly manners or pageantry, and books' that defy attempts to categorise early Scottish art and culture as philistine. During the Reformation many paintings and sculptures were destroyed in an attempt, it has been said, to 'wipe the cultural slate clean in a bonfire of vanities that has yet to be rivalled'. We know that we lost a great pre-Reformation Catholic-led inheritance, that many scores of music were burnt, and indeed that Thomas Wode, a composer contemporary, feared that 'music shall perish in this land utterly'. So it is literature alone that survived the religious wars and to this day gives Scots the most continuous source of stories about ourselves.[15]

The cultural writer Liam McIlvanney describes Scottish novelists as our 'unacknowledged legislators' and he is right that it is the most famous literary quotations that you can find chiselled into the walls of the Scottish Parliament for ever. But he is right in another way too: if you want to know what Scotland is like you need to understand the written word, our prose and poetry – and indeed the best of it.[16]

For while there has been a recent tendency to favour schools introducing pupils to the most contemporary and what is sometimes called the most 'culturally relevant' literature, nothing can surpass students being challenged by an early introduction to the highest-quality literary works. As I will suggest later, it was never a part of the Scottish tradition in education to dumb down or to patronise people by playing to the lowest common denominator. But nor is there just one uniform story being told in Scottish literature. As the poet Tom Leonard puts it, 'any society is a society in conflict and any anthology of the society's poetry that does not reflect this is a lie'.[17] After all, Hugh MacDiarmid said the job of the poet was to 'aye be whaur extremes meet'.[18]

My own view is that one of the most interesting 'extremes' and points of conflict in the Scottish psyche is between the particular and the universal. As a schoolboy the Scottish literature I was encouraged to read was not only the best but usually the most outward-looking. We were encouraged to be proud that the writers were Scottish, but proud most of all of how broadly those Scottish eyes scanned the world. Of course I devoured *Kidnapped*, *Treasure Island*, *Catriona* and the other books of Robert Louis

Stevenson, and watched all the films and TV series based on them that were shown as I grew up. I saw Stevenson as a cosmopolitan Scot who spent most of his life outside Scotland and who opened up the world to us through his books.

Burns was taught as part of our courses in English literature and then as a separate course when I was eleven. He came across not as a nationalist, but as an internationalist. I know how much effort has gone into making Burns the former: how on first crossing the River Tweed into England Burns is said to have shouted back to Scotland the last two verses of 'The Cotter's Saturday Night', beginning 'O Scotia, my dear, my native soil', seen by some as a prayer for Scotland's future. Of course Burns also wrote that the story of William Wallace 'poured a Scottish prejudice into my veins which will boil along there till the flood-gates of life shut in eternal rest', and he is also said to have uttered 'a fervent prayer for Old Caledonia' as he visited Bannockburn. The author of 'Scots Wha Hae', his connection to organised nationalism is asserted by his support for the pro-democracy group the Scottish Friends of the People, led by Thomas Muir.[19]

But the Burns I learned about at school was no narrow nationalist. Of course it matters little now that Burns used the pen name 'A Briton', even if it was employed in reference to a threat of British republicanism now mostly forgotten, or that he spent his working life in the employ of the Union. But we can see in 'A Man's A Man For A' That' the soul of an internationalist and an egalitarian, someone whose politics were at least as influenced by solidarity as by Scottishness. Whatever the truth, that is how we were taught to see him and I grew up believing that a love of Scotland's national poet was not at odds with being part of Britain.

One thing did strike me, though, growing up reading Scottish books. Just as Scotland had no Booth or Rowntree to chart in factual detail the condition of the Scottish working class, so too for almost all of the period of industrialisation we had none of the chroniclers that can be found in the fiction of England. We had neither a Scottish Dickens exposing the horrors of industrial society nor a Scottish Robert Tressell explaining the condition of the new working class, but instead novels not of urban squalor but of small town and rural life. Even John Buchan, author of *The Thirty-Nine Steps* and often regarded as a Kailyard author himself, was moved to criticise the narrow parochial view of Scotland spread by these writers in strong contrast to 'the nature of the real Scotland'.

Things changed as I was leaving school. At that point I was exposed to a different kind of twentieth-century literature, from books set in the inter-war years like *No Mean City* to the classic *Sunset Song* by Lewis Grassic Gibbon, and more contemporaneously the work of Archie Hind (whose *The Dear Green Place* is itself the story of thwarted aspiration) and much later James Kelman, Alan Warner, Janice Galloway, A. L. Kennedy, and Irvine Welsh's *Trainspotting* – as well as some of the great modern poets who are part of an exciting revival. Having met William McIlvanney just after his brilliant *Docherty* was published I marvelled at his ability to express what it was like growing up in the twentieth century in an industrial society; his novels always try to get to the heart of what it is to be human. I met the Scottish theatre group 7:84, and enjoyed working with the great writer John McGrath. I also met Hugh MacDiarmid (whose article on aesthetics I was not able to print in the *Red Paper on Scotland*, a collection of essays on Scotland's future that I edited in 1975). I found that in poems like 'Glasgow, 1960' and 'Edinburgh', MacDiarmid was at his best when challenging us never to accept the second rate and urging us on to test ourselves and our potential to the limit.

Running in parallel to this attraction to Scottish fiction was an interest in the writings of the Scottish Enlightenment, from the philosophical works of Smith and Hume right through to the interpretative studies of writers like George Davie with his book

The Democratic Intellect and more recently Nick Phillipson's brilliant work on Adam Smith.

I found that the greatest of these philosophical writers started from their experience of Scotland. As I said earlier, Smith was inspired in writing *The Wealth of Nations* by Scottish seafarers, but he did not write a book purely about or for Scots. Instead Scotland was a springboard from which he explored and analysed universal truths. All the great Scottish writers I read – whether of poetry, prose or philosophy – sought change not only because injustice offended Scottish sensibilities and would hurt the Scottish people, but because they believed the injustices they exposed offended values that mattered for everyone everywhere. It is this broad expansive view of the world and our place in it that has made stateless Scotland always seem bigger than any similar nation: it was as if they were telling us that our ideas were so powerful and we stood so tall that we never needed the trappings of an independent state.

The differences between Scotland and England were, however, apparent in even the most simple of events and activities. While England was on holiday on Christmas Day, much of Scotland was at work. The first day of the New Year and the night before, Hogmanay, was Scotland's time for its greatest celebration. Scottish newspapers were published on Christmas Day when the English printing presses fell silent, but on the first day of the new year Scots had only English newspapers to read. In our early years, my brothers and I had to wear kilts on special occasions. Ironically, some of the chief agents in the growing popularity of Scottish national dress and the Burns Supper in the nineteenth and twentieth centuries were British institutions, notably the monarchy under King George IV and Queen Victoria. But they alone could not have made the difference: in most cases the Scottish institutions we supported were ours and of our own choosing, institutions controlled by us and impervious to interference from outside.

But the whole story of my Scotland could not be told without recognising the importance of one other part of our wider culture: sport. Playing rugby for my school team, I was a regular visitor as a pupil and then later as a student to the Scottish rugby internationals at Murrayfield, including as an angry protester when sadly Scotland played the then apartheid South Africa.

Having run in the Scottish schoolboy championships I enjoyed athletics, where the story of Eric Liddell was an inspiration and we also could celebrate the contemporary success of champions like Alan Wells and Liz McColgan. I played tennis for Kirkcaldy's junior team against all the Edinburgh clubs. But football was always my greatest sporting passion and, I believe, the dominant sporting obsession of Scotland.

The first Scottish football team, Queen's Park, came in 1867; the first Scotland v England match, in 1872; and the formation of the Scottish FA with eight teams, in 1873. So football has been played as a national sport for almost 150 years now. And it has been so important to me personally that I tend to remember dates from my early life as a sequence of sporting moments: Scotland v England 1967, 3–2 with Jim Baxter taunting his opponents; the Lisbon Lions in '67; Rangers' victory over Barcelona in '72; the 1978 Gemmill goal after the hype and then the national disaster of the World Cup in Argentina; the David Narey 'toe-poke' (I was there) against Brazil in 1982 in Spain; and Aberdeen in Gothenburg in '83.

I remember well the great Scottish football commentator Bob Crampsey reminding us that for a time – with six first-division football teams – Glasgow could make a very plausible claim to be regarded as the football capital of the world. And William McIlvanney came closest to describing what I and others felt during the build-up to and in the ritual of the annual Wembley Scotland v England international: what may have seemed a mundane encounter for the English seemed more like a matter of life and death for Scotland, the match becoming a show of strength on the part, it seemed, of the whole country, with far too much invested in the outcome of the event.

As I grew up the preparations for – and then the emotional roller-coaster of – the annual Scotland v England match seemed to bring out – more than tartans, kilts, bagpipes or other forms of culture could ever do – just how strongly we felt our Scottishness. The 1961 international is etched on my mind as one of my earliest recollections of a big national spectacle: after an English goal in the seventh minute we conceded another eight while only scoring three. I remember goal after goal as I listened on the radio to the national humiliation being visited upon us. But the emotion of the 1961 defeat was such – and the humiliation so widely felt – that Scottish goalkeeper Frank Haffey emigrated to Australia. Thirty years later, it is said, Denis Law, then visiting Australia, was asked by Haffey if it was safe to come back, and Law responded that it was not.

It is the memory of 1961 that made 1967's 3–2 victory over England, the year after the same England team had won the World Cup, seem as though we had beaten the world.

The 1966 World Cup was seen by us as little more than the qualifying tournament: the Scotland v England match, we felt, was the real and final decider of who was best. But there were subsequent defeats: 5–1 to England in 1975 and then (I was there at Wembley as a supporter) in 1996 as Gary McAllister missed a penalty. The McAllister miss became one of the great 'what if?'s of Scottish history. I used to ask what if James VI had stayed in Scotland in 1603 and insisted on the capital of Britain being Edinburgh. I now asked – what if McAllister had scored? How far could we have progressed in Euro 96?

Football was so important to our sense of ourselves that the way we covered it on radio, TV and in the newspapers often mattered as much as the matches themselves. As TV grew in popularity, our fledgling TV sports programmes became national institutions in their own right. I started a Saturday night as a schoolboy listening to *Sports Report* at 6.30 p.m. after my father had bought my brothers and me at least two of the four Saturday evening sports papers sold in Kirkcaldy. Later as I grew up I watched *Sportsreel* – later *Sportscene* – and STV's *Scotsport* became one of the biggest events of the week.

I used to joke that if, as has often been unfairly said, English national identity was forged on the playing fields of Eton, then Scottish national identity flourished on the fields of Hampden Park and Wembley. I have followed Scotland teams everywhere, including to Spain, France and Italy for World Cup matches. What our players and fans did off the field in football could make us grimace – such as the follies of my Kirkcaldy compatriot Willie Johnston with the tartan army in 1978. But what we did off-field in football could also make us proud, like Celtic following up its victory in the European Cup in 1967 with a principled stance in 1968, refusing to play Ferencváros of Hungary, after the Hungarian government had been a complicit partner in the Warsaw Pact invasion of Czechoslovakia days earlier.

A recent study by British Future asked 'who will you support in the World Cup 2014?'. Around 40 per cent of Scots said they won't watch and 20 per cent of Scots said they will be neutral. But 10 per cent said they will support a team other than England and 15 per cent said they'd back England's opponents. Only 13 per cent of Scots say they will support England.[20] It suggests that in competitive sport – an endeavour which inevitably really *is* a zero-sum game – too much weight is put on thinking that Scotland's success comes at someone else's expense, and that expense should be paid down south by preference.

So sport bore a huge part of the burden of expressing what it was to be Scottish – perhaps too big a burden. As the football writer Hugh Keevins put it, 'football was there to enrich our lives, not to take the place of them'.[21]

If sport is one defining difference, however, we have known we were different, more than anything else, because of our separate religious institutions. For years the work of Knox and the story of the Covenanters – hunted down by their accusers – were as important to the national identity of Scotland as the heroic exploits of Wallace and Bruce. So it was in the church, above all else, that a non-political nationalism could be found. Colin Kidd makes the point best when he notes that, throughout most of our post-Union history, religion has been far more important to the day-to-day life of most Scots than politics.[22]

If the economic transformation of Scotland and the harsh working environment dictated the living conditions of Scots, it was religion that did most to determine our views and culture. It is simply impossible to understand the Scottish mind without first getting to grips with both Calvinism and Catholicism. I have perhaps a keener sense of this than others of my generation: from an early age I attended church twice on a Sunday and Sunday school too and our life as a family was built around my parents' commitments to the church and, through the church which was at the heart of the town, the community. I believe even those Scots brought up outside the Church are still influenced by its world-view. Calvinist notions of hard work, self-discipline and mutual obligation run deep in Scottish society, whether we recognise their theological inspiration or not.

I believe too that our Catholicism is also very Scottish. There is a significant Scottish pre-Reformation tradition that includes a strong commitment to supporting education and social engagement and is a defining feature of our ideas of civic society which became prominent in the eighteenth-century Enlightenment.

For both of these great Scottish religious traditions, government control of the Church is anathema. Both believe that the role of the Church is to speak truth to power, not to succumb to it. Again I can tell the story best through the experience of my ancestors. Their concern, it appears, was a common one of the time: it was not simply a demand that they have the freedom to practise their religion: it was an insistence that, as they discharged their inescapable duty to follow their conscience, the state should have no role whatsoever. The very act of standing up for their right to exercise their duty to their faith, free from state control, free from the influence of the establishment, free from any intermediary, led to regular secessionist movements from the established Church. There was indeed a pattern in an overly zealous country – a cycle through which sects that had once broken free from a Church deemed too close to the state were then accused of becoming too close to power themselves and they, in turn, became candidates for splitting into different breakaway movements.

THE SECESSIONIST BROWNS

The first post-Union religious rebellion came when the Union settlement, which contained guarantees of freedom for the Church, was modified by the Patronage Act of 1712. Under this Act, local lay patrons, gentry and landowners could appoint ministers in parishes, and by overruling the parishioners they seemed to break the guarantees of an independent self-governing lay-dominated Presbyterian Church. So this began what Kidd calls 'the long-running Scottish critique of the British constitution, and of Parliamentary sovereignty in particular, as a usurpation by the state upon the privileges of the Scottish Kirk'.[23]

After what was called an Associate Synod was founded in 1734 at Gurney Bridge in Fife, with the ideal of upholding the freedom to worship and doing missionary work with the poor, a secession Church emerged which itself eventually split into several groups: the Burghers and Anti-Burghers, the Auld Lichts and New Lichts and the Relief Kirk.

I believe that my grandfather's great-great-grandparents were part of the Lochgelly (Burgher) Associate congregation, which was formed in 1763, amassed its own funds and then in 1764 built its own church in Mid Street in the now expanding town of Lochgelly – the central market town for the area. It ordained its first minister in 1767. So even before the Great Disruption in 1843, when around two-fifths of Scottish ministers and their congregations left the Kirk to form the Free Church of Scotland, there were secessionist groups. In fact Devine estimates that before 1843 around a third of the members of the Church of Scotland had already seceded.[24]

And my ancestors were among those families swept along as secessions were followed by reunifications and then by further secessions. Indeed in 1820 the New Licht wings of both the Burghers and Anti-Burghers came together as United Secession, and then united with the Relief Church in 1847 to become United Presbyterians (UPs). Later the UP church became the United Free (Churchmount) Church when it reunited with the Free Church in the 1890s.

In many accounts, the Disruption and the prior secessions represented a split between those who were prepared to accept the domination of the laity by the aristocracy and those who rebelled against it. The Disruption was so cataclysmic for the official Church that in total 474 ministers left, losing among them £10,000 in stipends and Fife was at the heart of it. It was reported by Mark Bryden in 1869 that 'when the Disruption took place there was no locality in Scotland where the established church suffered more than Kirkcaldy'. Every church in Kirkcaldy, bar one, left, leaving only 280 Church of Scotland members in the whole town.

Across Scotland the religion of these rebels found a new energy with 743 new churches, 400 new manses, and new schools for 513 teachers and 44,000 children.[25] In the next fifty years the proportion of Scots confirming their religious adherence rose from 30 per cent to 50 per cent.[26] In 1851 (drawing from a

Scottish population of two million adults) the official Church had 400,000 members; and the Free Churches, around 270,000. By 1890 the dissenting Churches had 660,000 members as against 490,000 for the Kirk.[27]

But even with a range of sects to choose from, many felt excluded because of their poverty. In the official Church all were not equal: you rented your church seat or 'pew' – and after the Disruption working-class members found it difficult, because even in the Free Churches a rent was charged for a space in the church. Poorer members of the community were also discouraged by the expectation that you wore 'Sunday best' clothes. Early on in the 1790s in Edinburgh the Church of Scotland actually initiated evening services purely for servants and 'common people' and in Glasgow ministers and middle-class congregations petitioned the Town Council to discontinue services for workers and their families on the grounds of 'public hygiene'. Scottish working-class men and women often found a more comfortable home in the Baptist Church, which helps explain its doubling in size around this time.[28]

A pattern started to emerge: the Free Church was strong but flourished outside the urban areas. The dissenting Churches still had the farm workers, crofters and tenant farmers like my family and the industrial working class, while in contrast the Kirk Sessions of the Church of Scotland were, it appears, controlled by coal owners, shopkeepers and traders. And the connections between the official Church, imperial economic success and the Union can be illustrated by the career of Lord Overtoun, the Victorian owner of Scotland's biggest chemical works. My father told me when I was young that, even though Overtoun worked his men on a Sunday, he was the patron of the Lord's Day Observance Society and, while paying his workers poverty wages, he was a great charitable donor. When he died, one of his workers, angry at his hypocrisy, walked round Glasgow with a sign that read 'Consternation in Heaven: Lord Overtoun – Three days dead and not yet arrived'. But Lord Overtoun's views were typical of early-twentieth-century Scotland when, according to David McCrone, Scotland was marked out by the dominance of local and private capital, empire and Protestantism. In the spirit of this, in 1903, Lord Overtoun endowed a monument to the Scottish Covenanters, saying Scotland symbolised the 'priceless boon of civil and religious liberty'. The history of Scotland was, he said, 'the history of the Scottish Church up against fearful odds'.[29]

And there would have been no accommodation between Church and state and no reunification of the Scottish Churches in 1929 without the British state accepting that Scots Churches were guaranteed freedom from it. Indeed, we should recognise that reunification was only supported by the old secessionist sects because the Church of Scotland Act 1921 recognised that the Kirk would 'be subject to no civil authority . . . in all matters of doctrine, worship, government and discipline'.[30] It is a stipulation that would, at first sight, put the new law at odds with the conventional notion of parliamentary sovereignty – that no authority on earth could challenge the sovereignty of the king and that no legislation could ever bind successor parliaments – but it did help put to rest an issue which had caused tension in the Union from the outset, namely how to recognise the status of Scotland's national Church inside a Union which elided Anglicanism and the state. Kidd calls it a 'sort of concordat between state and the Kirk, a phenomenon unheard of in British constitutional practice'.[31]

But how do we measure the real strength of religion during these years? The 1851 census found that 33 per cent of the population worshipped in the morning, 21 per cent in the afternoon and 6 per cent in the evening, and in 1874 only 20 per cent had no Church connection. Yet the Churches weren't prepared to leave even that 20 per cent to it. Thus an evangelical Band of Hope was begun in the 1870s to rescue lost souls, not least from drink, and grew to 700 bands with 147,000 members by 1908. The Boys' Brigade was established in the mid-1880s and for adults there were the Home Missions, which were active in working-class areas and in mining villages. The level the Churches felt it necessary to go to deal with 'godlessness' can be gauged from the activities of the church my father led in a later time, St Mary's Free Church in Govan. In the late-nineteenth century St Mary's mission included the '1,137 children enrolled in its Sunday School, 493 in Bible class, 155 Sunday School teachers, a company of the Boys' Brigade numbering 58, Gospel Temperance Meetings with 420 members, a Penny Savings Bank, several branches of the YMCA, and 292 folk who had Home Mission workers'.[32]

Meanwhile, in Kirkcaldy, a Free Church commission of 1889 found that half of the town's young men had no connection with a church. Such was the concern of local ministers about the absence of churchgoing among these young men, mostly miners, that they formed the 'Hallelujah Chariot' to try to convert them, but their appearance in Cowdenbeath was said to have been greeted with rotten apples. People sensed that things were changing. T. C. Smout has written that at the turn of the eighteenth to nineteenth centuries the church minister and the parish was one and the same thing. A century later, in an increasingly industrial society, the ties between minister and community had been loosened, yet the parish infrastructure and leadership role of the clergy remained an important part of Scotland's civic society long after.

For whatever the real strength of religious conviction, the Church had influence far beyond its numbers. R. F. McKenzie, the radical and innovative headmaster who was a friend of my mother, wrote that the preeminent influence of religion meant that he was 'brought up to be respectable doing the right things' and historian Richard Finlay argues that there was 'widespread adoption' of the Kirk's definition of respectability which 'revolved round sobriety, temperance, thrift, hard work, religiosity and self-improvement'. Without a parliament or a separate state, the Church was the closest Scotland had to an authentic national voice. It also built the infrastructure of social welfare. The churches were the providers of Poor Law relief until 1845 and their influence in shaping social policy – the famous cleric Thomas Chalmers persuaded Scotland to see the poor not as the hungry to be fed and housed but as souls to be saved – continued long after. Schools only ceased to be church schools after the 1873 Act.

Until 1908, C. G. Brown writes, there had been at least a growing consensus in both the Church of Scotland and the United Free Church that part of their role was to agitate to improve social conditions and, wherever possible, to alleviate poverty directly. Under an informal agreement, social criticism had been left to the United Free Church with social welfare the responsibility of the Church of Scotland. But in the years leading up to the outbreak of the First World War, we saw what he calls 'the secularisation of social protest . . . the initiative in social and political action was passing out of the hands of activists inspired by religion and the bearers of social salvation were now trade union leaders, socialist intellectuals, and Labour politicians.'[33]

Then from the 1920s, when the Church played an inauspicious role in opposing the Scottish miners in the 1926 strike, it came to be more identified with establishment politics. But the Labour Party's Scottish members sought support from all Churches, Protestant and Catholic, and when elected in 1922 the Clydeside MPs left for London with a rally which included singing not only 'Jerusalem' but the 23rd and 124th Psalms. Their statement of aims – that they would 'bear in their hearts the sorrows of the poor, the aged and the infirm that they shall not be without comfort . . . [and] have regard for those fallen in the struggle of life' – owed more to the Covenanters than any Communist tract.[34] And influenced too by the Catholic priesthood the Independent Labour Party's Scottish faction had a highly moralistic streak, supporting prohibition, and dismissing cinemas and dancehalls as latter-day 'opium dens'. The ILP's *Forward* newspaper refused to carry adverts from advocates of birth control and in its 1918 manifesto for Scotland the Scottish Labour Party supported the prohibition of alcohol. When the Scottish Prohibition Party's Dundee MP Edwin Scrymgeour, who defeated Winston Churchill in the 1922 general election, proposed legislation that, if passed, would have imposed a five-year jail term on anyone trafficking in liquor, the bulk of his limited support in parliament came from the 'Red Clydeside' MPs.

So for nearly 300 years of post-Reformation history, the organisation of politics mattered less to the Scottish people than the organisation of religion. The Churches' influence could be felt in the beliefs even of those who did not profess a faith, and in the continuation of a Scottish national consciousness well after the Union of the parliaments. You could call this form of cultural distinctiveness a religious patriotism but while today, from the perspective of 300 years on, it is easy to view religion as yet another Scotland-versus-England issue and to write an account showing how the Scottish Church stood up for the Scottish nation against the British state, we should not forget that that was not how it was seen at the time.

We owe this important insight to the detailed work of Colin Kidd. In his book *Union and Unionisms* he shows that the most intense and highly politicised debates in Scotland for two centuries after the Union were not so much focused on a battle of 'Scotland versus England' but much more about 'church versus state'.[35] In the words of Jonathan Sumption, 'let us remember how the churches symbolise the important fact of Union: that the surrender of the Scottish state in 1707 did not entail the surrender of control of Scotland's civic society . . . Scotland could hold its head high because of the continued – indeed, guaranteed – autonomy of its civic institutions'. And it was this religious freedom from that state that church and chapel-going Scots were determined to protect.

Of course the churches stood alongside an impressive array of institutions that supported them and were supported by them. The Boys' Brigade was founded on 4 October 1883 in Glasgow. Its founder, William Alexander Smith, sought to instill 'Christian manliness' through sports, religious lessons and militaristic drills. It aimed to promote 'reverence, discipline, obedience'. In 1923 they were strong enough in Glasgow to have 10,000 boys inspected and in 1933 the future King George VI was greeted in Glasgow by 30,000 members. In the 1950s and 1960s I was a proud member of the junior arm, the Life Boys. Today, the Boys' Brigade has a smaller membership but still 430 companies.[36] Between them and the Scouts, which I joined later in my teens, and the Girl Guides they remain important organisations influencing young people growing up in Scotland today.

Scotland is the Orange Order's second biggest stronghold after Northern Ireland, with most lodges concentrated in west central Scotland. While no more than 2 per cent of adult male Protestants in the region have ever been members, six Orangemen were elected as Conservative MPs between the wars and even today the 'marching season' sows some seeds of division across Scotland. The Freemasons have been strong in Scotland, too.

Sectarianism is the darker side of Scotland's history of organised religion. After the establishment of Irish Home Rule, the Church of Scotland's Church and Nation Committee called for immigration controls and the deportation of unemployed Catholics to Ireland – a country most of them by then had never seen. Pressure from these sources led Ramsay MacDonald's National Government coalition cabinet to actively consider these proposals in 1933. Even in the late 1950s in Coatbridge and Airdrie the selection of a Catholic candidate, Labour's James Dempsey, led to the putting forward of a Protestant Rangers candidate, the sister-in-law of the player Alan Morton, who cut Labour's majority massively in 1959. Only gradually did Scottish institutions remove the shameful barriers to Catholic employment – one of the last being Rangers Football Club when their manager Graeme Souness signed the former Celtic player Mo Johnston in 1989.

FEATURES OF NATIONAL IDENTITY

And so, shaped by my background in Fife, and Scotland's religious inheritance, what did being Scottish mean for me as I was growing up? Everything and nothing. For me being Scottish was so innate that it shaped everything I thought, without itself ever being thought about terribly much. I didn't spend a lot of time working out what my Scottishness meant to me, because it *was* me. But of course now national identity is highly contested so every Scot is having to look anew at what it means to be Scottish. The writer Anthony Smith defines national identity as 'the process whereby a nation is reconstructed over time' – how a population conceived as many individuals constitutes itself as a people – through 'the maintenance and continuous reproduction of the pattern of values, symbols, memories, myths and traditions that compose the distinctive heritage of nations and the identification of individuals with that heritage and those values, symbols, memories, myths and traditions'.[37]

There is a tendency to think of identity as fixed, unchanging, sometimes even innate and ingrained. But history tells us that what looks permanent is often porous and subject to change. Nations are subject to the same ebbing and flowing, part of the tides of history. In a recent lecture in which he cited the French historian Ernest Renan's famous 1882 address 'What is a nation?', the UK Supreme Court judge Lord Sumption said that, while Renan was speaking at a time when nationalist sentiment in

Europe had never been stronger, he was prepared to subject to sceptical scrutiny all of the theories of national identity prevalent at that time. Many of the nationalist movements based their legitimacy on claims about racial, ethnic or linguistic distinctiveness. But Renan questioned the importance of both these ethnic and linguistic solidarities, arguing that the real identity of a nation was to be found in 'collective sentiment'.[38]

In other words, nations existed – and continued to exist – not primarily because their citizens met some objective criteria for membership but on the basis of the strength of attachment among their people, a phenomenon that was inherently changeable and amounted he said to a 'daily referendum' among the population. Sumption went further, saying that 'so far as existing national identities had any stability, this was due to the accumulated weight of historic myth'. 'A nation', Renan wrote, 'was the culmination of a long history of collective effort, collective sacrifice and collective devotion. It depended on a consciousness of having done great things together in the past, and wanting to do more of them in the future.'[39]

It is a reflection of his time that Renan's notion of these shared national stories is entirely bound up with war and conquest. Paraphrasing Renan, the Harvard political scientist Karl Deutsch observed, in language that has often been misattributed to Renan himself, that a nation is 'a group of people united by a mistaken view of their past and a common hatred of their neighbours'. Or, as Renan puts it, they are in 'possession in common of a rich legacy of memories' and at the same time also 'a shared amnesia, a collective forgetfulness'.[40] Attachment to one nation is underwritten by 'prejudice against others', showing that political nationalism can easily descend, as Yael Tamir suggests in her landmark study of liberal nationalism, to appeals 'in the name of God, Nature, History, Culture, the Glorious Dead, the Spirit of the Nation or any other such metaphysical entities'.[41]

Tamir, who has studied national identities and nationalisms all over the world, argues that: 'All attempts to single out a particular set of objective features – be it a common history, collective destiny, language, religion, territory, climate, race, ethnicity – as necessary and sufficient for the definition of a nation have ended in failure . . . no nation will have all of them . . . only one factor is necessary, although not sufficient, for a group to be defined as a nation – the existence of national consciousness.'[42]

In *After Independence: The State of the Scottish Nation Debate*, the writer and cultural expert Marc Lambert applies this sort of thinking to Scotland and asks: 'at what level of description are we to define sufficient Scottishness? Parentage? Birthplace? Accent? Education? Class? Cultural knowledge? Lengths of time spent in Scotland? DNA? Even if we were able to agree on a particular level of description, the idea that this is what defines us in total and happens to be the most important thing about us is to take part in a radically simplified national mythology which is both intellectually, existentially and historically dishonest.'[43]

With his popular and controversial histories *The Scots: A Genetic Journey* and *The British: A Genetic Journey*, Alistair Moffat offers a hotly disputed corrective to the idea of nations of 'blood and soil'. He finds that in a very real sense every Scot is an immigrant; until 9000 BC Scotland was empty of people and mammals, having lasted for 15,000 years with ice across the land. It suggests that, in this sense at least, we were a blank slate. He goes on to cite the controversial suggestion that most of us were briefly English, descended from bands of hunter-gatherers who walked across France, came up the Atlantic coastline and settled here between 9600 BC and 5000 BC. Of course this contention about Scotland is no different from what Daniel Defoe wrote about England three centuries ago: 'This from a mixture of all kinds began, that het'rogeneous thing, and Englishman.'[44] Thus Moffat too argues that despite clinging to a long-held assumption that our ethnic make-up is largely Scots, Celtic, Viking and Irish, we are in fact 'one of the most diverse nations on earth', with 100 different strands of DNA, and that 56 per cent of Scots in DNA tests are descended from these hunter-gatherers. As Moffat states, 'the explanation is simple. We are a people on the edge of beyond; on the end of a massive continent. Peoples were migrating north-west; and they couldn't get any further on the Eurasian land mass, and consequently we have collected everybody.'[45]

Moffat also reminds us that for most of our history the real division – along a cultural, economic and geological fault-line – has not been the border between Scotland and England but the one separating the Highlands and Lowlands. He claims that the elision of the two, into one Scotland, was made easier by two things: first, the rout at Culloden that began the long decline of the clan system and the Gaelic language; and second, the appropriation of an idealised Highland culture by Lowlanders which led to a kind of hybrid Scottishness, one that paid homage to the Highlands even as they were being cleared of their people. If he is right, and we can identify a kind of 'post-Culloden' Scottishness, what does it mean for a modern Scot whose relationship to the House of Stuart feels as distant as mine does to a man on the moon?[46]

Professor Craig Calhoun, who has studied three centuries of social movements, argues that the shared culture on which a sense of a shared national identity is built cannot ever be just some inheritance handed down from the past and passively accepted by each generation: it has to be a living culture which, subject to many global and cross-national influences, is being formed and reformed every day, continuously shaping and reshaping our sense of who we are. As recent studies suggest, national identity can be a shared belief among a group of individuals that they belong together that does not depend on ethnic roots.

So what do we conclude about the strength of national identity when we think of Scotland today? We think first of an ever-present consciousness among Scots of a distinct national identity. A sense that we have that membership in the nation is clearly important to the personal identity of each of us as Scots today. And far from being passive about that sense of national identity, Scots have always been willing to assert its importance. Moreover, we have championed and defended our own distinct public institutions – legal, educational, religious, cultural and sporting – as means by which we express our national identity, and, crucially, have always insisted that the British state respect the autonomy of these institutions. While the standard interpretation of our post-Union relationship with Britain is that we were culturally Scottish but politically British, ours was more than a claim for cultural independence (with a demand for recognition of a national language and body of literature and so on) and more like an assertion of 'national self-determination' in religion, education, law and social affairs. I will show in later chapters how what it meant to be Scottish and British has changed radically over recent periods of the Union and how the level of intensity with which we feel Scottish and British has changed over time.

A few Scottish intellectuals did indeed want to subsume our Scottish identity entirely into a British identity, believing that this would end civil war and violence, and some spoke of the 'civilising effect' of the link with England. And some of the reforms we adopted came from Scots who wanted to follow practices they saw in England. But many others were pushing in the other direction. 'The conviction developed that Scotland was somehow on the wane and might face a future as "North Britain"', the literary historian Robert Crawford writes. Sir Walter Scott fretted that 'what makes Scotland, Scotland is fast disappearing' while in 1832 Henry Lord Cockburn, the great Whig lawyer, worried that 'this is the last truly Scotch age'.

As Tom Devine puts it, 'the Scots in this view were becoming steadily invisible as a people as their ancient traditions, identities and institutions were diluted by the corrosive effect of close association with the world's most powerful state'.[47] Of course many of those most concerned about the dilution of Scottishness inside the Union were the very ones who most wanted the Union to survive. Industrialisation, urbanisation, dislocation and education made people want to think of themselves as part of communities with common traditions as they faced an onslaught of change. But an assertion of the distinctiveness of Scotland did not lead automatically to a subscription to political nationalism any more then than it does now.

To take just one example, Sir Walter Scott took great pains to stimulate a cult of William Wallace, being the first to propose a monument to him (and leaving £1,000 towards its construction in his will) and initiating a poetry competition to commemorate his 'guardianship' of Scotland. But for Scott, Wallace and Bruce were great Scottish heroes not because of what they did to the English, but because their victories against them enabled Scotland to join the Union not as a conquered nation but as an independent partner. His pilgrimages to Bannockburn did not, in his view, make him any less of a British patriot – they were in homage to one of the events which made the very idea of a peaceful Union between two separate and proud nations possible.

In 1823, Scott proposed a new popular history of Scotland that could be widely read and understood. Dissatisfied with the first volume that a fellow writer had done, Scott issued what he called *Tales of a Grandfather, being Tales taken from Scottish History*. His book, dedicated to his grandson, went on to be a wildly successful history for the masses. Later, in the mid-nineteenth century, a cult of Burns was born, driven by the creation of new popular magazines (like the *People's Journal*) that made for ready dissemination of myths and legends.

During these years new hero figures emerged, including the most famous Scotsman of the nineteenth century, David Livingstone. Dr Livingstone's Scottishness was central to his identity and popularity, and yet his simultaneous Britishness was demonstrated by the choice of his final resting place. Since the 1920s there has been a statute in his honour in Blantyre, Lanarkshire but his tomb has always been in Westminster Abbey, where he was buried with full honours.

In a recent study of Catalan nationalism, Laia Balcells draws a more general conclusion about nationalist uprisings by exploring why Catalans in Spain tend to support Catalan independence but Catalans in France tend not to. She explains three typical phases in nationalistic revivals: Phase A which she calls 'scholarly interest' led by intellectuals who discover and celebrate some lost or repressed identity; Phase B which she describes as 'patriotic agitation' where people become much more aware of the issues and more general nationalist sentiments surface; and Phase C, finally, is the 'rise of a mass movement' where collective action for national recognition and even independence takes place. She argues that just at the point that we shift from an oral to a literate mass culture and millions receive mass education, the very weak Spanish state was unable to prevent the teaching of Catalan nationalism in their schools but that France had created a very effective top–down state, imposed the French language and used the education system to socialise everyone into being French. But in Scotland, stage one, which went as far as the rediscovery of a lost identity, was seen to be compatible with being part of Britain.[48]

So, while romanticism was driving political nationalism across the rest of Europe, in Scotland it was being harnessed to the idea of a distinctive Scottish identity within the Union. Scott's idea of a uniquely proud but very Scottish civil society, whose distinctive institutions were so strong and exuded so much patriotic fervour that they did not even require a separate state, reshaped the Scots' sense of themselves. His public relations masterstroke was the adoption of Scotland and Scottish customs by the Hanoverian royalty, making him the first spin doctor of the modern age. King George IV's pageant in Edinburgh, his use of kilts, tartans, bagpipes and the gathering of the clans was of course exactly what Eric Hobsbawm has written of 'as the use of "invented tradition" . . . a set of practices normally governed . . . by tacitly accepted rules and other rituals of a symbolic nature which seek to inculcate certain values and norms of behaviour by repetition which automatically implies continuity with the past'.[49]

The result was that, while some worried about the 'Death of Scotland', as Devine states: 'what emerged by the Victorian era was the new dual identity of Scottishness and Britishness . . . The dual identity from then to this point, was never static, but constantly renewed and its markers reinvented for new times in the twentieth century.'[50]

Perhaps one of the reasons Scotland has always had this expansive streak that could accommodate being British is because we are a nation of emigrants as well as immigrants. Tom Devine shows us that while we have always thought of the Jews, the Irish, the Poles and the Italians as Europe's largest diaspora population, it was in fact the Scots. Over two million people, he says, emigrated between 1815 and 1939, a rate of outward movement that was 1.5 times that of England and Wales even before we include the 600,000 Scots who emigrated to England and Wales. Scotland, he says, was alone in experiencing at one and the same time large-scale industrialisation and mass emigration.[51]

This great scattering made Scots simultaneously cosmopolitan and nostalgic. Tom Nairn eloquently describes how it has led, amongst the Scottish diaspora, to 'the projection of imagined origins, a famously synthetic folklore of Auld Lang Syne, an identity deploying the most colourful items from successive wardrobes and cabin-trunks, with appropriate music and displays. The least home-bound population on earth has generated the most home-bound and nostalgic ideology.'[52]

That is perhaps understandable. All migrant communities have a tendency to eulogise a version of their country, not least if they were trying to proselytise for a country they believed was at risk of cultural assimilation with a much larger neighbour. But this was not like the Irish abroad, who proclaimed their political convictions in favour of independence. In Scotland's case it was a celebration of our distinctiveness in an apolitical way. As I will show, strong identities need not be exclusionary – and it is possible to feel proudly, particularly and indeed passionately Scottish, without feeling that such an identity must find its expression by breaking all political connections with the rest of Britain.

But what constitutes the modern Scottish national identity is now substantially different from that of the world of Burns and Sir Walter Scott. Perhaps it is not surprising that Flodden is thought of little. Some historians trace the end of Scotland as a separate political entity from the Battle of Flodden in 1513, arguing that from Flodden onwards any dream of Scotland standing alone as a big European player was gone. Scotland, some suggest, never recovered.

James IV was a monarch with European ambitions: seizing his chance to invade England while Henry VIII was fighting in France. The Scots crossed the Tweed at Coldstream, looped down to Flodden, but held the ridge above Branxton which made the battlefield a bog, removed the advantage that their encampment had given them, wrongly used siege cannon (which fired over the English and did not hit them) and fell victim to English bills (short, savage weapons converted from the humble agricultural billhook). When England's archers attacked, the Scots were routed: James IV died alongside 10,000 others. But what commemorates these 10,000 war dead?

The 500th anniversary led to the erection of a set of gates (with a design of Scots pikes, English bills and longbows, and the royal symbols of the two countries). There was a Flodden exhibition at Coldstream Museum, a Flodden marquee set up in Branxton village, a '500 Years to the Hour' battlefield walk, a weapons demonstration, a commemorative service at the memorial in the evening and a service at St Giles' Cathedral in Edinburgh. There was even Flodden marmalade made with blood orange.

But the 500th commemoration was a low-impact affair compared with the more poignant, dignified and sombre ceremony at the 400th anniversary. Back then there was a dedication to the Brave of Both Nations, with a stark granite memorial cross, funded by public subscription. It is said that the modern equivalent, with its emphasis on Scottishness rather than sorrow, simply did not inspire the people of Scotland to take part.

Bannockburn, meanwhile, was a great Scots victory worthy of celebration because it was by an army outnumbered two-to-one. It is too early to say what will happen in the summer of 2014 at the 700th anniversary of Bannockburn but so far the commemoration has not evoked the outpouring of national sentiment predicted. The proposed gathering of Scottish clans has been cancelled, the Bannockburn re-enactment scaled back and audience numbers reduced.

In neither case have the people of Scotland shown an obsession with or even a huge appetite for revisiting a time when our Southern neighbours were enemies instead of family and friends, suggesting that Scots have moved on from the Walter Scott era when, alongside the kilts, tartans and clans, we conjured up as our national symbols the wars, battlefields and armies of the past.

I began this exploration by trying to work out what gives a nation an identity. Every generation of Scots has had to think through our relationship with England, and no generation has had to engage in more reflection and reappraisal than this one. In my lifetime we have seen the loss of the British Empire, the changing status and competitive strength of the British economy, our new role in Europe, and the onset of globalisation, so it is hardly surprising that sentiments about identity and nationalism are in flux. What has happened to our sense of identity and the changes in the way we think of ourselves is the backdrop to the current debate on Scotland's future, and the theme of the next chapter. I grew up in the post-war years aware that Scotland and England were different even if they were no longer separate. As a country we were distinct from England but when we looked round the world we resembled it most; however, if what it means to be Scottish has been expressed in different ways at different times we should not forget one truth: the belief among Scottish people that being Scottish is important has not changed and I don't believe it ever will.

CHAPTER 2

The Changing Face of Scottish Identity

A few months ago I attended a school prize-giving in my constituency in Fife. No one will be surprised that I was welcomed in the familiar Scottish way – to the sound of bagpipes playing the school's anthem, 'Highland Cathedral', and by pupils dressed in kilts and tartan. But what would have struck a casual observer from outside the area was that there was nothing that was remotely or distinctively British about the occasion. No national anthem. No reference to anything British, or anyone like the Queen. And when the references were made to parliament they were not to the UK Parliament but only to the Scottish Parliament. We could easily have been living in a post-independence Scotland.

A few weeks later I attended my village's children's gala near my home in Fife. Waiting for the procession at the top of the hill, I could see the Saltire and Lion Rampant on display but not one Union Jack was in sight. This, a big change from a few years ago, is part of a pattern, not too dissimilar to the pictures I saw of a recent visit by the Queen to Edinburgh. A few years ago the flags on display in the Royal Mile would have been the Union Jacks that dominated the Olympics coverage, or we would have had Union Jacks mingling with the Saltire or the Lion Rampart. But not this time.

I made a decision when I became Prime Minister in 2007 to display our United Kingdom flag on public buildings. I had been struck how, in every other country I visited, the national flag was on permanent display – to the extent that in the USA millions of people had the Stars and Stripes on poles in their gardens. So I decided to change the arcane rules that assumed the Union Jack was for royal occasions and special days and instead allowed all government buildings to fly the flag. Of course the new SNP minority administration in Scotland refused.

Today it is hard to find Union Jacks flying in Scotland other than at UK government offices, on some famous landmarks like the Bank of Scotland's HQ on the Mound in Edinburgh and at Standard Life in Edinburgh's West End. Edinburgh Castle, which used to fly a large Union Jack, has downsized to one so small I cannot see it from Princes Street. St Andrew's House has four flagpoles, all flying Saltires. And of course there has been a long-running battle in Stirling about which flag to fly. And when you drive south, there are three flags flying as you enter England – the Union Jack, the Cross of St George and the old Kingdom of Northumbria flag – but if you enter Scotland, travelling up on the northbound lane, all three flagpoles are flying the Saltire.

Does any of this matter? According to a recent study by Peter Kellner for British Future, 61 per cent of English adults associate the St George's Cross with pride and patriotism, but that figure jumps to 80 per cent for the Union Jack. The figures are quite different in Scotland. Here it is the Saltire that evokes Scottish national pride and patriotism for 84 per cent of the public. Only 25 per cent of Scots saw the Union Jack representing a modern diverse Britain (compared to 37 per cent in England), while it is the St Andrew's Cross that evokes the values of modernity and diversity for a full 58 per cent of Scots. Instead for Scots the Union flag has very distinct associations with the monarchy (80 per cent), with the armed forces (70 per cent), with the sacrifice in the world wars (55 per cent), and with Team GB at the Olympics (65 per cent, compared to 75 per cent in England). If the Union Jack now means very different things north and south of the border, it clearly cannot play the unifying role it did in times past.[1]

There has also been a distinct shift in the popular taste for national anthems. I remember John Smith, who loved the anthem 'Jerusalem', changing the famous phrase 'to build Jerusalem in England's green and pleasant land' when he sang it, to say Scotland instead, arguing that England should not have a monopoly on its utopian ideals. He wasn't alone in that view, of course. As I noted earlier, the radical Clydesider MPs sang 'Jerusalem' at St Enoch railway station before they left for Westminster. But it doesn't solve the problem of what the national anthem is. In the opening match of the 1998 World Cup, when Scotland played Brazil in France, I was fortunate enough to be the guest of the French government. Seated near me was the Duke of Edinburgh. I could see his surprise as he stood for the national anthem only to discover we were to sing not 'God Save the Queen' but 'Flower of Scotland'. Now in rugby, football and athletics, 'Flower of Scotland' has replaced 'God Save the Queen' whenever Scotland plays.

Donald Dewar had the idea that we might replace both 'Flower of Scotland's talk of sending folk homewards and 'God Save the Queen's chant about crushing the rebellious Scots with a non-military anthem, 'A Man's a Man for A' That', and have it sung at the opening of the parliament. It was to no avail.

While these are recognisable symbols through which we manifest our Scottishness, they are of course ultimately superficial and in this chapter I want to look at whether anything more substantial lies beneath the changing fashions for flags and anthems. Having painted a picture in the introduction of the world I grew up in the 1950s, and ended the last chapter by questioning how salient the appeal to past glories really now is, I want to focus on what the enormous changes to working, family, religious and community life in Scotland have meant for me and mean for Scottish identity today.

Of course Scotland's contemporary experience is paralleled in other countries that have also moved from the 'industrial' to what is often called the 'post-industrial' economy. While fifty years ago most of what we produced, bought and sold were products made in and for national markets, now every advanced industrial country sources many of its goods and even some of its services from cheaper-labour locations round the world. There are now a billion home owners and a billion car owners around the world; by 2025 there will be two billion car owners and home owners. It's a global revolution in which more and more people are entering an international 'middle class'. And these global trends that have increased consumer power have impacted on Scotland too: we have never had greater access to cheap goods, and overseas holidays are now the norm for Scottish families.

A recent survey has shown just how much more prosperous Scotland now is. Little has changed over fifty years in the balance between city, town and rural areas. Some 69 per cent live in urban areas, 12 per cent in small towns and 19 per cent in rural and remote areas and when asked where they lived, one third of Scots normally describe their residence as urban or city centred, one third town-centred, and just under one third village and rural. But there are signs of change all around. Sixty-nine per cent of Scots have had a foreign holiday in the last three years, including half of Scots in semi-skilled and unskilled jobs. And in 2012, the last year for which figures are available, there were 480 foreign holidays for every 1,000 Scottish people. In a far cry from my youth, more than 80 per cent of 16–25-year-olds have travelled abroad in the last three years. Over one fifth of households own two cars and in total 70 per cent have a car, again a level of mobility that was unheard of in the 1950s. And as another signal of a social revolution, 62 per cent of Scottish households are now owner-occupied, with 28 per cent of homes being owned outright.[2]

But, at the same time, globalisation has seen Scottish jobs in heavy industry and manufacturing move eastwards. The West collectively now only makes 40 per cent of the world's goods and there has been a big 'hollowing out' of the semi-skilled jobs in the middle of the economy, creating a big gap between the very well educated and those left behind with few skills or opportunities, the private sector being unable to create sufficient well-paying jobs. Once we include universities, the NHS, police, local government, armed forces, the nationalised banks and public corporations, over one fifth of working Scots are part of this wider public sector.[3]

Scotland is at the sharp end of this global transformation in a very real sense, because it is hard to pinpoint many countries where the economic change in fortunes has been faster or more extreme than here in Scotland. Brilliant academics from Ernest Gellner and Craig Calhoun to Tom Nairn and David Marquand have shown us how globalisation – the waves of economic and social change which have followed the opening-up of the world economy to the free flow of capital goods, services and people – has led to the shaking-up of traditional societies and identities everywhere; and explained how many countries have responded to their buffeting at the hands of what often seem invisible and alien forces, seeking to protect, shelter, insulate and cushion themselves from change – suffering, in its wake, crises of confidence about their role in the world, sometimes over-emphasising their sense of being different, and on occasion embracing populist parties.

Thus the writer Gellner suggests that it is wrong to explain political nationalism purely as some kind of throwback or reversion to tribalism at the time it faces being wiped out at the hands of universalising progress: he sees it as a demand for 'a renovated collectivity' or what is sometimes called 'a new imagined community', strong enough to bear the huge stresses and disruptions of modernising change.

Scotland is unlikely to be an exception from these responses to – and expressions of resistance at – global change, not least because Scotland is one of the countries that have changed faster than other parts of the industrialised world.

Today 81 per cent of Scottish jobs are in the service sector.[4] In 2014, the typical Scots employee is a young woman in a bank, an insurance company, a contact centre or in one of our schools or hospitals or working in social services, rather than a miner or boilermaker. Employment in the service sector – health, education, retail, and home care – has grown almost threefold from 1951. We have seen a threefold increase in the number of Scots in professional and technical jobs over the same time frame. Now the typical Scottish trade unionist is a female graduate working in health and social work (where women are more than four in every five of the workforce) or in education (where women are three in every five of schools and college staff).[5] The collapse of our industrial identity has coincided with shrinking levels of religious affiliations, leading in turn to huge changes in our family lives and in levels of enthusiasm for traditional institutions in Scottish life. The Scotland of 2014 is a million miles away from the old Scotland, which was in many ways more industrialised, more religious and more traditional than any comparable country in the developed world.

If I think of just one town, Kirkcaldy, and one county, Fife, the speed and scope of the change becomes apparent. What used to be one of the world's strongest coalfields, employing nearly 30,000 men, barely exists today on the mining map. The textiles industry has virtually disappeared. Electronics came in huge numbers and has gone. The biggest employers apart from the health service are a call centre and the local further-education college. Fife has moved from its reliance on heavy industry to a service economy, benefiting on the way but only in part from three large areas of growth in the Scottish economy: North Sea supply work, spin-offs from Edinburgh's financial services sector and the era of the Silicon Glen triangle from Inverclyde across to Dundee. Over the last fifty years Scotland's professional workforce has been transformed, trebling in size to half a million.[6]

At the same time, an astonishing two out of every three manufacturing jobs have been wiped out. From a total of over 900,000 jobs across manufacturing and mining in 1951, we have just 199,000 now. No country started the post-war years with such a big a share of its workforce in these heavy industries and hardly any other country now has so small a share. At their peak the great manufacturing nations – America, Japan, Germany, Italy and France – had 30 per cent of their workforces in manufacturing and mining while Scotland's share peaked at 40 per cent. Today 19 per cent of the German and Italian workforces are still in manufacturing and mining while in Japan it is 16 per cent. In fact only 7.7 per cent of Scots work in manufacturing today, and manufacturing workers now represent a smaller share of the workforce than in England, Wales or even Northern Ireland.[7]

Table 1: Working population of Scotland by broad industrial group: 1951

	Number (thousands)	Percentage of total for all industries
Manufacturing	804.2	36.6
Agriculture, forestry, fishing	162.4	7.4
Mining and quarrying	99.5	4.5
Service trades (including building)	1,128.6	51.4
All industries and services	2,194.7	100.0

Source: House of Commons Library

Table 2: Industrial share of employment (per cent), Glasgow and Scotland, 1951–2011

	Glasgow	Scotland
1951	50.2	42.2
1961	46.0	
1971	38.7	35.2
1981	27.9	
1991	19.2	20.9
2011	5.5	7.7

Source: *The Moral Economy of Deindustrialization in post-1945 Scotland*, Jim Phillips; and, for 2011, House of Commons Library

Table 3: Employment in railways and coal in Scotland, 1951–91

	Railways	Coal
1951	55,393	89,464
1961	53,990	80,410
1971	22,910	34,315
1981	19,380	25,180
1991	11,870	2,370
2011	7,913	1,362

Source: *The Moral Economy of Deindustrialization in post-1945 Scotland*, Jim Phillips; and, for 2011, House of Commons Library

Of course if you travelled through the Scotland of the 1950s you would have met hundreds of employees of the public corporations everywhere. From British Gas to British Rail and the Post Office we had plenty of organisations that had a strong British identity because they delivered a unified network of rail, postal, gas, electricity and telecommunication services. In the 1950s, one in every five Scottish workers were employed by the state-owned British public corporations but today they sustain only a fraction of the old jobs. Railway employment alone has fallen from 55,000 in 1951 to less than 10,000 now.

Patterns of rural employment have changed fast, too. Scotland is a third of the land area of Britain and hitherto employed a disproportionately large share of rural workers. But having seen employment across agriculture, forestry and fishing fall dramatically from over 170,000 jobs in 1951 to just 60,000 now, we now offer little more chance for employment on the land or at sea than most other Western economies.[8]

Taking all these once-dominant Scottish sectors together – we find that employment across manufacturing, mining, utilities and agriculture has dropped from 56 per cent of the workforce to just 12 per cent. Or, to put it another way, almost one *million* traditional jobs have disappeared.[9]

So at least half of Scotland's families have been directly hit by waves of industrial change; there will not be an extended family in the country that has been unaffected as male manual workers have been pushed off the land, taken out of the deep mines and thrown out of the factories and workshops that for a whole century and a half were at the heart of Scotland's industrial life.

That huge shift in our economic life has been mirrored by new arrangements in our personal lives. Over one third of adults over sixteen described themselves in the 2011 census as single, another fifth said they were separated, widowed, divorced or in a civil partnership – and only half the adult population were married, a distinct change from the 1950s.[10]

I mentioned in an earlier chapter my mother's own experience of work and home and how she was expected to stop working when she got married. In 1901 women formed 28.7 per cent of the Scottish workforce; by 1951, women still accounted for only 40.2 per cent of the workforce. Indeed in the post-war years the typical age at which women married actually fell – to 24 compared with 30 today – and yet the traditional notion that a marriage, even at such a young age, meant the end of a career for a woman persisted far longer in Scotland than across the border. In 1951 only 15 per cent of married women went out to work and the vast majority of women only had children after a marriage that typically took place in church, with religious ceremonies accounting for 85 per cent of weddings even in 1960.[11]

Things could not be more different now. While only 5 per cent of Scottish children were born to unmarried parents in 1951, today it is half of Scotland's children. Whereas religious ceremonies accounted for 85 per cent of weddings as recently as 1960, half our marriages are now civil ceremonies. Today 75 per cent of married women – and 70 per cent of married mums – work outside the home. From a handful of divorces each year before the early 1950s, and just a few thousand in total for the whole of the first half of the twentieth century, one million Scots have been divorced since 1951.[12]

I am not passing any judgement on these new trends in family life and, indeed, I think we should welcome the connection between greater workplace flexibility and women's empowerment at home and, crucially, at work. But change there has been, and it is dramatic.

In the 1920s only one in seven Scottish trade unionists was a woman, and most trade unionists were men working in private-sector heavy industry.[13] In the 1950s one in three was a woman. Now half the trade unionists of Scotland are women. Gone are the days when I could hear one of my trade-union colleagues talking of 'the Scottish working class and their wives'.

From a peak of 1.2 million Scottish trade unionists just twenty years ago, there are now 635,000 and, while they represent a larger share of the workforce in Scotland (35 per cent) than England (29 per cent), Scottish trade-union membership has been falling at twice the rate of English membership in the last ten years.[14]

When the trade unions in Scotland started off as distinctively Scottish organisations, they were slow to get off the ground. The entire affiliated membership of the Scottish Trades Union Congress stood at just 135,000 in 1909 and, while it doubled to 225,000 by 1914 and then doubled again to 500,000 post-1918, Scottish trade unions, especially in rural areas, were much weaker than in England.[15] Indeed the now-legendary strength of Scottish trade unionism happened only as Scottish trade unions merged into British trade unions. One by one, in the years after 1918, the iron moulders, tailors, steel workers, plumbers, cabinetmakers, dockers, gas workers and municipal workers amalgamated into British unions. The last Scottish-only industrial union to merge into a British union was the Scottish Horse and Motormen's Association, led into the Transport and General Workers' Union by Alex Kitson in the 1960s. In 2000 only 4 of the 46 unions affiliated to the separate, distinctive and well organised Scottish Trades Union Congress were exclusively Scottish, 3 of them teaching unions, reflecting the ongoing separation of the education system.[16]

The unification of Scottish and English trade unionism reflected a growing realisation that, employed by British firms and often by the British state, trade unionists were better off bargaining together. Indeed Scotland produced many of Britain's best-known trade-union leaders, from Alexander MacDonald, the leader of the first British miners' trade union, and his successors Robert Smillie and Keir Hardie (who started as a miners' leader), right through to famous modern British leaders from Scotland like Lawrence Daly, Mick McGahey, Jimmy Airlie, John Boyd, Alex Kitson, Sam McCluskie, Jimmy Knapp and many others. None of these men saw a Scotland-only road to socialism as the sum total of their ambitions. Believing that Scottish interests and ideals were best secured through and not in opposition to the Union, they argued for UK-wide improvements to working conditions and, in so doing, raised the levels of pay and protection enjoyed by Scots from 90 per cent of average UK wages in 1951 to near parity today.[17]

So even though the heyday of Scottish trade-union strength

may have lasted only for the sixty years from the great amalgamations in the 1920s through to the 1980s, those successes did a huge amount to shape our identity and to drive forward real improvements in the living standards of Scots.

Then, of course, most Scots worked for British-owned companies, British public corporations or the British state. Today many Scots who work in the private sector are employed by non-Scottish and non-British companies and, since devolution, most Scottish public-sector workers are employed by Scottish-run, rather than British-run, agencies of the state.

We will look in a future chapter at how Scotland remains bound into a social settlement which started with the UK-wide Factory Act and goes right through to a common UK minimum wage, but it would be hugely surprising if the changing nature of trade unionism (with the shift from male to female majorities, and from private to public sector), in combination with the changing nature of Scottish employment (with far more working for Scottish rather than British agencies in the post-devolution state), had *not* had a huge impact on how effective trade unionism could be as a vehicle for maintaining a sense of British solidarity.

So, if our work and home lives are very much in flux, has that other great anchor of Scottish identity – the church – fared much better at giving Scotland a sense of stability in unsettling times?

Alas (at least from my point of view) the answer to that is no. Perhaps the most striking feature of contemporary Scotland is that religion matters so much less to the everyday lives of Scots than ever before.

Today, more Scots have no religious beliefs than identify with the Church of Scotland, the largest religious denomination. In total, 54 per cent of Scots identify themselves as Christian but the number of people with no religious beliefs has grown from 1.4 million to 1.9 million in the space of a decade. With the exception of their weddings (half of Scotland's brides and grooms are, as I noted, married in religious ceremonies), their funerals and what happens in schools, most Scots have no contact with a minister, priest or any religious leaders or institutions. The downward trend in religious affiliation set out in the introduction – that church membership has fallen from two million in the 1950s to no more than 400,000 now – looks even more dramatic when we discover that the Church of Scotland has lost 50,000 in the last three years. If this pattern continues then the membership will halve again in just over a decade.[18]

Of course the decline in religious commitment and attendance is being reported everywhere – even in America. But while America has suffered a small fall in adherence, and their different denominations still pride themselves in confidently celebrating the American way of life, Scotland's massive fall in such a short time represents one of the most dramatic declines in any country I know. Only eleven new ministers were ordained by the Church of Scotland last year.[19] And with its new priests coming from Poland and Africa as recruitment from Ireland dries up, the Catholic Church in the west of Scotland is being reorganised to cater for new times.

Religious leaders have taken comfort from the findings of the 2011 census in which more than half of the people of Scotland spoke of their positive identification with the Christian faith. More people, they say, attend Sunday church services than Saturday football matches.[20] But while we once thought of ourselves as 'the godly commonwealth' and 'the covenanted nation' – and the Church still thinks of itself as 'the keeper of the soul of Scotland' – the words of a former Church of Scotland Moderator, Professor John Baillie, that 'the life of the Scottish community has largely slipped its Christian moorings', uttered first in 1943 as a warning, are surely relevant as a description of fact now.[21] Even though it is recognised that in many communities faiths provide 'spiritual capital' that is part of the social capital that makes them tick, Scotland is now sadly – in my view

– defined as 'secular', 'post-Christian' and sometimes 'post-secular'. All parties are committed to upholding the freedom of religious conscience and I, like many, want to end anti-Catholic and gender discrimination in the laws of succession.

It may seem uncontroversial that the Scottish government would not ask a new monarch to swear loyalty to the Church of Scotland nor seek to uphold the Church of Scotland as the national church even though this is currently enshrined in UK law. But it would have been unthinkable fifty years ago that any Scottish constitution would be a secular one and not acknowledge that 'human realms are under the authority of God'. It would have been equally unimaginable that there would not be a positive response to the unanimous request of Scotland's very diverse faith groups that the contribution of faith to Scottish society should be properly recognised in the constitution.

Scots churches may be paying a price for being too slow to embrace a more tolerant society. For many years until the mid-1960s the Church of Scotland Assembly summarily rejected well-argued proposals from women to admit them even as elders.

And in 1983, when I first stood for parliament, the Catholic Church's uncompromisingly tough stand of banning all abortion led to priests denouncing candidates like me at the Sunday services. Even as recently as 2009 the then head of the Roman Catholic Church in Scotland, Cardinal O'Brien, hired my father's old church to make a speech attacking my stance on embryology.

On gay rights too, Scotland's history is one of religiously inspired moralising. It was a Scottish voice, that of James Adair, a former procurator-fiscal for Glasgow, a Church leader and the head of the YMCA in Scotland, that was the only one raised against the otherwise unanimous and humane recommendation of the Wolfenden Committee that 'homosexual behaviour between consenting adults in private should no longer be a criminal offence'.[22] And while the Church of Scotland committee reported as early as 1957 in favour of decriminalisation, their proposal for reform was rejected by both the prestigious Church and Nation Committee, and then the General Assembly, after Mr Adair delivered an inflammatory speech arguing that 'it would no longer be unlawful for perverts to practise sinning for the sake of sinning' and that under the new law homosexuals would be soliciting on the street.[23]

Kenneth Roy's chronicle of the times records how he was supported by all the influential newspapers of the day. The *Glasgow Herald* said that 'it is much more important that medical and psychiatric research should be intensively directed towards discovering a cure for or a socially accepted palliative of homosexuality than ... public order and decency should be risked even to a minor degree by premature changes in the law' while a *Scotsman* article declared that it was 'no solution to any public problem to legitimise a bestial offence'. A *Daily Record* poll found 85 per cent of Scots resisting decriminalisation, a much higher degree of opposition to reform than found by its sister paper the *Daily Mirror* in a similar poll south of the border.[24]

So, when the 1967 Sexual Offences Act was passed for England and Wales, Scotland was excluded not because it had its own laws that were to be liberalised nor because of a dispute over whether sexual 'offences' were more appropriately regulated at a Scottish level, but because the proposed new law was deemed too liberal for Scottish opinion. We can be proud that, like England, Scotland has recently legalised same-sex marriage but we should not forget that until 1980 homosexuality was still criminal in Scotland and that, even as recently as the year 2000, Wendy Alexander's brave attempts to repeal the law which prohibited discussion of homosexuality in schools were opposed by a multi-million pound, privately organised referendum campaign that exploited people's prejudices and fears.

All these debates spoke to a wider social conservatism, with a small 'c'. I remember how every year when I was growing up a notorious Edinburgh councillor, John Kidd, was dragged out at the time of the Edinburgh Festival to savage anything considered avant-garde; how every year at the time of the General Assembly there was always a well-publicised denunciation of our nation's declining moral standards; and how even in the 1980s and 1990s when I was dealing with personal cases as a constituency MP I was shocked to find so many people who had been sexually abused, subjected to domestic violence or been victims of prejudice and discrimination, feeling ashamed to come forward in a Scotland where judgement and blame were so often our dominant responses to complex social issues.

Of course in Scotland today many youth organisations still thrive, many churches flourish, some after declining and then being born again, and one-third of Scots today do voluntary and charitable work. The Scots response to worldwide appeals against hunger, illiteracy and disease is impressive. But have we finally seen the passing of what the writer Gerry Hassan called 'high Scotland' – or what I might call 'high and mighty Scotland' – which was 'a managed, ordered society of closed elites and professions who until recently faced very little public scrutiny or criticism' and who championed a puritanical, moralistic and authoritarian Scotland that, he says, knew your best interest better than you did, that preached at you while rarely listening, that was quick to judge, and that required you to have permission to act? And if the old order has passed, what, if anything, might fill the space in which the Churches, trades unions and civic organisations used to be predominant?[25]

As so often in the past it is to literature that we turn in our search for clues about the new Scotland. In the late 1970s, the literature top ten would almost certainly have been Scottish classics from Burns, Scott and Stevenson to J. M. Barrie and John Buchan. But in 2003, in a Scotland traumatised by deindustrialisation, the top-ten list chosen by Scots demonstrated, according to the head of the Scottish Book Trust, that 'drug addiction, crime, fantasy, murder and broad comedy are the literary topics which best represent contemporary Scotland'. The choices of *The Crow Road* by Iain Banks, *Morvern Callar* by Alan Warner, *One Fine Day in the Middle of the Night* by Christopher Brookmyre, *Not for Glory* by Janet Paisley, Dave Brown and Ian Mitchell's *Mountain Days and Bothy Nights* and Des Dillon's *Me and Ma Gal*, were said by the *Herald* newspaper to represent 'a grim Scotland brought to book'. All were fiction, with no room in the Scotland of Scott and Burns for history or poetry, although *The Broons Annual* made it, suggesting there's still a little bit of *Sunday Post* Scotland left after all.

Scotland had rebelled, concludes Robert Crawford in *Scotland's Books*, against the 'narrowly middle-class, residually Presbyterian assumptions that still governed the Scotland of the 1950s and 60s when these writers were growing up'. In place of 'rural parochialism', Scotland now embraced 'the brilliance of a backlash' devoted to the 'sub-cultural experiences' of characters like those in *Trainspotting*.[26] They were what Alex Niven calls 'sullen portrayals of a dilapidated Britain riven by Thatcherism and failed by a decrepit counterculture . . . a Thatcherite scorched earth in which nothing was worth working for and the simulated escape route offered by drink and drugs seemed like the only option'.[27]

'We must be honest about the problems in our midst' wrote Alasdair Gray, the author of the landmark novel *Lanark*, saying 'people endured hellish industrial conditions. Their lives were scarred and shaped not just by poverty but by pronounced inequality.'[28] Or, as 1994 Booker Prize-winner James Kelman put it: 'what I want to do is to write as well as I can from within my own culture and community, always going more deeply into it . . . using the living language and it comes out of many different sources including Scotland before the English arrive'.[29] According to the literary academic Alex Thomson, the new literature is about 'preserving the idea of a national literature operating in advance of political structures'. It is 'the forerunner of and inspiration for a new kind of "self-affirmation" by the Scottish people and the manifestation of more profound upheavals at the level of national self-consciousness'.[30]

Liam McIlvanney, on the other hand, argues: 'It would be wrong to reduce the novelists to the cheerleaders of a resurgent nationalism' and A. L. Kennedy has asserted that we can exaggerate 'Scottish traditions of writing' as they are 'an irrelevance with most Scottish writers'.[31] Perhaps James Robertson, the first writer-in-residence of the Scottish Parliament, who had traced a nationalist awakening in his novel *Voyage of Intent*, gets nearer the truth when he wrote in 2005 that while Scottish literature must be aware of and understand our history because it is the story of who we have been and where we have come from, it need not be restrained by it.[32]

My own view is that Scottish writers are still trying to answer the question 'wha's like us?' with a defiant 'damn few', but I do not believe that the distinctively dark image that modern Scottish literature conveys is the settled story of post-industrial Scotland. Perhaps the extreme puritanism of the old could only be met with the extreme hedonism of the new and Irvine Welsh's may be the only kind of voice brazen enough to attempt to drown out John Knox. But if those modern literary traditions are the antithesis of our older ones, I do not think we yet have a synthesis that explains the Scotland of today. Now playing down, contrary to our public image abroad, appeals to the old mythology of clans, tartans and ancient battles, we have come a long way from what W. B. Yeats called 'an immature cultural nationalism' to becoming a culturally mature nation; and, thanks to historians like Tom Devine, modern Scotland has started a reckoning with our past – with our role in empire and the slave trade, with anti-Irish racism, with sexism and homophobia, sectarianism and violence – as well as the old moral authoritarianism.

But I don't believe either of these processes – the historical re-evaluation or the literary renaissance – is in itself enough to fill the vacuum where once the organisational strength and popular resonance of the church used to sit, expressing and shaping our national identity. Even our media are no longer as able as they were to shape the kind of national conversation we need at this time of transition. The popularity of STV and of the Scottish opt-outs by the BBC from the 1950s onwards was important to consolidating and shaping our Scottish identity, but for a century until recently it was the printed press – from the old Scottish *Daily Express* and then the *Daily Record* (which beat the world for its national penetration as a daily newspaper) to the million-selling *Sunday Post* – which really marked the Scottish media out as different. But today our best-selling papers, the *Daily Record* and the *Scottish Sun*, have seen their sales halved in just a decade to just over 200,000 each.[33]

So we find ourselves on the brink of a decision which could draw to a close 300 years of history, and yet without the sense of national certainty and a clear view of our national destiny which a decision of that magnitude would normally entail.

In the past we have seen how our Churches and civic organisations were Scottish without ever being anti-British. Our workplaces and in particular our trades unions were seen as part of Britain while drawing on the best of Scottish traditions and values. But traditional Scottish institutions – our churches, companies like RBS, trades unions, local councils, voluntary bodies, sporting institutions, government and media – seem less able to express and shape Scottish identity than before. Take football: while the national team is recovering, some of Scotland's greatest football institutions – clubs like Rangers, Hearts and, in my home county of Fife, Dunfermline – are going through the same crisis of confidence that has overwhelmed other traditional Scottish institutions. The truth is that these old once-authoritative institutions no longer provide a settled home for our sense of national identity nor command the loyalty they once did and their weakening has left a vacuum which new forces are seeking to fill.

One sign of the emergence of a modern Scottish identity would be gender equality. A strong women's movement is growing but, as Carol Craig has documented in her highly successful book *The Scots' Crisis of Confidence* and its sequels, most recently *The Great Takeover*, the position of women in Scottish society is yet to undergo the fundamental change that could allow us to talk meaningfully of genuine equality achieved.[34]

Much is, of course, different. Today the Labour and Conservative parties in Scotland have female leaders; the SNP has a female deputy leader and has just announced two new female cabinet ministers. Women account for over half the workforce. Girls have been outperforming boys in Scottish schools and women now comprise the majority of students in professional subjects like law, accountancy and medicine. Important feminist demands, from a focus on domestic violence to new rights to childcare, rightly attract huge support and public funding. Excellent enterprises have begun to write a women's history of Scotland and to acknowledge the importance of women in Scottish life.

But as Carol Craig points out, a typical meeting in Scotland of head teachers, company chief executives and church ministers will still be dominated by men.[35] And while women are as likely to be trade union members as men, the leaders remain predominantly male. The voices of women, which are so critically important to the future of Scotland, are still not heard as loudly as they should be. 'We need women who can speak for Scotland, who can tell us not just what Scotland is or was but what it might yet be', wrote the former *Herald* editor Harry Reid in 2010. Or, as Craig puts it, making a more general point about aspirations and confidence: 'What was most troublesome was that very few women's voices were being heard in the media, at events and on public platforms . . . In a culture which undermines rather than builds individual self-confidence and which expects people to conform to rigid norms of behavior, Scottish women have had good reason not to feel ambitious for themselves and to conform to the limited life which has, at least until recently, been on offer.'[36] The old Scotland has gone but the new Scotland is yet to arrive.

So is it any wonder that, in this time of great flux, there is a vacuum in which political nationalism can appear to offer simple answers to the question of how we might both shape and express our sense of ourselves as Scots today?

On every measure, the polls now show that Scottish identity trumps all else. When forced to choose just one national identity out of an array of possible identities including Scottish and British, Scottish identity has been far more popular throughout the last forty years: 65 per cent of respondents said they were Scottish and 31 per cent said that they were British in 1974.[37] This had shifted to 72 per cent and 25 per cent in 1992, went as high as 80 per cent and 13 per cent in 2000, and was most recently 66 per cent and 24 per cent in 2013.[38]

In response to the more elaborate 'Moreno question' – named after its author who presents five options to gauge the relative weighting of an individual's Scottish and British identity – the proportion of respondents who have said that they were either solely Scottish, more Scottish than British or equally Scottish and British was 84 per cent in 2009 and 83 per cent now. Those who feel solely Scottish or more Scottish than British accounted for 61 per cent of respondents in 1997 and 53 per cent now. There is no doubt that Scottishness is the predominant identity now.[39]

But for me the more subtle and interesting change is in what has happened to our sense of Britishness. Some Scots, a small minority, are anti-British (or even anti-English). That has always been the case, but Scots' commitment to a British identity was seriously eroded during the years of Conservative government at Westminster from 1979. So how many people are prepared to accept a British dimension in their lives and at what level of intensity or detachment? Ten per cent of people feel British not Scottish or more British than Scottish. Around 30 per cent feel equally British and Scottish. And around another 30 per cent feel more Scottish than British but not exclusively Scottish. That leaves 25 per cent or so (it peaked at 36 per cent in 2001 just after the Scottish Parliament was created and reached a low of 23 per cent last year) who feel exclusively Scottish and therefore feel no affinity to Britain.[40]

Those who feel exclusively Scots do not feel this way because of our distinctive religion – people saying they are solely Scots are more likely to be agnostic – but men and women in the lowest-income group were more than twice as likely as those on the highest incomes to describe themselves as Scottish not British. Yet what is most striking is that less than half of those who feel solely Scottish want independence. The Scottish Centre for Social Research found that 'national identity does make a difference to people's views about independence . . .', but the effect is nowhere near as big as we might imagine. Of course those who, on the Moreno scale, say they are Scottish not British are much more likely to support independence than those who put themselves at the other end of the spectrum, and yet only '46 per cent of those who say they are Scottish and not British support independence'.[41]

What may have changed, according to John Curtice, is that in recent years people have become less likely to think that Scotland gets a raw deal from the Union. The gap between those who feel that England's economy fares better from the Union than Scotland's does is small, 28 per cent to 22 per cent. 'By far the most widespread perception nowadays is that both countries derive equal economic benefit. In the early days of devolution, in contrast, the view that England's economy benefited most from having Scotland in the UK was quite widespread.'[42]

There is one very real sense in which Scots feel detached from Britain and the importance of the finding cannot be underestimated. The most recent polls suggest that more Scots feel that most English people look down on them. This sentiment is obviously felt strongly by those who support independence – and may be one of the reasons why they do so – with a large majority of them holding this view. But it is also felt by many people voting No (one quarter) and even more so by undecided voters (around half). And very few people are prepared to disagree with the sentiment that most English look down on the Scots: only one in six of Yes voters and one in four of undecided voters. The feeling is particularly strong amongst lower-income voters, the majority of whom agree that most English people look down on them, with only one in four taking the opposite view. The feeling is also more prevalent amongst men than women. This does not bode well for good relationships between Scotland and England.[43]

But we have to put this in proper perspective. As the British Social Attitudes Survey concludes from its longitudinal study from the 1970s, '[o]nly a minority of around a third in each year regard themselves as exclusively Scottish . . . Most respondents recognise a British identity besides their Scottish identity and do not regard them as mutually exclusive.' According to John Curtice: 'Older people are much more likely to have a strong sense of British identity; over half of those aged over 65 give themselves a score of six or seven on our Britishness scale, compared with just 14% of those aged 18–24. They do indeed seem to be still carrying the outlook and sympathies of a more unionist age.'[44]

When it was recently reported that 62 per cent of people living in Scotland now said their national identity was 'Scottish only', Professor Tom Devine rightly challenged the credibility of the 'forced choice' question which gave rise to these headlines, on the basis that it is 'set in such an "either/or" fashion that it cannot capture the full complexities of duality'. And either because of a residual sense of affection or a hard-headed calculation, the vast majority of Scots have not yet written off the British connection.[45] Perhaps after 300 years of Union there is at least a submerged or latent attachment to a British dimension in most of us.

I think of my own family – the war experience of my mother, who worked in London, my brothers working in England, my wife born in England and having an English family, and the time I have spent working in London – and conclude that my family's story is not that unusual.

Today with half of all Scottish families having relatives in England, many Scots working for British companies and many with British connections through voluntary organisations, the armed forces and regular travel, most people do not see our Scottish identity and a British dimension to our lives as mutually exclusive. While older people may be more strongly British, many younger Scots see their Scottishness as compatible with or even complementary to a whole host of other cross-cutting identities. Douglas Alexander MP has made the acute observation that younger voters, the so-called 'nationalist generation', are in fact the networked generation, whose regular internet contact and mobile communication with people across the world has changed their view of what national identity is. As Salman Rushdie says, young people are attracted not just to 'home' – the dream of roots – but to 'the away' – the mirage of the journey. They do not see themselves as one-dimensional figures but as people with multiple links and loyalties and world-wide connections. Alexander cites Barack Obama's conclusion in his memoir *Dreams from My Father*, which highlights the limits of a politics of identity and ethnicity: 'Our sense of wholeness would have to arise from something more fine than the bloodlines we'd inherited ... It would have to find root in ... all the messy, contradictory details of our experience.'[46]

It is thus Alexander's argument that 'dual identities come easily to these dual screeners. They fear a separate Scotland would be a narrowing, not a broadening, experience. And they see the forced binary choice of Scotland or the UK as last-century, not this-century, thinking ... The polls show consistently that the Network Generation recognises that they and future generations have the most to gain from remaining part of the UK and the most to lose from walking away.' So in addition to those still influenced by the shared experience of war and the success of building a welfare state, even if we were too young to have been directly part of either, there are the children of globalisation, completely confident in multiple identities and attuned to the opportunities which being part of a leading world player still brings.[47]

We should not be surprised that Scots have a sophisticated account of their identity in a time of globalisation as we have so often shown ourselves highly adaptable in the past. Indeed the Moreno statistics I have quoted have led Tom Devine to argue that: 'From the late 18th century, Scots, who were citizens of a historic nation, albeit a stateless one after 1707, developed a dual identity, a complex mix of Scottishness and Britishness which has endured to a greater or lesser extent to the present day. In the Victorian era and during and after the Second World War, Britishness was in the ascendancy. More recently, however, Scottishness has become much more dominant. Nonetheless there is little sign ... that the dual identity has finally been shattered.'[48]

So the Scottish identity may be in flux with a new identity yet to crystallise, but it is not yet an identity that excludes Britishness, even if it wishes to downplay it.

An even earlier Scottish thinker helps explain why that might be. Adam Smith wrote in 1759 about the extent and limits of the empathy we have in common with people in other regions, countries and continents, of a world of concentric circles – of an inner circle of relationships where there is a stronger empathy broadening out all the time into an outer set of circles where the feelings of solidarity may be weaker, but can be made to be real nonetheless.[49]

Smith takes an example of his peers' lack of interest in the victims of a Chinese earthquake to say that people felt little concern for the fate of distant strangers because they knew little about them, had little capacity to help them and, ethics aside, recognised no shared purposes with them. As Fonna Forman has shown, they were, in Smith's time, beyond the circles of knowledge, capacity and interest, but Smith believed that, if these obstacles could be overcome, our moral sense could be engaged.[50]

So Smith does not base his idea of empathy on racial affinity but founded on knowledge, contact and the education of the moral sense and, crucially, he suggests that the loyalties we feel are not permanent, fixed and unchangeable but can alter over time: we can develop feelings of empathy towards others once we know more about them, are in regular contact and communication with them, and educate our moral sense about what we have in common.[51]

This is precisely what has led millions of Scots to participate in campaigns like Make Poverty History, but also precisely what has meant that bonds of Britishness may not be so easily severed as we travel and communicate across the border with ever-greater regularity.

In the next chapter we are going to look at whether there are distinctive Scottish values, but we have seen how a set of dramatic economic, social and cultural changes helps explain why the question of who we are is being asked so insistently today and gives the questions we will address in Chapter 3 a very special urgency.

CHAPTER 3

Are there Scottish Values?

You never forget your teachers and in a very real way your education shapes your life. I can list each teacher I had from the day I started at primary school, aged four – Miss Mason was followed by Miss Donaldson and then Mrs Monroe and so on. The secondary school I attended, Kirkcaldy High, is one of the oldest schools in Scotland and is the direct heir of the Kirkcaldy Burgh School that the world-renowned but unmistakably Scottish economist Adam Smith attended in the eighteenth century.

Smith always acknowledged the debt he owed to his Burgh School in Hill Street, only a few yards from where he and his mother lived. He had one of the best educations that any young man of the time could have, at one of the best schools of its day in Scotland. Local people continuously searched for the best teachers to bring to Kirkcaldy. In Smith's day that meant bringing in a schoolmaster from nearby Cupar, but by the nineteenth century it meant hiring the great writer Thomas Carlyle. That restless drive for improvement ensured the school was always changing. The building in which Smith learned has been knocked down and, in the course of two centuries, the high school has been moved from its second location, near the seafront, to the centre of the town and then, from the 1950s, to the outskirts.

I've started this chapter with the story of Kirkcaldy High not out of sentimentality, but because I believe the values represented by my school are illustrative of what I mean by a distinctive Scottish tradition in education. The school's educational philosophy is summed up in a book written at a time of great change in education, 1944, by the then headmaster, Dr Frank Earle. His theme was extending educational opportunity to all by providing what he called an 'omnibus school' or 'universal school'. He ran Kirkcaldy High as a precursor of the comprehensive ideal which emerged in the sixties, believing that individual development would be promoted best by the 'congregation, within one school, of pupils whose varied aims, ambitions, abilities, interests, tastes, temperaments and characters reflect those of the community to which they belong'.[1]

While he believed in academic streaming, he did not believe in academic selection and instead argued that the separation of children into different schools both thwarted the ambition of the least able and ensured that the most gifted lost the chance to develop the leadership skills they'd need in adult workplaces where people have mixed skills and abilities.

The idea of mixed comprehensive or universal education was not, of course, distinctive to Scotland and educational reformers in England were having similar ideas at the time Dr Earle began his 'omnibus' experiment. But what was, I believe, a distinctively Scottish strand could be found in the determination that all children should be introduced to the very best of what might be called 'high' culture. This mentality saw schools as more than servants of the economy and believed that even those who would be unable to secure top professional jobs nonetheless had the right to learn how to think critically and to access the entire cultural and intellectual heritage of our country.

This idea, sometimes called 'the democratic intellect', was taken further in Scotland than anywhere else. Another term for it was the 'lad o' pairts' (a talented youth who could rise through the system despite humble origins), which was radical for its time although it did not, as it should have, include the lass o' pairts too.

These two strands of thinking – that local schools should combine universality with excellence – came together forcefully in Fife. The Fife education authorities were determined to have as many pupils from as many backgrounds as possible studying together, so our secondary schools were far larger than the average in Scotland. And my school motto – 'I will strive my utmost' – says everything about the high ambitions the teachers had for every child.

My education was distinctively Scottish in other ways too. The Scottish education system was founded on offering the widest possible educational curriculum, so I now know why I studied for such a wide range of Highers (seven in all) in contrast to the narrow specialism of A-levels, even if I did not fully comprehend why at the time. Indeed, when I went to university I did not really appreciate the deeper reasons that led me to being offered a course in mathematics even when I was taking a degree in history, nor why I was drawn to taking an ordinary MA degree with moral philosophy at its core before I specialised in history, taking an MA Honours degree.

Education specialist Professor Lindsay Paterson explains that Scottish curriculum design began from the idea that 'the only educational preparation that will enable people to develop a critique of traditions, rather than unthinkingly be absorbed into them, is through the academic study of the main disciplines of thought ... Philosophy provided the common language that enabled the dialogue to take place: in the Scottish tradition, general education sought to instil in its students a familiarity with abstract reasoning even at the expense of detailed knowledge.'[2] Professor William Storrar has called it a philosophical 'cast of mind that establishes first principles as the root of all branches of knowledge'.[3]

So what I realise now is that what I was studying reflected a strong Scottish tradition – that philosophy is the essential tool of learning and that a Scots education is not about rote learning but about developing all the critical faculties of the mind.

CRITICAL MINDS

I have written in earlier chapters about the distinctive traditions of Scottish religion and that while our faith has often led Scots to be puritanical, it has just as regularly led to the rebellion by critical minds against any attempts to insert a layer of authority between the individual and their God. That same dissenting tradition runs through our educational philosophy and practice. Together, they form the basis of what are, I would argue, distinctive Scottish values.

This is fiercely contested terrain in the independence debate. In a controversial book, Lesley Riddoch says that between Scotland and England we find 'two sets of values grinding away at each other in almost every aspect of life', while two thinkers who are otherwise opponents – Douglas Alexander and Nicola Sturgeon – are agreed that we should be wary of the 'cultural conceit' which says Scottish values are both separate and superior.[4] I believe the truth will always be contested but most will agree that in values, as in much else, Scotland feels different from England but is more like England than anywhere else.

I write elsewhere about the power of the idea that animates our Union – that we should share risks and resources and provide the same rights and social protection to citizens of each of the four home nations. But in this chapter I want to look more closely at whether we can trace a distinctively Scottish strain in the formulation and execution of that idea.

The suggestion, of course, that the Union would not be structured in the way that it is without the inspiration of Scottish values need not lead us to the conclusion that it is *solely* a product of Scottish values. We have been much enriched, for example, by the English ideas of rights and the responsibilities of rulers, as well as the very English idea of tolerance that, you might suggest, had to be taught to us Scots. The peculiarities of the English Reformation created a deep-seated English pragmatism that is still to be found in English law, with its focus on the application of precedent to specific, modern circumstances, and in the very quiet and peaceful way in which constitutional innovations are incorporated into the way we govern ourselves.

So it is perfectly possible to believe, as I do, that Scottish values are meaningfully distinct, but that they benefit from cross-fertilisation with the ideas of our neighbours. Sometimes we choose to reflect our shared values in shared institutions like the NHS and sometimes we choose to assert our differences through separate institutions like the different Scottish and English legal systems. That system might not be perfectly neat, but it is perfectly practical.

The creation of a separate Scottish Parliament is perhaps the most significant point in the development of this argument in my lifetime. Those of us who fought for a Scottish Parliament did so because we wanted Scotland to have control over those of her affairs where power was most appropriately located closer to home. We thought an institution in and of Scotland could reflect distinctive Scottish concerns and values, but that those differences were not so great that total separation from our neighbours was the answer. I remember a conversation with Donald Dewar about the importance of the choice of words engraved on the head of the ceremonial mace of the Scottish Parliament – not the words of 'Flower of Scotland' but, as he insisted, the words 'Wisdom, Justice, Compassion and Integrity'. These reflected, in his view, distinctive Scottish ideas.

Ideas about society, of course, don't really mean anything – distinct or otherwise – if we can't imagine a practical way in which they might be expressed. But I believe that in this instance we can trace those Scottish values that Donald so cherished, through our history, and in the development of our Union. Two in particular stand out. The first is the idea, discussed above, of the democratic intellect. The valorisation of the critical mind – and the sense that God gave one to each and every one of us – has been reflected throughout the history of Scottish religion and Scottish education.

The second is the idea of civil society – that we can build together institutions that reflect not just rights enjoyed but obligations owed, and that those obligations can exist at one step removed from the blood ties of family and the enforcement powers of the state. That idea found its earliest modern expression in the period of the Scottish Enlightenment.

I believe that these two notions – Scottish in source and inspiration – have determined not just what makes us distinctive as Scots, but the nature of the unique Scottish contribution to Britain and the world. We discussed in earlier chapters why that might be. The fixation on the individual and their critical faculties has its roots, I believe, in the Reformation – in the determination that Scots would be a people of the Book. The second, as discussed, perhaps emerges from the peculiarity of the Scottish situation of being a society without a state. Perhaps only a stateless people could develop ideas about 'social capital' while having no political capital of their own. Whatever the reasons behind it, historians generally agree that the development of both education and civic life has been different on each side of the border.

Why does any of that matter today? For me the question of whether there are distinctive Scottish values is important because it helps us to determine what the independence fight is really all about. If we reduce the conversation simply to a cost-benefit analysis of who gets what, when and how, then I think we do a disservice to Scotland's long and proud history as an independent nation. But if we simply assert that there is an inevitable link between the distinctiveness of Scottish values and the need for a separate state, then we obscure what is in fact the most exciting fact of Scottish history: that we have maintained our distinct identity not in *spite* of the Union, but *through* it. Scotland's genius has been to resist assimilation into a bigger identity while ensuring that the wider British state bears a distinctively Scottish stamp.

Looked at in this way, who is talking Scotland down: the No campaign, which simply wants answers to specific questions about the practicalities of separation? Or the nationalists, who believe Scotland is so weak she has been quite unable to exert her power inside our family of nations and has nothing to show for 300 years of intellectual and political agitation in the service of her values?

For me any honest account of Scotland's future needs to begin with knowing ourselves, and that starts with understanding how our education has shaped our mentality.

In the town in which I grew up, education was always valued as a route out of the pits and into the professions. The miners' leaders who ran our county council and thus our education system prided themselves on the high standards of local schools and in helping young people from poor backgrounds to succeed. The suggestion that you would 'dumb down' education to make it more 'accessible' to the working class was totally alien to them – as it was to legendary local trade unionist Lawrence Daly.

Daly was both a young miner in Fife and on the board of a highbrow publication, the London *New Left Review*. He would correct and comment on the proofs of this literary magazine on his breaks while working down a mineshaft, sending his thoughts back to the London literati covered in coal dust.

So in Scotland the democratic intellect was not a focus on the intellect without a focus on democracy – which owes more to the elitism of the English public-school system and to Oxbridge – but neither was it a focus on democracy without a focus on the intellect, which would have undervalued the importance of education itself.

Instead my generation was simply the latest in a long line of Scottish children encouraged to believe that every single person has a talent and should be stretched to the full. As Jimmy Reid said in his rectorial address at Glasgow University, 'the untapped resources of the North Sea are as nothing compared to the untapped resources of our people. I am convinced that the great mass of our people go through life without even a glimmer of what they could have contributed to their fellow human beings. This is a personal tragedy. It is a social crime.'[5]

There are plenty of others who share this form of egalitarianism, of course, and there is no doubt that in England educational reformers like R. H. Tawney, Harold Laski and G. D. H. Cole held as radical if not more radical views about reform. What is interesting about the Scottish experience is the coalition that united behind these ideals. North of the border bold ideas about the rights and potential of the poorest children weren't simply held by left-wing intellectuals, trade unionists and Labour politicians, but by the teaching professions and the clergy too. Go back a few centuries – whether it was 1494, when the aristocratic lords were called upon to take responsibility for education; or the 1560s, when the *Book of Discipline* demanded education for every child; or 1696, when a law was passed requiring village and burgh schools to be set up in every community – and Scotland pioneered a belief in social inclusion through education.

The work of historian Rob Houston has, however, shown in great detail that the Reformation ideal of universal literacy (so that all people could study the Bible, leading to 'a priesthood of all believers') was honoured more in its neglect than in its observance. In 1834 the Rev. George Lewis wrote about Scotland as a half-educated nation and in 1857 it was found that only half of 5–10-year-olds attended school in Glasgow. While primary-school education was made compulsory in 1872, 90 per cent of boys and girls did not attend secondary school and, even when the school leaving age was raised to fourteen, you could go half time at the age of ten.[6] And the high achieving schools from the eighteenth century onwards that were feeders for the universities were the burgh and city grammar schools, rather than the parish schools.

While Scotland had university places for one in 1,000 adults in contrast to one in 5,800 in England, Robert Anderson shows us that Scottish students were still overwhelmingly drawn from the upper, middle and skilled working classes; and Ian Carter has highlighted the low levels of social mobility in rural areas.[7]

But the expansion of education did nonetheless pick up pace from the late-nineteenth century onwards. The notion that education was the obligation of the state, and one it owed to all children equally, reached fulfilment with the 1918 Education (Scotland) Act, passed a quarter of a century before England's Butler Act. The provisions in the Act that ended discrimination against Catholics ensured it was lauded by T. C. Smout, one of my history professors, as one of the great advances in the history of Scottish human rights.

It is worth noting, however, that the drive for equal opportunities never equated to a belief in equal outcomes in Scotland. Calvinism is too hard-wired into the Scottish psyche for us to welcome an end result in which hard work and individual effort have played no part. But the drive for education was nonetheless radically egalitarian and inspired by the idea that all Jock Tamson's bairns had the right to fulfil their true potential.

So the split, found elsewhere in the UK, between a social elite of classical scholars and a barely educated populace was, as George Davie, author of *The Democratic Intellect*, wrote, 'utterly alien to the intellectual democracy of Protestant Scotland, where the elite was cultural, not social – a matter of trained minds rather than of privileged status – and the mass of society, even where impoverished and materially powerless, still was expected to engage with the great questions debated each week from the pulpit or in the school'.[8]

It is important to understand the social dimension of this 'democratic intellectualism'. The point is not simply that all aspects of learning and culture should be opened up – without being dumbed down – to people of all classes and abilities. It is also that people of all classes and abilities are then expected to play an equal part in the deliberations of the community. The development of the critical faculties was not enough – Scottish education sought to engender the active *application* of first principles about right and wrong in the life of the nation.

There is, of course, a tension here, between the authoritarian and dogmatic side of Calvinism's theology, and the anarchic and disputatious side of its congregations. In my view it is in that tension that much of the creativity of Scottish culture can be found. On the one hand, we are a puritan people with deep fixations on hard work, delayed gratification and long-term rewards. On the other, we are magnificently inventive, spectacularly stubborn and willing to throw everything up in the air if appeals are made to unearned status. Perhaps it is not so surprising that the tradition of Enlightenment education, which took an aggressively secular turn in France, made a happy accommodation with a Scottish Presbyterian tradition which built democracy and debate into the very structure of church life.

My thinking on Scottish education has been deeply influenced by the work of Professor Paterson and his argument that while each of the three aspirations for Scottish education – that it promotes individual opportunity, assists economic development and creates better citizens through a wide liberal-arts curriculum – are not in themselves unique to Scotland, they have combined together here in a unique way.[9]

I have spent the first section of this chapter really looking at only two of Professor Paterson's Scottish educational imperatives. I believe it is clear Scots always valued education for its role in helping each person develop their talents, and that we had and have a distinctive view about its role in creating good and critical citizens. But what of the other idea – that Scotland has always worried about how education will provide each generation with the skills of the future?

I have written earlier about living in a town of mass unemployment as the industries of Fife fell away. But what I want to explore now is whether there was something more than material hardship at stake. Because I believe that what united the community of Kirkcaldy in solidarity with the unemployed was not simply the belief that it could soon enough happen to any one of us, but also a sense that worklessness offended our values. We didn't just worry about our friends and family on the dole, we felt affronted on their behalves. Why was that?

I have spoken before about my parents' consternation on returning home to find I had invited a well-known local housebreaker in for a cup of tea. But I was only following their example – nobody who knocked at the door of the manse in need of help was ever turned away. My parents never encouraged us to pity any of those people – we were taught to see them as our equals, even if they were struggling at a time when we were not. In part that was because of how we thought about unemployment. We didn't think of it as something that *might* happen to any of us, but as something that *was* happening to all of us – because we were all part of the same moral community.

The flipside of the Calvinist obsession with the obligation to work was an equally vehemently held belief that people had a *right* to work – that access to jobs was even more important than access to services. So when the Upper Clyde Shipworkers held their work-in in the 1970s, it was no surprise to me that they got as much support from the local church and civic groups as they did from friends across the labour movement.

Or that when Donald Dewar, John Smith and I joined the March for Jobs it did not look like a typical left-wing protest, but more like the whole of Scotland including middle Scotland on the move.

By the time I entered the Treasury, I'd had thirty years as a foot soldier on the front line of the fight for jobs. The employment figures were always the ones I studied most closely and they still are. My focus at the Treasury was always on work as the best route out of poverty. We set up the New Deal to get young people into work, the tax-credit system to make work pay, and the most ambitious work programme any government anywhere enacted to meet the great recession of 2008, the Future Work Programme. In the thirteen years I was in government, Scottish unemployment decreased until the great recession. For most of this period it was around 5 per cent, getting close to what economists define as 'full employment'. These are figures that Britain had not achieved since the 1960s, but targets we hit in most of the years after 1997.[10]

The idea that all people and not just the elite should have opportunities to learn and to get a decent job is not, of course, a uniquely Scottish proposition. But I do believe that the idea of the democratic intellect and the Calvinist notions of worship through work do combine in a unique way there.

So if Scotland has a unique sense of both the role and the power of education, is that enough for us to conclude that there are such things as distinctive Scottish values? I do not believe so – not on its own at any rate.

THE SCOTS IN SOCIETY

To find the true source of Scotland's distinctive values, I think we need to look at our views about education in combination with something else: our views about civil society.

Looking back on my youth, our lives revolved around not only the home but also the school, the church, the youth club, the local football and rugby teams, the local tennis club, the uniformed organisations – the Scouts and Boys' Brigade – and other organisations as varied as the Royal National Lifeboat Institution, the St John's and St Andrew's Ambulance Brigades and the annual Christian Aid collection my mother helped organise.

I remember vividly the first game of football I played for the local Life Boys team and my jitters the night before on being handed the blue V-neck strip of the first team. I remember too the day I was given the yellow goalkeeper's jersey – then all goalkeepers' jerseys seemed to be yellow – and the feeling that I was being recognised as important to the team by being asked to play in goal. I also remember the first-aid certificate I won through classes in the station waiting room and the stamp collection – including stamps of the defunct Saar state – that was assessed as valuable by a local expert at the local stamp club on the promenade. Likewise I remember the music lessons I received, my time at the running club and the bob-a-job tasks I did for charity with the Scouts. All of these things were possible because youth leaders, church elders, sports coaches, Scouts and Boys' Brigade helpers, fundraisers, secretaries of local associations and other volunteers all pitched in to help for free.

It is easy to romanticise it now, and certainly attendance in formal community activities from church congregations to political parties is on the wane. But if you ask any MP or councillor in Scotland and they will tell you the same story – about communities held together by folk who'd never dream of calling their way of life 'volunteering', but who got on and did their best and their bit nevertheless.

People will rightly point out that you can find this same sense of neighbourliness all across the rest of the UK and indeed the world too. I don't dispute that, but I do want to suggest that Scotland should have a special place in the affections of the world for the role it played in helping us make sense of these instincts of compassion and care that we have as a species.

For it was Adam Smith who helped us to understand that human societies may find their affairs guided by the invisible hand of market competition, but they need the helping hand of social cooperation too. So often held up as the classical hero of selfish individualism, Smith in fact believed that 'to restrain our selfish, and to indulge our benevolent affections, constitutes the perfection of human nature; and can alone produce among mankind that harmony of sentiments and passions in which consists their whole grace and propriety'.[11] His fellow Enlightenment thinkers were likewise obsessed with the question of how true benevolence – that which is neither bought by the market nor compelled by the state – could be realised in society.

Smith, unlike Hume, saw our responsibilities to others arising out of more than enlightened self-interest, reciprocal altruism or empathy, but out of duty. In his *Theory of Moral Sentiments*, Smith wrote: 'Kindness is the parent of kindness; and if to be beloved by our brethren be the great object of our ambition, the surest way of obtaining it is by our conduct to show that we really love them'.[12] He and Adam Ferguson and others were engaged in a searching discussion of an idea that went variously under such headings as 'moral sense', 'sense of duty', 'moral faculty' – and 'common sense'. But the big Scottish idea underpinning this was that of a civic society, as something more than a mechanistic, or random coming together of a few individuals, but, instead, a highly moral public sphere which emphasised social responsibility and justice. Out of this the very idea of 'social capital' and indeed the discipline of sociology was born.[13]

We have talked earlier about the theory that this conversation started in Scotland precisely because we are a stateless nation. On this account, theories about civil society are Scotland's reaction to the paradox of being a society without a state. At this point I should also say that the Scottish academic Nicholas Phillipson, whose *Adam Smith: An Enlightened Life* adds to a long list of books and essays he has contributed to our understanding of these times, argues that Smith was largely untroubled by Scotland's peculiar constitutional status. Indeed he argues that Smith believed that social improvement, promoted by responsible citizens, was only possible in a reasonably stable polity, which was something he thought that Scotland had gained from the Union.[14]

So Scotland inherited from her Enlightenment both a set of ideas about mutual obligation, but also a distinctive understanding of how these ideas might be realised by smaller units of 'civil' government in the absence of a state. Thus in the seventeenth and eighteenth centuries it was not the state but the Church, the leader of civic society, which contributed to a school in each parish and to poverty relief. And as the Church gave way, the view grew that teachers, doctors, nurses and trained experts with their own professional ethics, supported by the government of the day, should be at the heart of the relief of poverty and destitution. So when I talk about Scotland's ideas about civil society, I do not mean that we think voluntary associations should somehow substitute for public services or universal guarantees of the provision of the essentials of life. Instead we mean the idea that people might recognise and fulfil obligations that are not legal duties we owe to the government but moral duties we owe one another that we undertake freely to fulfil.

Indeed I would argue that it was her disdain for the very idea of public service – and indeed the idea that some communities of professions have their own ethos and obligations and measures of professional pride and distinction beyond profit and loss – which in part explains the breach between the government of Mrs Thatcher and Scotland's middle class. We should not forget that the idea of Scotland as a 'Tory-free zone' is a relatively recent one. In the 1950s the *Scotsman* and *Glasgow Herald* were both Conservative papers and the *Daily Record* advocated a

Conservative vote in 1955. Moreover, the Conservative Party is the only party ever to have secured more than 50 per cent of the Scottish vote, achieving 50.1 per cent in 1955 when the Liberals earned only 1.9 per cent and the nationalists 0.5 per cent. So Scotland's lawyers, doctors, accountants, teachers and local-government officers have not always supported Labour, though I am delighted so many of them do now.

But do these two ideas – about a distinctive Scottish approach to education, and a distinctive notion about how mutual obligations can be realised in civil society – together add up to something we could point to as 'Scottish values'? I would say that they do – and we will look in a future chapter at the extraordinary success Scotland has had in shaping the British state so it can serve those values.

We should be wary, however, of pushing this argument beyond what the evidence will bear. It has become a common assertion in the independence debate that distinctive Scottish values stretch well beyond the democratic intellect and notions of civil society to encompass all sorts of left-of-centre views on every topic from redistribution to immigration.

Professor John Curtice, whose Scottish Social Attitudes survey is the largest source for polling material, challenges the idea of a uniquely socialist Scotland. While noting that 78 per cent of Scots (compared to 74 per cent of English voters) say the gap between high and low incomes is too high, only 43 per cent of Scots (compared to 34 per cent in England) believe that government redistribution is the right way to rectify it.[15] Scots may care (marginally) more about inequality than English people, but they don't appear wildly more enthusiastic about traditional left-wing ways of solving it.

In his recent report entitled 'Is it really all just about economics? Issues of nationhood and welfare', Curtice reports that the proportion of Scottish people who now think that unemployment benefit is too high is greater than it has been at any time since the advent of devolution, having risen from 33 per cent in 1999 to 52 per cent today. Overall, just 42 per cent of people would now like to see government spending increase, compared with 60 per cent in 2002. If the number of Scots who wanted to increase taxes to pay more for social spending reached its peak in 2001 when we won support for a National Insurance rise for the NHS, it has fallen from that high of 63 per cent to just 42 per cent today. While spending to support disabled people and pensioners remains relatively popular in Scotland, we have not in general been immune from a UK-wide trend towards tougher attitudes on welfare. However, when it comes to attitudes to privatisation and indeed to private schools, opinion polls show a significant difference between Scotland and England, with greater support in Scotland for publicly run services and collectivist institutions.[16]

So I want us to be honest when we talk about distinctive Scottish values. If we look at the North of England and Wales we find left-of-centre views on social issues very similar to those of Scotland. But while rejecting any airs of superiority it is not a total fantasy to believe that there is special commitment to social justice that stirs the Scottish heart. William McIlvanney, in his book *Surviving the Shipwreck*, recounts a French friend telling him that 'for you Scots it's always justice. It always comes back to justice.'[17] And the writer Milovan Djilas said that the difference between Jennie Lee, who came from Scotland, and her husband Nye Bevan, who came from Wales, was that, while he wanted to get on with the action of implementing change, she kept bringing things back to principle, always wanting to work out what was just before she tried to work out what was possible.

I believe that the defining events of Scotland's early modern history – the Reformation and the Enlightenment – have hardwired this quest for justice into Scotland's national life. Its manifestation in our distinctive education system and our complex web of civic institutions has helped keep Scotland different, but not so different that we must restrict the circle of our compassion only to those found north of the Tweed. Indeed I believe that Scotland's belief in equal opportunity – in the democratic intellect and in institutions of mutual obligation – has helped to shape the Union into what it is today. In a later chapter we will examine whether our modern partnership, built on sharing resources in the interests of social justice, is not perhaps the most powerful testament to Scottish values of all.

CHAPTER 4

Scotland and the Union

A few months before I completed my years as Chancellor, the head of the Royal Mint came to see me because he wanted to strike a commemorative coin to mark the 300th anniversary of the Anglo-Scottish Union. Little did I realise that it would be just about the only celebration of the historic date.

The anniversary fell two days before the Scottish Parliament elections on 3 May 2007. While the Scottish Executive had held a number of commemorative events through the year, none attracted much attention. An education project led by the Royal Commission on the Ancient and Historical Monuments of Scotland was followed by an exhibition of documents about the Union at the National Museum of Scotland. There was also an exhibition of portraits of people associated with the Union at the National Galleries of Scotland. The public seemed content to let these commemorations slip past, just as they thankfully largely ignored the Orange Order's march in Edinburgh.[1]

As I looked into it, I discovered that was not a one-off. The anniversary in 1807 also passed with little celebration, in contrast to George III's Golden Jubilee three years later in 1810. Even in 1907, the high point of the Union's popularity, there was little public celebration.[2]

In this chapter I want to look at why that might be and trace how the Union of 1707 changed, in a way that has transformed Britain from the image it created after 1707 – that of the unitary state of undivided Westminster sovereignty which at the same time provided for substantial civic and social autonomy for Scotland – to a more diverse UK with the Westminster Parliament complemented by a Scottish Parliament and two assemblies in Wales and Northern Ireland.

What we call the United Kingdom is, as Linda Colley reminds us in *Acts of Union and Disunion*, the product not just of one union but of a series of unions: between England and Wales in 1536–43, between England and Scotland in 1707, and between Great Britain and Ireland in 1800–1, the last ending in bloodshed and bitterness with the withdrawal of the Irish Free State in 1922 and its reconfiguration as a union with Northern Ireland only.[3] But the conventional view of the absolute concentration of power in Westminster was of course challenged in 1953 in a famous judgment of the Scottish courts by Lord Cooper, an eminent legal historian and a former Unionist politician, who argued that the principle of unlimited sovereignty was a distinctively English principle which had no counterpart in Scottish constitutional law: 'Considering that the Union legislation extinguished the parliaments of Scotland and England and replaced them by a new parliament, I have difficulty seeing why it should have been supposed that the new Parliament of Great Britain must inherit all the peculiar characteristics of the English Parliament but none of the Scottish Parliament, as if all that happened in 1707 was that Scottish representatives were admitted to the parliament of England.'[4]

Of course in a modern world where sovereignty is now seen as derived from the people not from the monarch, as stated in the all-party 1989 Claim of Right, few would agree with the 1707 theory of sovereignty. Indeed the vexed relationship between

Church and state in post-Reformation Scotland meant that the relationship with the monarch was more like a contract than a surrender to divine or dynastic rights.

The modern reinterpretation of the Union, however, goes beyond a reappraisal of ideas of sovereignty. The constitutional expert Professor James Mitchell has recently described the complex, post-1997 arrangements for devolved government between the core of the UK and the three non-English parts of the state, as 'a state of unions' and suggests that the idea of the UK as a union state 'fails to appreciate the variety of unions that created the UK and the persistence of their legacies in its development'. This leads him to conclude that 'the UK now has a system of government that is asymmetric with diverging trajectories and although the Westminster model remains important' ours is now 'an even looser union'.[5]

What really matters is the distribution of powers between the centre and the different parts of the Union, and thus the idea of the UK as a unitary state fails in another respect, leading the political scientists Stein Rokkan and Derek Urwin to offer an alternative characterisation of the UK as a 'union state'. They argue that while unitary states are built around a clear, dominant political centre, which 'pursues a more or less undeviating policy of administrative standardisation', the UK is different. They observe that 'while administrative standardisation prevails over most of the territory, [we see] the survival in some areas of pre-union rights and institutional infrastructures which preserve some degree of regional autonomy and serve as agencies of indigenous elite recruitment'. Territorial variations in the administration of decision-making, they argue, were sensitive to and reflected the nationhood of the component parts of the Union. Because Scotland was not conquered, the Treaty guaranteed the status of the separate Scottish legal system, the jurisdiction of the Court of Session and the independence of the Presbyterian Kirk and while the Great British Parliament retained the power to legislate on all issues, it had no intent to administer in law, religion, education and social policy.[6]

This is, of course, of more than historical interest. Indeed I believe we can only truly understand the choice facing Scotland now by understanding the historical evolution of the Union, and learning from our experiences in it to build a Union fit for the globalised age. So let's look at the three distinct phases in Scotland's relationship with the Union, which were each, I believe, underpinned by a set of common themes.

The first phase, from the inception of the Union until the early-nineteenth century, was a period during which security and economic policy were centralised but in almost all other areas it was an era of non-intervention by the British state. With the exception of the period between 1710 and 1714 and then the period after the 1745 Jacobite rebellion (when the British government moved against what was seen as a backward-looking Scottish feudalism) Scotland's autonomous institutions evolved without much interference. Indeed, in controlling the administration of the Scottish Poor Law and education system, mainly through the organisation of all-powerful local church leaders, Scotland resembled what has been called a 'parish state'.[7]

While maintaining the autonomy of our own civic institutions, Scotland also sought to benefit from the British Empire, from the wars with France and from the growth of commerce. And yet in the eighteenth century, the focus of most Scots commentators was on how the Union benefited the individual by providing liberty and security, rather than on how it impacted on Scotland itself. From Hume and Smith right through to Scott there was a belief, in Nicholas Phillipson's view, that the Union offered the possibility of political stability and national regeneration under the leadership of a patriot elite prepared to exploit the opportunities the Union offered. This explains the rebuilding of civil society in Scotland in the century and a half after the Union and the belief on the part of many senior lawyers, clerics, intellectuals and politicians (who contributed to the ethos of public service and professionalism that became so important in the civil service of the late nineteenth and twentieth centuries) that to engage in this was the essence of modern patriotism.[8] In fact, as Lindsay Paterson has observed in *The Autonomy of Modern Scotland*, Scotland enjoyed more autonomy in the nineteenth century than many states that were notionally independent. It should therefore be no surprise that, when state power began to increase from the late-nineteenth century onwards, the issue continually arose as to whether power should be centralised or devolved.[9]

The second phase, which covers most of the nineteenth century, is the age of industrialisation that spawned the growth of towns and cities, created social unrest in its wake, spurred the demand for representation (the electorate grew from 4,000 to 65,000 in 1832) and, in many other countries but not Scotland, ushered in periods of political nationalism. Facing the upheaval of industrial change, Scotland was still managed through its own distinctive civic institutions, through a reformed Poor Law and later a reorganised education system that was run locally but supervised by Scottish-administered boards. But Scottish identity was expressed in new ways, through a revitalised sense of nationhood in part attributable to the romanticism of Sir Walter Scott and Robert Burns, and later through some pressure for decentralisation of decision-making to Scotland. Both forces helped cement the idea of a distinct Scottish community inside the Union.

The third phase – that is the era of the twentieth-century welfare state – saw the build-up of British central government, which in turn created pressure for devolution. While Scotland rejected keeping the Scottish Poor Law in favour of creating UK-wide institutions, it did demand some local say in economic policy through the decentralisation of its administration. As the century proceeded, Scots started to take the view that, if large amounts of public money were being spent in Scotland, Scots should decide how it should be spent. Thus out of an initial desire for decentralisation and then administrative devolution, the demand for political devolution was eventually realised with the creation of the Scottish Parliament in 1999. But at all times until very recently Scottish national identity was expressed through distinctive and autonomous Scottish institutions with which the Union rarely interfered.

HOW THE UNION EVOLVED

When James VI of Scotland became James I of England in 1603, Scotland and England were still foreign countries to each other and the Union of the Crowns did little to change that. The St George's cross was laid over the St Andrew's saltire to create the Union Jack, but even that was merely a royal stand-ard, not a national flag. In his first address to the English House of Commons, King James VI/I made no secret of his determin-ation to unite Scotland and England more fully: 'Do we not remember that this Kingdome [England] was divided into seven little Kingdomes, besides Wales? And is it not now the stronger by their Union? And hath not the Union of Wales to England added a greater strength thereto? . . . I desire a perfect Union of Lawes and Persons, and such a Naturalizing as may make one body of both Kingdomes under mee your King. That I and my Posteritie (if it so please God) may rule over you to the World's End.'[10]

There was in fact little desire on England's part for that 'perfect union' – or even for a full political one. That desire did not increase even after Cromwell had incorporated Scotland into his protectorate in 1652. Anglicans were worried about the threat Calvinist influences posed to their state Church and resisted any suggestion that Scots might have a vote in a parliament of both nations on English religious issues. There was also (justified) concern about the weakness of the Scottish commitment to English ideas of liberty. In Scotland, even the Union of Crowns was becoming less popular as the Stuart monarchy became ever more dictatorial and absolutist and did nothing to modernise the more feudal seventeenth-century Scotland.

It took a common anti-Catholicism and the threat from France to bring the two nations closer. Outside of parts of the Highlands and north-east lowlands, Catholic practice had disappeared in Scotland more completely than in England. By 1688, both England and Scotland had each renounced their allegiance to the Catholic James II and both had independently invited the Protestant William of Orange and his Stuart wife Mary to occupy the throne. But despite this common commitment to the Protestant faith, there was no emotional pro-Union tide, no shared British nationalism and no real popular pressure for a new arrangement.

What happened next was more of an elite bargain than a public settlement. England was starting to focus on expansion to create an overseas empire and it could pursue that quest more effectively without a threat from its northern neighbour. For their part, the Scots needed access to England's rapidly growing domestic and colonial markets. England's Navigation Acts, backed up by the English navy, reserved colonial trade to English nationals and English ships, thus excluding Scots from lucrative trade opportunities with the English colonies in the Caribbean and North America. The Darien Expedition of the 1690s was Scotland's own independent attempt at colonisation, but it had exposed Scotland's weakness and foreshadowed the difficulties it would face as a small country if it continued to try to build an empire on its own.

The interests of the wealthy in both countries were starting to align. As Christopher Whatley, a historian of the Act of Union, points out, this was 'an age of muscular mercantilism'. In his article 'Taking Stock: Scotland at the End of the Seventeenth Century' he concludes that 'no matter what legislation was passed however, the story was the same', that the Scottish state was insufficiently strong to support its legislative goals with the authority of legal, fiscal, military or naval force available to others. 'Scotland,' says Whatley, 'was vulnerable to English political decisions whether they were consciously designed at the Scots or unintended side-effects.'[11] Scotland was 'an ungovernable kingdom with an unmanageable Parliament', another historian, Maurice Lee, has argued, 'and a paralysed and useless Privy Council'.[12]

And yet Union was not inevitable. In the years immediately leading up to it, anti-English feeling in Scotland was probably stronger than it had been at any time since the Anglo-Scottish wars of the Middle Ages. In 1703/4, in anticipation of the death of Queen Anne, the Scottish Parliament passed an Act reserving the right to choose a different monarch from England unless arrangements were made, as they put it, to secure 'the religion, liberty and trade of the nation from English or any foreign influence'.[13] Both sides agreed something needed to happen to cool tempers, and a joint commission was created to review the relationship. Meeting behind closed doors, the commissioners drafted articles of Union strongly to the benefit of Scotland's landed, legal and commercial classes, and in particular giving solace to those who had invested in the Company of Scotland and the Darien Expedition.

The Union took place without a war but there was no popular enthusiasm for it. So while the Scottish authors of the deal might have been patrician, they weren't daft, and they built into the bargain financial provisions for Scottish institutions in the hope that it might popularise the new arrangement.

The first annuity of £2,000 per annum was to promote the Church of Scotland's work in the Highlands and Islands to convert Catholics and thus remove a shared 'security threat'. The second provided financial support for the four Scottish universities, St Andrews, Glasgow, Aberdeen and Edinburgh, and reflected the Treaty's restatement of an earlier Scottish law that the four Scottish universities 'shall continue within the Kingdom forever'. The third was designed to compensate for the loss of Scottish revenue from harmonising custom duties: within a generation £1,000 per annum was paid to a Board of Trustees of Manufacturers for the encouragement of the woollen trade, and such 'other manufactures and improvements as might conduce to the general good of the United Kingdom'. Part of this annuity – by the end of the eighteenth century £1,000 per annum – was applied to promote the fishing industry, an important source of income and employment along Scottish coastal communities.[14]

Almost immediately there was English pressure to replace Presbyterianism. From 1710–14, the British state introduced measures including the Patronage Act 1712, Toleration (of Episcopalians) Act of 1712 and the Yule Vacance Act 1712 designed to support episcopalianism and undermine the guarantees given to the Church of Scotland by the Union. The Patronage Act – which imposed lay patronage on the Church of Scotland, whereby local landowners instead of congregations appointed ministers in parishes – seemed to Scotland to be a particularly offensive violation of the Union measures guaranteeing the autonomy of the Presbyterian Kirk. And the Union would not have survived easily had not the demand for episcopalianism been withdrawn, replaced by a concordat established between state and the Kirk, which led eventually to the 1921 Act under which the British state granted freedom to the Church of Scotland. 'In so far as there had been irritants in the Anglo-Scottish union these had been ecclesiastical rather than political', concludes Kidd. 'It was ecclesiastical issues which had hampered the generally smooth processes of Anglo-Scottish integration.'[15]

In the eighteenth century and for long afterwards, religion

mattered more than politics. For most of the post-Union period in Scotland, an all too present Church was to act as a substitute for an absent state. But the autonomy of the Churches also sent out a message that the dissolution of the Scottish state in 1707 did not entail the surrender of Scotland's civic society. Pro-Unionist politicians understood that this fact, true well into the nineteenth century, was the main reason for Scotland's acquiescence in the Union. There was to be no integration of religion, law, education or social policy. The Union was in fact a partial union, akin for a time to what Tom Devine has called 'semi-independence'.[16]

While the Westminster Parliament retained the power to legislate on all issues, it had no intention to administer law, education, social policy and – with a few notable exceptions in the early years of the Union – religion. It meant Scotland and England remained substantially foreign to one another, so much so that the novelist Daniel Defoe could write that the first town you entered after crossing the border was 'perfectly Scots, as if you were a hundred miles north of Edinburgh; nor is there the least appearance of anything English . . . in their way of living, eating, dress or behaviour'.[17]

The test of a state's viability and endurability, many historians have written, citing the American revolution as an example, is its ability to raise taxes from the people. While there was some trouble in 1725 as Scots rioted in protest against the UK government's attempt to impose the 'malt tax' on Scotland to pay for war against France, there were few tax rebellions that took a nationalist form.

And while there was a post-1745 attempt to repress dissent and reform the old Scottish feudal system in the aftermath of the failed coup d'état by Bonnie Prince Charlie at Culloden, generally England felt that, having established the security it sought on its northern border, it could afford to let Scotland go its own way within the parameters of the Union. Alvin Jackson has described this approach as a posture of 'benign neglect' but in retrospect it is worth celebrating this flexibility as one of the defining achievements of the Union.[18] It meant that England felt able to leave the administration of law and order – the courts and policing – in Scottish hands, which seems remarkably risky if we compare the Scottish situation to that of its nearest comparator, Ireland.

I remember well that even in 2009 a proposal to devolve the administration of law and order to local Northern Ireland control was highly contentious because some people felt they didn't have an assurance that it would not be administered in a discriminatory manner. So while the devolution of powers to Northern Ireland was extensive in social and economic affairs, even to the extent of cross-border agreements aimed at diminishing the likelihood of a return to violence, it was impossible to get an agreement about how policing would operate. But 300 years earlier, Scotland and England had been content to let each other get on with it: nobody worried that Scottish justice would discriminate against English citizens, and while the repression after Culloden was brutal, nobody in England demanded the ordinary day to day matters of law and order be taken out of the hands of the Scots themselves.

Other than in 1710 and in the years that led to the Disruption Scots were not generally forced to adopt – against their will – English practices, in law, education or, by and large, religion. For most of the time nobody on the English side felt much moved to push the matter. The contrast is our then enemy France, where a national strategy was pursued centrally by the state to socialise everyone into being French, not least through a common education curriculum designed to 'convert peasants into Frenchmen'.[19]

In other countries where integration occurred, promises that civic autonomy would be maintained and upheld were not honoured; in the United Kingdom they almost always were. So, with the administration of law and order retained in Scotland

– and with education and social policy still under Scottish control – an incomplete, partial Union was one that suited both Edinburgh and London. Some English ideas were embraced by 'modernisers' in the Scottish establishment who wanted Scotland to move from its semi-feudal status. Colin Kidd has reminded us that the Scottish legal establishment itself *decided* to accept the House of Lords as a court of appeal – it wasn't pushed upon us by the Act of Union or any other law. Indeed, if Scotland had wanted to keep the Scottish Poor Law or a version of Scottish social policy into the mid-twentieth century, it could easily have done so and, as we have shown, England was willing to give assurances to the Church of Scotland in 1921 that stood well outside constitutional convention.[20]

The question is whether we could ever hope for more than a degree of flexibility on both sides that enabled two distinct peoples with different institutions and a proud heritage to rub along. Could Britain ever become more than a marriage of convenience? Were there not ideas and institutions that could bind the nations more closely together?

BUILDING BRITAIN

We have spoken in earlier chapters of how deeply Scots held on to the distinctiveness of their Presbyterian faith and how fiercely they protected the rights of the Kirk to manage her own affairs. But the location of Presbyterianism inside the wider family of reformed and anti-Catholic faiths did help to cement a cross-border identity in the early days of Union.

Though the Presbyterian form of church governance and Calvinist theology came to distinguish most Scots Protestants from their English counterparts, and though Catholicism became a powerful presence in the west of Scotland in the nineteenth century, a common commitment to the Protestant religion bound the peoples of Scotland and England against much of the rest of Europe – particularly Catholic France, with whom we were at war on eight occasions from the Act of Union in 1707 to the Battle of Waterloo in 1815.[21]

The division between British Protestants and British Catholics was of course enshrined in law. From the late-seventeenth century until 1829, British Catholics were not allowed to vote and were excluded from all state offices, both Houses of Parliament and, as they shamefully still are, from the monarchy. For much of the eighteenth century, Catholics were subject to punitive taxation, forbidden to possess weapons and discriminated against in terms of access to education, property rights and freedom of worship.[22]

It is impossible to understand how such grotesque discrimination could be popular without first grasping how important security had become to the shared British identity. In 1708, 1715 and again in 1745, expeditionary forces in support of the Stuart claimants to the British throne landed in Scotland, with the intention of marching south to capture London and thereby the entire island. While a successful Stuart restoration would have meant the replacement of a Protestant monarchy with a devoutly Roman Catholic dynasty, it also meant foreign control and perhaps even a foreign army of occupation, for the Stuarts could never hope to get back into power without substantial French or Spanish military and financial aid.[23]

Despite the ties of the 'Auld Alliance' between France and Scotland, France had come to be seen as profoundly 'the other', not simply because of their Catholicism but because the French were perceived, in the words of Lord Sumption, as 'the servile helots of a privileged aristocracy and an absolute King'.[24] Britain regarded itself as an entrepreneurial country of liberties and laws and saw France as unreformed, backward-looking and weighed down by an old corrupt elite.

In fact right until the end of the nineteenth century, many

politicians, military experts and popular commentators continued to see France as Britain's most dangerous and obvious enemy, and for good reason. For much of time France with a much bigger population – 27 million in 1801 against Britain's 10 million – was Britain's greatest commercial and imperial rival, and her powerful army regularly showed itself able to conquer large tracts of Europe.[25]

But Britain's emerging identity was being secured by pride in her improving track record in war. From the fifteenth century to 1688, England and Wales, like Scotland, had been peripheral kingdoms in the European power game, wasting their energies in war with each other. When they did engage with the Dutch, or the French, or the Spanish, they were not very successful, except under Oliver Cromwell. And yet now a succession of Great British continental adventures – the Nine Years' War with France, the War of the Spanish Succession, the wars of Jenkins' Ear and Austrian succession, the Seven Years' War and the wars against Revolutionary and Napoleonic France – brought military and naval victories where territories were won and trade routes gained.[26]

At the same time, the benefits of a single all-British market were slowly being realised. By the time Samuel Johnson and James Boswell made their tour in 1773, recorded in *A Journey to the Western Islands of Scotland*, Johnson was able to say that Scotland was 'a nation of which the commerce is hourly extending, and the wealth increasing', and Glasgow in particular had become one of the greatest cities of Britain.[27] Scotland after an uncertain start reaped significant economic benefits from the Union, and rapidly made the transition from a rural subsistence society to become by the 1820s second only to England in the global league of industrial countries.[28]

Why this should be so has been a matter of debate. Some have argued that Calvinism – Scotland's 'character reference' in McCrone's phrase – is the answer, with Smout arguing that 'Calvinism seemed to be released as a psychological force for secular change just at the moment when it was losing its power as a religion'.[29] Others have argued that Scotland's pre-existent assets – a relatively high standard of literacy and education and a generous endowment of natural resources, particularly coal as well as water and power – explain our rise. But access to the domestic and international markets of England was indispensable, establishing Glasgow and Clydeside as a major European centre for transatlantic trades and one of the greatest centres of heavy industry in the world.

And so too it was the opportunities provided by the Union that enabled Scotland to benefit disproportionately from an empire she would not have been able to build on her own. Sir Charles Dilke, an observer on an imperial tour in the 1860s, commented that 'for every Englishman that you meet who has worked himself up from small beginnings, without external aid, you find ten Scotchmen'.[30] And accounts of the era cite the Scottish-born American steel baron Andrew Carnegie remarking that America would have been a poor show without the Scots. He was of course referring to himself.[31]

However, the Empire not only transformed the prospects of Scottish emigrants but also transformed Scotland's view of itself. Devine is right to say that the Empire 'was the means by which the Scots asserted their equal partnership with England after 1707', gaining benefits seen first in the Scottish role in the Atlantic trade and then in the Scottish part played in the construction of the Empire's infrastructure, including railway engines, rail tracks, harbours and ships.[32]

Some have tried to distinguish between empire 'traders' and empire 'warriors', a myth that tries to separate off good Scots from bad English. Yet through meticulous research Tom Devine has shown that Scots and English folk alike were both warriors and traders and that the traders benefited from the warriors, especially via the Navy fighting wars in the West Indies and Caribbean to advance British interests.[33]

Scotland also supplied a disproportionate number of the Empire's soldiers and administrators – between 1850 and 1939, a third of all British colonial governors were Scots – and Scots were among imperialism's most prolific and successful settlers, missionaries, engineers, traders and industrialists.[34] In 1901, at a time when the Scots were about 10 per cent of the population of the United Kingdom, they accounted for about 15 per cent of the British-born population of Australia, rising to 21 per cent in Canada and 23 per cent in New Zealand.[35] Indeed Professor Devine has argued that it is when we compare Scottish enjoyment of, with Irish exclusion from, imperial opportunities that we can best understand why the Union between Scotland and England is so enduring and that between England and Ireland so fleeting.[36]

Scotland's enthusiasm for empire should surprise no one. Small as it was, Scotland was a seafaring and trading nation that had tried to expand its interests overseas even before the Union. Scotland had long been a nation of both immigrants and emigrants and British imperial ambitions offered a means by which Scots could spread their distinctive educational, religious, cultural and political ideas across the globe. Indeed when the Enlightenment was at its height its leading Scottish figures applied themselves to debating universal moral laws and not simply the most parochial questions of their day.

So the Empire provided both the incentive and the means for Scots to think in terms of 'British' and not simply Scottish interests. The integration of Scottish soldiers into a British military that fought their eight massive eighteenth- and nineteenth-century continental conflicts, ending with Trafalgar and Waterloo in 1805 and 1815, helped to entrench that sentiment. A quarter of the Duke of Wellington's army at the Battle of Waterloo fought in regiments raised in Scotland, at a time when only about one in seven of the population of the United Kingdom lived there.[37] During the Napoleonic Wars the Highlands supplied some

74,000 men to the army, out of a total regional population of 300,000.[38] The endurance and fierce loyalty of the Highland regiments became legendary and their martial exploits on behalf of the Union were celebrated just as surely as the glories of the Wars of Independence and the Covenanters before it.

The bonds cultivated in the eighteenth and nineteenth were strengthened in the twentieth century as, in two traumatic world wars, the country united around not just a common enemy but also shared values to which the vast majority could subscribe. Unlike the Ireland of 1916, where many people were not prepared to fight for Britain, and the India of the 1940s, where there was a large anti-war movement, there was little dissent when Scotland joined the war.

The recruitment for the British Army between July 1914 and November 1918 included 557,618 volunteers and conscripts from Scotland, out of a total of just less than five million from across the UK.[39] While the Scottish rate of recruitment – around 24 per cent of the male population – was matched by a similar response from England, Scottish casualties were much higher, at a rate of about one in four and twice the average for the United Kingdom as a whole.[40] Later, in the Second World War – with bombings hitting Clydebank in Scotland in the same way that they hit Coventry and London in England – people felt tightly bound in one war effort not just on the front line of Europe but at home.

And thus both wars cemented a common sense of Britishness as people of diverse class and regional backgrounds found themselves fighting side by side. Just as the First World War ushered in new British institutions like the UK Ministry of Pensions (for war widows and war wounded) and a UK Ministry of Reconstruction, the Second World War brought the Beveridge Report for a British welfare state and, in 1948, a British National Health Service. Both were signed up to with enthusiasm by Scotland.

So the history of the Union from its very beginnings to the

middle of the twentieth century was one of two nations becoming ever more tightly bound through ties of trade, empire, war and welfare. And it is a story of Scottish success – in industry, imperialism and the intellectual life of the country. It was not only a Scot who had formed the Bank of England before 1707 but a Scot, James Thomson, who authored 'Rule Britannia' in 1740; a Scot who formed the first British trade union, the London Corresponding Society; a Scot who formed the National Union of Mineworkers; a Scot who led the formation of the British Labour Party; a Scot who became the first Director-General of the BBC; and a Scot who became the first head of the Open University. One-third of Prime Ministers have been Scots.

THE DECLINE OF BRITISHNESS

But notwithstanding this degree of Scottish success inside the Union, enthusiasm for it is in doubt. Linda Colley is the author of the most influential book in this field. In *Britons: Forging the Nation 1707–1837*, Colley contends that the historic basis for Britishness has now been eroded: 'The factors that provided for the forging of a British nation in the past have largely ceased to operate. Protestantism, that once vital cement, has now a limited influence on British culture, as indeed has Christianity itself. Recurrent wars with the states of continental Europe have in all likelihood come to an end, so different kinds of Britons no longer feel the same compulsion to remain united in the face of an enemy from without.'[41]

If she is right, then Scotland's ties to the Union are weakening not because, as nationalists might argue, Scotland is now ready to reverse our 'annexation', but simply because the quite specific historical events which brought us together no longer feel relevant to our sense of ourselves in 2014. The last half-century has seen the waning of Protestantism, the end of the Empire and with it a diminished global status for what was once the world's premier power. Long periods of peace have gradually undermined the rationale for British unity, argues Colley, with no common foe to sustain British national solidarity.[42] Today our identity feels more closely reflected by events at the Scottish Parliament than what happens in Westminster and Whitehall, and the drive for devolution has undoubtedly played its own part in loosening the attachment of Scots to institutions based down south.

There were other forces binding us together as partners in the same island. Britain was also being shaped in its early days by other common experiences – the growth of roads and communications, a common system of economic administration, a shared pursuit of trade and commerce, and – outside the Highlands – a common English language alongside the healthy persistence of local dialects.

In the late-nineteenth century, Britain was being remade as an integrated industrial economy with the growth of postal services and then telephone communications that inevitably linked us closer together, and then increasingly by intermarriage and mobility between the two countries, and by the growth of British companies and British institutions. The first halting steps were also taken towards a common social provision – with the same rights to education albeit under different laws, the same protection of children in the workplace under the same law and a growth in similar systems of public health. But, as we have seen, Scottish legal, educational and religious institutions were enhanced by the cultivation of a distinctive Scottish culture just at the time pressure started to grow for a more distinctive system of Scottish administration.

Britain was again remade in the twentieth century not just by the collective experience of shared sacrifice in two world wars, and the collective provision of the British welfare state which brought into being a modern concept of British citizenship, but also through the growth of a British-wide network of radio and television and through all-British trade unions that were built from strong class-based loyalties at the workplace, a strong layer of identity which like our religious affiliations stood between the individual and the state.

As the twentieth century ended, Scotland's relations with the Union changed yet again. New forces were at work, including globalisation and modern ideas of human rights. The worldwide triumph of ideas of popular sovereignty – that power derived from the people not from the monarch – led to the global expansion of democracy and the spread of national self-determination. This, and the shift from an industrial society to a post-industrial society, together with the erosion of old collective loyalties, forms the background to demands for a new Scottish relationship with Britain.

DECENTRALISATION AND DEVOLUTION

For most of the history of the Union, government intervention was limited and, in the eighteenth and nineteenth century, parliament rarely intervened on Scottish issues unless invited to do so. While responsibility for administration lay until 1885 with the Home Secretary in London, in practice the Lord Advocate continued to control from Edinburgh key policy areas including law enforcement and policing. The everyday work of managing Scottish domestic affairs took place in local boards and bodies and these institutions, proud of their own autonomy, would go directly to the Treasury for funding, whether it be for grants for harbours and piers or art galleries, and then the Chancellor would consult its Scottish representative, the Queen's and Lord Treasurer's Remembrancer (based in Edinburgh) and the Home Office.

So distinctively Scottish institutions had a direct line to

Whitehall and, while it was part of the pattern for Scots – and this remains an element of the nationalist rhetoric today – to complain at one and the same time about legislative neglect by the UK Parliament *and* over-interference by it in Scottish affairs, Scottish legislative needs were addressed in a manner that sought to be sensitive to the demands of Scottish institutions in three 'light touch' ways. First, where Acts of Parliament covered the whole of the UK, as in trade, industry and finance, Scottish 'application clauses' took account of Scotland's different legal and institutional framework. Second, there would be scope for Scotland's own local and national institutions – including the cities, the royal burghs and eventually the counties – to put forward their own private legislation. Third, separate Scottish Bills, often following an English measure, would deal with health, welfare and education, giving us separate Scottish laws for the Poor Law, lunacy, public health, universities and schools.

Before 1845, as Ian Levitt and T. C. Smout have shown, the unreformed Scottish Poor Law was run by the Churches – by Kirk Sessions which found they could not cope with the influx of Irish Catholic immigrants and the fall-out from the Disruption. Additionally, as Rosalind Mitchison has pointed out, the Scottish Poor Law was already a patchwork of different regimes, with the south-east of Scotland relying on 'legal assessments' to levy money and the rest of the country relying on voluntary assessments, or in some cases on a form of 'licensed begging'.[43] So Scotland had a unique and uniquely ineffective system in need of reform. But the reforms that came were still uniquely Scottish, giving power to Scottish administrators working through distinctively Scottish institutions that were seen as the best way of representing Scottish opinion. These included the powerful Scottish town councils set up by the Scottish Burgh Reform Act of 1833 and the growing number of Scottish supervisory boards, which grew up from the 1840s onwards.

The tendency was to encourage Scottish day-to-day control by a new professional class staffing a bureaucracy whose inspectors were Scots doctors, lawyers, surveyors and engineers. As a result the number of civil servants employed by the Home Office for Scottish administration totalled no more than fifty in 1850 and they worked as service regulators rather than service providers, doing little more than sending out circulars to local boards and doing so in a semi-judicial capacity. This board system was supposed to encourage local decision-making. So even in the 1890s, when the UK government wanted to give relief to Scots who were unemployed, it felt unable to override the local boards who objected to relief for the able-bodied workless: the convention was that the state should consult with and be led by representative opinion in Scotland before acting. The Scottish public would see the boards and the local councils, rather than the distant Whitehall and Westminster, as responsible for the routine government of Scotland.

It was not until the late-nineteenth century after the passing of the Education Act 1872, and the extension of the franchise to the working class, that there was a decisive movement towards the creation of a more centralised British state. But the more this happened the more the pressure for administrative decentralisation and for some recognition of the Scottish dimension in government grew, Rosebery admitting in 1881 that 'the words home-rule have begun to be distinctly and loudly mentioned in Scotland . . . it is a significant sign of the times that in the present circumstances it should be heard'.[44] However, still Gladstone felt confident enough to turn down a proposal to designate a Scottish Under-Secretary at the Home Office, rejecting also the case for a House of Commons Select Committee on Scottish Affairs, arguing that 'the grievances of Scotland are not more real to Scottish members than the grievances of England are to English members'.[45]

Even though Disraeli wanted to appoint a parliamentary undersecretary at the Home Office to conduct Scottish business, he was easily dissuaded by his Scottish supporters, who told him this would challenge the position of the Lord Advocate.[46]

In 1885 an all-party measure restored the post of Scottish Secretary, whose primary functions were to promote Scottish legislation, control the Scottish boards (and serve as Vice-President of the Scottish Education Department), take responsibility for law and order, and of course manage Scottish patronage. From then until the 1920s the Irish question came close to creating a Scottish question as Gladstone, who had committed to treat all nations including Scotland in the same way, had to promise that his Irish Home Rule Bill would be followed by a Scottish Home Rule Bill. This led directly to the creation of the Scottish Home Rule Association in 1886 and the conversion of Scottish Liberals to home rule in 1888.

The Scottish Secretary was not yet a member of the British Cabinet by right. With the full elevation of the post to cabinet rank in 1926, the first Secretary of State, Sir John Gilmour, immediately proposed an end to the boards system that encouraged local representation in the administration of social policy and its replacement with a departmental system run by professional civil servants. The board system had been administered in Scotland by Scottish representatives and so it was agreed that the departments – education, health, home, including industry and agriculture – would be established in Edinburgh not London. But when the Scottish Office conceded in 1948 that much of the expansion of domestic administration was conducted in a haphazard way and not necessarily in accordance with Scottish sentiments, they were accepting that the process of decentralisation to respond to Scottish needs and opinion was bound to continue. And political devolution was on the agenda with the support of the Liberals, Labour – who sponsored numerous home-rule bills in the inter-war years – and on occasion even Unionists, with

Churchill telling Edinburgh's Usher Hall in 1951 that 'I do not . . . wonder that the question of Scottish home rule and the movement of Scottish nationalism has gained strength with the growth of socialists' authority and ambition in England'.[47]

But if one side of the coin was the pressure for decentralisation, another was the demand for an equitable system for financing the meeting of Scotland's needs. Looking at the debates on finance over two centuries, the term 'equivalence' appears and reappears to justify the allocation of finance to Scottish services. Yet equivalence was not to be seen as an allocation of resources simply on the basis of our share of Gross Domestic Product or a similar indicator of the size of the Scottish economy, nor was it seen as justifying a simple calculation of, say, the numbers of poor or sick or disabled in need of assistance. Achieving 'equivalence' meant equal status for Scotland and in practice it came down to estimating the Scottish contribution in taxes to the UK Exchequer and, once that base figure had been established, an understanding that if expenditure in England rose so too should Scotland's from that baseline by the same proportionate amount.

In addition to compensation for the Darien fiasco, Scotland received four annuities in the Union of 1707. Each evolved over the next two centuries to become more generous than the initial guarantees. While the first annuity – £2,000 per annum – was to promote the Church of Scotland's work in the Highlands and Islands, as Ian Levitt's recent work has shown, it rose dramatically after it was accepted, as one Scottish official noted, that 'the Highlands and Islands were not a Scottish but a national concern and the money required to develop them should be altogether that'.[48] In an era of market economies and fast communications it was important to incorporate the Highlands and Islands into the Union in exactly the same way as the Lowlands. Gladstone's Liberal government of 1880–5 extended the offer, supporting a regular Highlands mail service through a subsidised ferry service and providing support for telegraphic services (this time on the basis of supporting the fishing industry).

By the end of the nineteenth century, the Highlands and Islands were receiving in excess of £40,000 per annum, covering subsidised ferries, harbour construction, telegraphy and road improvements, well in excess of their original guarantee of £2,000. Here 'equivalence' meant doing something to equalise economic opportunity for those areas that lay on the periphery of the UK commercial marketplace.[49]

While the second annuity of £2,000 expressly covered the four Scottish universities – St Andrews, Glasgow, Aberdeen and Edinburgh – this grant-aid was 'distributed through various channels and on diverse grounds', a Treasury phrase used to indicate that Scottish universities were a pressure group who might deploy any plausible justification in their demand for subsidy.[50] Not surprisingly, in the 1880s the Treasury tried to roll the subsidies back, but officials received a one-line minute from Gladstone, then both Prime Minister and Chancellor of the Exchequer, simply authorising a grant of £40,000 per annum. And in this way Scottish universities continued to be 'protected' by the Treaty, with one grant of £25,000 received by Edinburgh University bigger than all the help available to all the English universities combined.[51]

The third annuity of £1,000 a year – originally paid to Scottish woollen traders – was first abolished and then in 1847 restored and doubled under a new pretext for 'the purpose of education in the fine arts generally, and in decorative and ornamental art, and in taste and design in manufacture'. Scottish lobbyists had seen the then government's subsidies for London's National Gallery and Museum and demanded finance to create Scotland's own cultural institutions that could rival London's in status. Whatever the Treaty had meant by 'equivalents', Victorian Scotland interpreted it as the right of Scotland to enjoy provision matching that down South.[52]

And the fourth annuity – aid for the fishing fleet of £1,000 – became much more than that: finance for the improvement and maintenance of the fishing ports meant that by 1900 the original £1,000 had become a total of £560,000 spent on financing loans for harbour improvements, most notably at Leith, Dunbar, Arbroath and Wick.[53]

By the late-nineteenth century the UK government was however under pressure to do far more than merely extend these annuities and had to introduce the first significant and sizeable series of grants-in-aid for education and other public services. But there had to be a financial basis on which this was done. The 1888 Budget proposed a series of grants, mainly for schools, based on the amount generated by an existing tax, probate duty – the tax raised on wills. The figure for Scotland turned out to be 11/80ths of that generated in England, or 13.75 per cent. So the formula, the rough equivalent to Scotland's contribution to British wealth, was calculated at 11 to 80, with a further assumption that any future grant would now be increased on an 11-to-80 basis in proportion to any increase in England.[54]

The grants that followed in the succeeding years, again using the 11/80th formula, became known by the name of the then Chancellor of the Exchequer, Goschen. Some other taxes raised north of the border, such as that on spirits, raised a higher percentage than 11/80 and others like income tax raised slightly less, making the Goschen formula seem balanced and fair. Of course Scotland received more than 11/80ths of spending because neither Goschen nor succeeding Chancellors applied the formula to the amounts distributed to the Edinburgh art and museum galleries (which more than doubled), the universities, (whose grant also doubled), the fishing industry (which received 70 per cent of all UK improvement grants), or the Highlands, which also received grants well above what civil servants now called 'the Goschen line'. In practice the Goschen line became the floor and never the ceiling for Scottish requests and often when the Scots saw Irish MPs winning extra resources, further demands were made. Indeed the financial provisions contained within the Treaty of Union were never abandoned but retained, the distinctiveness of the terms of Union ensuring that 'equivalence' went beyond a simple set of financial formulas and was instead seen as a guarantee of equality of consideration and status.[55]

So in 1923, with Scotland facing high levels of unemployment, the Prime Minister, Stanley Baldwin, accepted that, though the population ratio had now dropped below 11:80, the Goschen formula should be retained for 'its rough justice'. It led eventually to the Barnett formula of 1978, described by Iain McLean as 'a new Goschen for modern Unionists', meaning that, while allocation was to be justified on the basis of 'need' the formula that decided 'need' started with what had been previously guaranteed on the basis of 'equivalence', with the year-to-year sums adjusted in line with Scotland's declining share of the UK population.[56] Indeed the Barnett formula was an attempt to bring public spending under control at a time when the Scottish public-expenditure figure had risen to being 20 per cent more per capita than the British figure.[57] By adjusting future increases in expenditure the Treasury brought the gap down to 15 per cent. Some say it is now nearer 10 per cent but, in his study of the economics of independence, one of Scotland's leading economic experts, with experience in government as well as out of it, Gavin McCrone, suggests that when a comparison is made of the same categories of identifiable spending as in the 1970s it is probably around 14 per cent.[58]

Thus, even as the British state took responsibility across ever wider economic affairs, the Scottish dimension was strengthened by both administrative decentralisation (and new arrangements for funding its decentralised services), and then eventually by a Scottish Parliament. The exception was in social welfare, where Scotland argued not for a separate pensions or social security system or for a separate system of health funding but for a UK-wide system. In economic policy, however, substantial devolution was sought. Scotland's negotiating power came in part through the building of a Scottish consensus which was at its most pronounced when Tom Johnston, wartime Secretary of State for Scotland and Churchill's 'King of Scotland', brought together both businesses and workforce representatives and on occasions all political parties on a non-partisan basis. As Lindsay Paterson puts it, there was 'a forum of unobtrusive nationalism that involved having to present a united face to London in order to extract resources for the social welfare on which the Scots agreed'. And we should not underestimate the importance of a professional class of Scottish-born civil servants who saw public service as the means by which they helped Scotland.

The creation of the Scottish Parliament in 1999 was, therefore, built on Scotland's post-1707 history of decentralisation and administration of Scottish affairs through Scottish boards, departments and committees. The difference was that Scotland now had a directly elected Scottish authority vested with wide-ranging powers, a tax-raising authority and, perhaps most importantly, a sense that it spoke for Scotland. But as we shall see later, the transfer of powers was incomplete. Schedule 5 of the enabling statute, the Scotland Act 1998, specified those areas of policy not devolved to the Scottish Parliament, calling them 'reserved matters'. And, while the Scotland Act 2012 amended the Scotland Act 1998 to devolve further powers to Scotland following the recommendations of the Calman Commission, the constitutional fiction of a unitary state has been maintained in law: in theory Westminster can continue to legislate for Scotland on devolved matters, and even abolish the Scottish Parliament by a single Act of Parliament. But as we shall see in Chapter 7, the reality is rather different and it is time for the constitutional theory to catch up. In England, of course, the sovereignty of parliament still corresponds to a genuine supremacy over 'all persons, matters and things' and Westminster can legislate on all matters as it wishes, subject to the European Communities Act 1972 and the Human Rights Act 1998.[59] But over time Westminster has accepted in the Sewel Convention that it will not normally legislate on devolved matters without the consent of the Scottish Parliament. Thus, in practice, it is the Scottish Parliament which alone legislates on matters devolved to Scotland and it is recognised that Scottish powers cannot simply be removed unilaterally by Westminster but require the consent of the Scottish Parliament.

Moreover, over the fifteen years of the Scottish Parliament's life, the UK Supreme Court has adjudicated on disputes between the UK Parliament and the Scottish Parliament, including its decision in *Axa General Insurance Limited v The Lord Advocate* (2011) and are also likely to include the challenge by the Scottish Whisky Association to the Scottish government's plans to set minimum prices for alcohol.

The Supreme Court's power to resolve constitutional disputes, and the mechanism through section 30 of the Scotland Act 1998 that allows for further devolution under Orders in Council, appear to challenge the old notion of Westminster sovereignty. Now that the relationship between Scotland and Britain has changed, it looks set to change once again.

OVERVIEW

For most of the first part of the history of the Union, the freedom that mattered most to Scots was the freedom to practise their religion. With London pursuing its imperial ambitions, the British state was otherwise occupied anyway and the pressures to integrate and become North Britain were never strong enough to rid Scotland of its distinctive legal, religious, educational and social institutions.

As long as Scotland did not threaten England, it was free to go its own way when it wanted to. And even if some could attribute England's acquiescence in the autonomy of separate Scottish legal, social and educational traditions to the desire for an unobtrusive unionism or even to indifference on its part, what mattered more was the determination of the Scots to retain their autonomy and the flexibility of the arrangements. The autonomy of the Church and the law made it much easier for Scottish people to support – or at least acquiesce in – the Union and feel they belonged to Britain.

And so if we look more deeply into the deals that were done and how they were seen, the Union is best likened not to an annexation or assimilation, and certainly not a colonisation, but to an international agreement between two nations that each seemed to find benefit in exchanging the constant threat of war for the long-term promise of peace and stability. It enabled England to focus on trade and empire and Scotland to share in the spoils of this, while also retaining a strong national identity, a distinctive set of values and autonomous civic institutions that made a strong sense of Scottish patriotism possible within the Union. Over time, as government became more complex, new machinery for government had to be created and at each stage the choice was whether to centralise or devolve.

But we should not underestimate the complete makeover of the Union in the last hundred years. The twentieth century turned the old arrangements made in 1707 on their head. Decentralisation and then devolution happened in the very area where integration had once been the key to the Union – economic affairs – and centralisation happened in an area hitherto left to Scotland's own devices – social welfare. Scotland was to abandon any claim to a separate social welfare policy and instead argue not for a system of Scottish social rights but for UK-wide social rights. It changed the whole nature of the Union, making the Union of 2014 fundamentally different from that of 1914. And it is this twentieth-century innovation – the pooling and sharing of resources and risks across the whole of the UK to ensure equal social and economic rights for all irrespective of nationality – that is now the core of the Union and central to its very existence. It is to this innovation that we will turn in Chapter 6, but first we are going to look at what being British really means.

CHAPTER 5

A British Identity

Just under fifty years ago in 1965 when Winston Churchill died, there were commemoration services around the country. I remember well what happened in Kirkcaldy. I was just fourteen, but like many others I attended a special memorial service in our local church on a Sunday afternoon. This flag-filled event brought together all the uniformed youth organisations like the Life Boys, the Boys' Brigade, the Scouts, the Brownies and the Girl Guides. Members of the Royal British Legion in Scotland were there in uniform displaying their war medals, joining representatives from the army, the navy and the air force. Not just the National Anthem was sung, but 'Land of Hope and Glory' too. Churchill had organised his funeral years before he died – entitling the plan 'Operation Hope Not' – but while the funeral service itself was the most elaborate seen in the country, with the gunboat sailing down the Thames, the significance of the church services held in towns and cities across the country was that this was an all-British commemoration representing a high point in the life of the Union.

It now feels like something from another age. I cannot imagine a similar outpouring of 'Britishness' for any political event or figure happening again in my lifetime. And I want to discuss how what it means to be British has changed and kept changing. First a common identity was forged in a surge of imperial pride that was buttressed by anti-French and anti-Catholic sentiment as we fought a series of continental wars. Then in mid-twentieth-century Britain our identity, shaped by the shared sacrifices on the battlefield and home front and by the desire for a common British National Health Service and welfare state, owed more to ideas of equality and fairness than hierarchy and empire. In recent times what belonging to Britain means has been changing yet again as we come to terms with a more diverse culture, the levelling processes of globalisation and the reality that people's identities and loyalties are multiple and multi-layered.

So the story I want to tell is about a British identity that is neither unchanging nor set in stone. A successful refashioning of our British identity is not inevitable. Indeed, more than ever, our British identity is just one of many identities each of us has. From a time when it was Scots who were the most aggressive proponents of the idea of Britishness, because they felt it kept them safe from being overshadowed by or considered part of England, it is Scots who are today least attracted to being British. But I will show that there is still a British dimension to Scottish lives that matters, one that is founded on a common culture, shared values and institutions that reflect these values as across four nations we share the risks and resources of our country in a way no other multinational association in any other part of the world has ever done.

One feature of these times stands out: Britishness has not had a good time since that high point of Unionism in 1965. Coincidentally that is also the year when Mr Churchill's party in Scotland changed their name, the Scottish Unionist Party, to become the Scottish Conservative and Unionist Party. Two years later in 1967 the first peacetime Scottish Nationalist MP was elected. By 2007 the nationalists were forming a government in the Scottish Parliament.

But more important than the year-to-year changes in the political fortunes of parties are the shifts in the long-term identification people have with Britain. From that high point of Britishness, there has been a distinct shift: English people now feel more English, the Scots more Scottish and the Welsh more Welsh than any of those groups feel British. But it is in Scotland where the decline in a sense of Britishness has been fastest. Today there are far fewer Scots who will tell you they feel more British than Scottish and, while many say they feel equally Scottish and British, the majority of Scots feel more Scottish than British or not British at all. Indeed, if asked to make a choice between being Scottish and British, only 24 per cent of Scots now choose British.[1]

So the mid-century years were the high point of Britishness in Scotland but also a 'turning point', according to David McCrone, an acknowledged expert on understanding Scotland. He argues that 'an emphasis on our Britishness in the years after the war has given way to a more recent emphasis on Scottishness, although not to a desire for outright independence'. And this drift from our previously strong identification with Britain has a social-class dimension too. Being British now seems to matter less to Scots on lower incomes. Christopher McLean and Douglas Thomson have found that Scots in the lower quarter of incomes were less likely than those in the highest quarter to mention being British (49 per cent compared to 71 per cent) and more likely to mention Scottish as their national identity (85 per cent compared to 77 per cent).[2] Ipsos MORI research for British Future similarly found that a poorer Scot was twice as likely to reject the idea of being British than a wealthier counterpart.

Of course a lot has changed that helps explain why that sense of Britishness has dimmed. If I had been an MP in the first half of the twentieth century I would not have had to put a question mark over Great Britain's future. Any suggestion that Britain would not last for ever would have been treated as one step away from common sense and by some as the equivalent of treason. We were talking of the Britain that could legitimately make claim to be the first country in the world to reject the arbitrary rule of monarchy; the Britain that was first to make a virtue of tolerance and liberty; the Britain that was first in the Industrial Revolution; the Britain that was centre to the world's largest empire; the Britain that had the imperial mission which made us a world power and then gave us a mission for the 'defence of the West' which appeared to justify a continuing sense of ourselves as a world power; the Britain that – unlike America – did not feel its exceptionalism called for any statement of purpose, or defining goals, or explicit national ethos. It was a Britain, in short, that was assured of its own continuing relevance and power.

Those days are gone for ever. The old pride in the Empire has gone and the old symbols that characterised British unity – the Union Jack and the national anthem – are already much less popular in Scotland than in the days of 1965 when, as I have shown, hundreds of flags were unfurled at one ceremony in one small town. The change has come as a quiet revolution: there has been no burning of British flags, no blowing-up of British monuments and no recent bombing of postboxes. Public displays of anti-Britishness are also rare: when Joan McAlpine MSP claimed that Glasgow's remembrance week was 'a cynical attempt to boost Britishness ahead of the referendum' and argued that 'the outburst of hysterical patriotism in 1914 represented the worst of British – arrogance, self-delusion and a desire to dominate on the world stage', she was widely condemned.[3]

So there is no evidence of a huge outbreak of hostility to Britain and it appears more like a quiet drift into indifference. Indeed, whether through abbreviations – BA, BT, BBC, BHS and so on – or through dropping the 'British' prefix, the word British appears out of fashion. But in a recent break with the post-1965 pattern, there was a new enthusiasm in 2012 for one very British enterprise, the British Olympic effort, which the

Scottish public were as happy to applaud and support as the English and Welsh. We were enthusiastic too about what Danny Boyle achieved when he choreographed an opening ceremony that presented Britain – our history, culture and ideas – to the world. In the months before the Olympics, the nationalist MP Pete Wishart had claimed they were 'a games for London and the South East' only and argued that Scotland would 'get absolutely zilch' from the London Olympics.[4] Some had even predicted that Scots would support only the Scots athletes. But crowds turned out in Scotland to witness the torch relay and there was no support for Mr Salmond's attempt to rebrand Scotland's members of Team GB as 'Scolympians'. In fact, most Scots agreed with Chris Hoy – the gold medal-winning cyclist whose Olympic team trained at a single, well-endowed, UK-financed centre in Manchester – that Scots did better because they had the whole resources of Britain and an expert all-British support team behind them.

I wanted to persuade the Scottish football authorities to endorse a UK-wide Olympics football team, both a men's and a women's team. I had hoped to assuage their worries that an all-UK Olympic football team would undermine Scotland, Wales and Northern Ireland's distinctive status as single nations within world football's governing bodies. I wanted an agreement on a UK team because, to me, it seemed strange not to have a team in the sport that we invented. So I used what authority I had as Chancellor and then as Prime Minister to push for a British team. I talked to Sebastian Coe, and suggested he invite Alex Ferguson, the best-known Scot, to be the manager. When I raised it with Alex in 2009 and 2010 he was very positive, with one caveat: he did not know where he would be in 2012. I then met Sepp Blatter specifically to ask him to sign a waiver that FIFA would never use Scotland's participation in the Great Britain Olympics football team as an excuse or pretext for denying Scotland full status as a nation in its own right in European and world tournaments. He instantly agreed to my request, he and the FIFA board signing the waiver. But with the SFA still reluctant to offer support, the British team was primarily an English squad, without, of course, the crucial addition that could have made it Olympic gold medal winners – Alex Ferguson as manager.

I have talked to Danny Boyle on a few occasions since the Olympics and discussed the brilliance of his opening ceremony, which painted a progressive history of Britain. His *Isles of Wonder*, which started with the shipping forecast and included 'Danny Boy' and 'Flower of Scotland', was a celebration not so much of our ancient institutions as of our shared qualities, in particular our inventiveness and industriousness, and our values, not least our belief in social justice and fair play. He illustrated the work ethic of a British people who were the first to create an Industrial Revolution; he focused on the creative genius of scientists and engineers who made Britain the most innovative country in the world right up to the invention of the world-wide web by Sir Tim Berners-Lee, who appeared on his Olympic stadium stage; he used modern British music starting with the Beatles, British fashion starting with Carnaby Street and British literature right up to J. K. Rowling to suggest that this dynamic, creative Britain was not just a historic achievement of a past that has gone but very much part of what it means to be British today. And he highlighted the NHS as a shared endeavour of doctors, nurses and the general public that is loved by the people of Britain. His portrayal led the Culture Minister of the time to let slip his view that there was 'too much NHS and not enough armed forces', but I think Boyle got the balance right.

But when in February 2014 the current Prime Minister returned to that Olympic stadium to conjure up the Olympic spirit in support of Britain staying together, reminding us rightly that the Olympic success was a shared one, and emphasising his view that Britain was held together by family ties, our shared history, and pride in Britain's pre-eminence in the world, his speech made little impact. Why? Some might say it was because the Olympics were just a moment in time and might cite the recent poll that only 29 per cent of Scots wanted an independent Scotland to be part of a future Olympic Team GB.[5] But perhaps there is a more profound reason, that Danny Boyle had got closer to the essence of modern Britishness than any politician or writer has managed, presenting a picture of Britain quite different from the traditional story conjured up of empire and war.

Of course when you ask about an individual's sense of belonging, many things come to mind. When in 1999 the Smith Institute asked people what sources of identity gave them a sense of belonging, 45 per cent said it was their religion or faith, 69 per cent said it was their ethnic group, 78 per cent felt a sense of belonging to their local community, but 80 per cent identified with Britain.[6] At least in 2000, Scottish and British identities were not seen as alternatives but ideas that could coexist. And when this poll was repeated by the Ministry of Justice under Michael Wills's leadership in 2009, similar results were reported with 81 per cent in England feeling a strong sense of belonging to Britain, compared with 87 per cent in Wales. The figure was 75 per cent for black and minority ethnic respondents. It was 70 per cent in both Scotland and London – a weakening of Britishness, yes, but still a significant majority who felt they belonged.

But even since 2009 attitudes have been changing fast. When asked to define Britishness in the most recent British Social Attitudes survey, most thought it was best represented by the monarchy, the rule of law and the armed forces. Yet these symbols did not make the majority 'very proud of Britain'. While more than eight out of ten people say they are at least 'somewhat proud' to be British, there has been a marked decline in the proportion who say they are 'very proud' to be British, down from 43 per cent in 2003 to 35 per cent now – a change which, partly because of the debate on the Union, has not occurred in Scotland. This contrasts unfavourably with the 77 per cent of Americans, over

70 per cent of Latin Americans and 66 per cent of Australians who are very proud of their respective countries.[7]

'For some people, greater exposure to other countries through budget travel and a wider digital community can lead them to query what it means to be British', the author of the study, Penny Young, has said. 'The big unknown is whether today's young people will grow more proud of their British heritage. Even if pride increases with age, there is a lot of ground to make up and as a result we would envisage a continued decline.'[8] Indeed, commenting on the recent figures, the Director of British Future, Sunder Katwala, has said that the changes reflect a shift towards Britishness becoming a secondary identity: 'Britishness is still there in the background and we will come together for events such as the jubilee or the First World War centenary but the other nationalities are gaining ground. In England, as well as in Scotland and Wales, British is becoming the second identity.'[9]

In this chapter I suggest that over the three centuries of the Union, what we mean by Britishness – and what impact it has had on our sense of identity – has continued to change and adapt and indeed it is in the process of changing once more. I suggest that while identities in the global era are now always likely to be multiple and multi-layered, a modern British identity can still be an important part of being a proud and patriotic Scot. And yet I want to highlight a danger too.

I tried while Chancellor and Prime Minister to persuade people that we should unite on a non-partisan basis to debate the values that matter to Britain – and agree where possible on what Britishness meant. Throughout my thirteen years in government I made speeches, held conferences, wrote articles and indeed encouraged a book on the subject, yet the Conservative Party were determined to prevent Labour ever being identified with putting patriotic British values on the agenda.

If we missed one opportunity in the first decade of the century to debate and define what holds us together as a nation, the failure is a long-standing one. England was of course not just the first country to industrialise but thought of itself from the sixteenth century onwards as the 'first born' nation, a view reinforced in the seventeenth century by its defeat of absolutism in favour of a commercial revolution. So there is some truth in the view that, already possessing a sense of its uniqueness, England did not ever feel the need to be as self-conscious as the newly created America or revolutionary France in building national unity by asserting its ethos. Neither written constitutions nor grandiose statements of purpose are seen as necessary foundations for legitimacy and popular support when you are pre-eminent. So England has spent little time in debating its ethos or purpose either before or within the Union.

But our failure to be explicit about what we mean by belonging to Britain – or even being willing to debate the question – has created a vacuum that everyone from UKIP to Welsh and Scottish nationalists are now trying to fill.

BECOMING BRITAIN

Great Britain long predated the parliamentary Union in 1707, coming with Scottish James VI's accession to the throne of England in 1603. And the writer John Mair, a Scottish university principal who had started off teaching in Paris, had already called for the term Britain to be used when talking of the union he championed as early as 1521, pleading with the monarchs of the day to unite the two kingdoms. Mair represented a strand of Scottish opinion that sought union *with* England as an alternative to assimilation *by* England. Indeed there is some evidence that the use of the term 'British Empire' denoted support for an Anglo-Scottish project before the Act of Union.

After the Union it was Scots who first wanted to use the term Britain, as James VI did himself, to describe Scotland's part in a venture bigger than England. They feared that the real alternative to talking of Great Britain would be to talk of the new kingdom only as England. To talk of Great Britain gave Scots a place in a land otherwise dominated by the size of one nation. There was another reason too – some were worried by the potential for a retreat into Scottish parochialism and so stressed an ideology of Britishness and energetic participation in the new British state and later the Empire to help Scotland become more outward-looking.

Indeed there is some evidence that Scots were pressing the use of the term 'Britain' while English voices resented it as the term to describe their country. The English novelist Horace Walpole had come to despise the word Britain precisely because it was being used in preference to 'England'. When a London-based Scots writer, Tobias Smollett, became editor of a magazine that he named the *Briton* he was mocked by his opponents who said it should be entitled the *North Briton* (which was, ironically, the name of the magazine's rival, owned by John Wilkes). Indeed we find Smollett highly conscious of the English reaction to him when he starts his novel *The Adventures of Roderick Random* with the words 'I was born in the northern part of this United Kingdom'.[10] Smollett was also sensitive to English prejudices, as his characters remark: 'you Scotchman have overspread us of late as the locusts did Egypt' and 'what between want of curiosity and traditional sarcasms, the effect of ancient animosity, the people at the other end of the island know as little of Scotland as of Japan.'[11]

So in the early days of the Union Britishness was not only an identity still in the process of being constructed but also a hard sell in England. James Boswell describes how, in his early twenties, around 1760, he went to the theatre at Covent Garden and the audience shouted 'No Scots' and 'Scots, out with them'. This experience led him, normally a proud Unionist, to write: 'I hated the English; I wished from my soul that the Union was broke and that we might give them another battle of Bannockburn.'[12]

So British names were introduced and gained traction only

slowly. The Bank of England had been formed in the 1690s before the Union and Scotland did not use its currency for some years afterwards, so even though it was founded by a Scot it was to remain the Bank of England. In 1997 I wanted to change the name to the Bank of England, Scotland, Wales and Northern Ireland but I was frustrated by age-old legal precedents that made changing the name through legislation even more difficult than making the institution independent. However, because the British Linen Bank was created after the Union, the Scots who founded it named it the British Linen Bank, and gradually references to Britain and Great Britain – and, after the union with Ireland, the United Kingdom – became a more popular way of expressing our identity. Britain, wrote T. C. Smout, 'became now to many Scots the name of the theatre where Englishmen and Scots acted out, independently or together, their roles on the life stage. Of course, it did not replace Scotland in their consciousness but it formed the outer circle of a concentric loyalty.'[13]

But, as he said, a British identity meant different things to the Scots than to the English: 'At this point Scottish people internalised the notion of Britain, as the English never did and never have. For the English the usual name for both their state and for the theatre of their lives was, and still is, England: the Empire might have been British but the homeland was England, as it has been from Saxon times.'[14]

Smout cites the comments of English writer A. N. Wilson that: 'Britain is only a term the English use for their country when they remember to be polite to the Scots,'[15] a sentiment put over more unkindly by an Oxbridge academic who responded to a Scot's comment that 'you must think of we the Scots as abrasive' by saying 'we do not think of you at all'.

So although it is the Scots who now show the least affinity with Britain, it is arguably the Scots who worked the hardest at constructing a British identity. It was the Scots who insisted on talking of Britain first, whose feelings were best assuaged by referring to Britain, and who first saw Scottishness and Britishness not as stark opposites but complementary.

As Linda Colley's landmark history *Britons* has shown, between the Union in 1707 and the mid-nineteenth century a common British identity was constructed. We may have shared the same islands and were part of the same common market but the sense we all belonged to Britain did not just happen by accident: a nation's sense of itself is not – and cannot be – created overnight. It is a product of a complex pattern of shared experiences over many years. Indeed, as she demonstrates, a patriotic pride in being British was forged in unique never-to-be repeated circumstances. Colley is conscious that Britishness can never be based on a common ethnicity: unlike ordinary nation states Great Britain brought together three ethnic groups and then added a fourth. Colley identifies three historical forces at work – a common Protestant faith, and a fear of Catholicism; a common enemy in France; and the perceived mutual benefit in exploiting the opportunities afforded by the Empire.[16]

Indeed, the Empire, which had started off with English not British colonies, might easily have been labelled early on as the English Empire but instead it became known worldwide as the British Empire. 'Mobilising the whole of the islands towards the imperial project necessitated creating an identity whereby one could retain one's distinctiveness in ethnic and even national terms', concludes Krishan Kumar in his book *The Making of an English Identity*, 'yet at the same time share in the political identity made possible by the formation of the new British state.'[17]

But if a common religion, enemy and empire brought Britain together then they cannot do so now: no one can contemplate rallying people to the common cause of Britain today by attacking the Catholic religion, by parading the benefits of a long-gone empire and by simply whipping up anti-French sentiment. In the absence of these unifying forces, the story of Britain – and a clear picture of what Britishness means – has to be updated to meet the needs of our times. And we have been slow to do so, says Krishan Kumar: 'the symbolic resources upon which a non-British non-imperial identity could be formed (important for the prospects of a potentially post-British post-imperial identity) were late in coming and weak when they did appear.'[18]

So what is it that holds the United Kingdom together today? A person? An institution? An idea? I want to first look at the state of our common institutions and ask whether they are a sufficiently strong adhesive to hold the country together and give it purpose.

OUR SHARED INSTITUTIONS

Any assessment of British institutions should start with the monarchy – not simply the first institution of the Union, but also in many ways the most visible. The first days of the new united monarchy did not serve Scotland well. James VI visited Scotland only once – seventeen years after ascending to the English throne. The first three king Georges did little to counteract this long history of neglect and, while George IV engineered, thanks to Walter Scott, a brilliant public-relations coup with his pageant in Edinburgh, he failed otherwise to cement the monarchy's links with Scotland.

It was Queen Victoria who ended the benign Hanoverian neglect of the country. In fact, Queen Victoria offered Scotland the first sustained royal presence since 1603. Not only did she visit regularly, set up a home at Balmoral and run her royal court from there for weeks every year, she also tried to recast herself as part of a continuous chain in Scottish regal history. She claimed in her Journals that she had Jacobite blood, described Mary Queen of Scots as one of her 'poor ancestors' (another, of course, that she falsely claimed to be her ancestor was the childless Elizabeth I, who signed Mary's death warrant) and restored the tomb of the Scottish King James II, engraving on it that the work had been done 'By Victoria, A Scottish Descendant'. She also visited Bannockburn and, with little basis in history, claimed that the two combatants, Robert Bruce and Edward I, were both her ancestors.[19]

Things went backwards under her successors Edward VII and VIII but relations improved again when George VI and his Scottish wife took over in 1936. An early blunder by their daughter the new Queen Elizabeth – she made the mistake of saying in a Christmas broadcast that she would visit New Zealand as Queen of England – was repaired completely by the solicitous way that she, her mother and later her children have regularly visited Scotland, made their summer home there and identified with all things Scottish. There has been but one instance of abuse during a visit to Scotland, the infamous Stirling University opening in 1972, and there has been one singular embarrassment, when the crowd booed the singing of 'God Save the Queen' in Princess Anne's presence and demanded a Scottish national anthem be played at Scotland's rugby internationals against England. But with Princess Anne patron of the Scottish Rugby Union, Prince William a graduate of St Andrews and Prince Charles regularly holidaying in Scotland, no one can begin to argue that Scotland is neglected or ignored by the royal family today.

And yet Scottish people do not embrace the monarchy in the same way as the English. When asked by British Future 'Are you very proud of the Queen?', 50 per cent of English respondents said yes and 30 per cent more said they were fairly proud. But in Scotland those who say they are very proud of the Queen amounted to only 15 per cent, with fairly proud at 26 per cent. A total of 55 per cent of Scots compared with just 17 per cent of the English said that they were 'not proud'.[20]

These figures should be put in proper perspective: the Queen is almost universally popular and appreciated in every part of Scotland and today 62 per cent believe that an independent

Scotland should 'definitely' or 'probably' continue to share a monarch with England. While they want the Queen to be head of state rather than sovereign, the nationalists have been shrewd enough to assert that an independent Scotland would retain the monarchy.[21]

But if there is a continuing affection for the Queen, there is little left for Westminster.

An in-depth survey commissioned in 1999 showed that the House of Commons was deemed very important to our identity by only 33 per cent of Scottish people – and that finding was before the expenses scandal. Now, according to the Scottish Social Attitudes survey, Westminster is trusted by only 18 per cent of Scots. This is not a complaint against all parliamentary institutions, as the Scottish Parliament and Scottish government were trusted by 71 per cent of people.[22]

Yet voting has declined at all elections. From a peak of 81.2 per cent in 1951 we are down to 63.8 per cent Scottish turnout at the last UK elections, yet the Scottish Parliament elections have never managed a turnout of more than 58.2 per cent (in 1999). In fact, since the Scottish Parliament began it has consistently failed to rival the turnouts at UK elections: in the 2011 elections, where the SNP won a majority, the turnout was just 50.4 per cent, 13 per cent less than the turnout at the UK election the year before. It seems that even if their voting record is only based on an instrumental decision – that the elections matter for our economy – Scots turn out in greater numbers for UK elections than for Scottish Parliament elections and, while they see the parliament in Scotland as more in tune with their sentiments, they are voting with their feet, recognising that the UK elections are still of importance to them.

But a higher turnout does not necessarily mean that Westminster enhances our sense of being British, for there is another dimension in Scottish attitudes towards the institutions of Britain. Indeed, government from the centre is so unpopular that people talk of 'London rule', 'London mismanagement' and 'Whitehall rule'. Westminster is often described as if it is a foreign place. Thousands visit the Scottish Parliament every year – yet only a fraction of Scots visit Westminster. If we were serious about wanting to explain the importance of the House of Commons to the Scottish people we would make it possible for thousands of school children to visit the UK Parliament as well as the Scottish Parliament and offer a far more tangible outreach, with MPs visiting schools and undertaking a major educational programme about where the UK Parliament fits into our constitution. But Scots might also find it more relevant to their identity if we reform it – answering a demand that comes from all parts of the United Kingdom.

Of course Britain now has a Supreme Court but while, in the last resort, we find that people support the judiciary as a bulwark against an overbearing state, the English judiciary is neither important enough to Scotland – Scotland has its own laws and system of justice – nor is there any real understanding that it performs the role normally ascribed to federal states. While the UK Supreme Court containing Scottish representation arbitrates on issues of dispute between the Scottish and Westminster parliaments and governments it is not, like the US Supreme Court, seen to be an ultimate arbiter for the country as a whole.

The armed forces fare much better as a unifying institution: 51 per cent of the Scottish public say that the armed forces help express and shape our British identity, and a deep sense of reverence and respect for the war dead is still as likely to be expressed with dignity in Stonehaven as Southampton. A quarter of a million Scots joined the army in the post-war years when we had conscription, and regular commemorative events and well cared for memorials indicate the deep respect and admiration people have for our armed forces. In every part of Scotland there are memorials to the fallen and to the wounded of the First and

Second World Wars and on every Remembrance Sunday people still come together en masse to pay tribute.

Time that has distanced us from the events of 1914–18 and 1939–45 has not diminished the power of these British occasions and the genuine mourning for the dead. The Scottish National War Memorial was opened at Edinburgh Castle a decade after the war and became a scene of mass pilgrimage. And such were the deep connections between our military and community in Fife that our first community centres were 'war memorial and miners' institutes'.

Fife is also home to a memorial garden for those who fell in the Iraq and Afghan Wars. And I was proud to be present in Kirkcaldy the day the Black Watch received the freedom of Fife in 2006. Seeing them march through the streets of the town to respectful and affectionate applause, you could appreciate the strong connection between a very Scottish regiment and local citizens: it was not only families and friends of servicemen and women who came out to applaud them but an entire community. I favoured the award of an HM Armed Forces Veterans Badge to thank all those who have served our country and I have had the privilege of witnessing their patriotic pride at first hand when awarding the badge to hundreds of constituents. For five years now events that highlight the achievement of the armed forces have been held across the UK and there is no suggestion that the events are any less popular in Scotland. I attended privately the Armed Forces Day in 2011 in Edinburgh with my children, not asking for any role, but simply to be there.

The respect and admiration we have for our armed forces has always been expressed most strongly in time of war. And while recent wars in Iraq and Afghanistan have been more controversial in Scotland, the SNP's plan for separate Scottish armed forces – 5,000 army, 5,000 navy and 5,000 air-force personnel – is neither appealing, with Scotland losing the benefit of the collective strength of Britain's 200,000 servicemen and women, nor adequate.[23] Indeed, only 27 per cent of the Scottish public believe that an independent Scotland should have its own army, navy and air force, while as many as 67 per cent believe it should combine its armed forces with the rest of the UK.[24]

I, like many others, wish to see nuclear weapons removed as part of an agreement for multilateral disarmament but the Scottish National Party wish to write in to a new Scottish constitution a unilateral 'ban on nuclear weapons being based in Scotland' while still seeking to join the nuclear weapon umbrella of NATO.[25] But a recent poll finds that 37 per cent of Scots are 'strongly' or 'somewhat' in favour of Britain having its own nuclear weapons, while 46 per cent are opposed. On the other hand, 41 per cent agree that, 'if Scotland becomes an independent country, Britain's nuclear-weapons submarines should continue to be based in Scotland', slightly more than the 37 per cent who disagree.[26] Reflecting on SNP demands to remove nuclear weapons from Scotland and to have our own independent army, the Scottish Social Attitudes survey concludes that 'neither stance is, though, overwhelmingly popular'.[27]

But of course the British army cannot be the force it was in the days of conscription or all-out war. Some may remember the campaign to save the Argyll and Sutherland Highlanders, which gained more signatures than any other petition in Scotland in my lifetime. But the eleven Scottish regiments have now amalgamated into one Regiment of Scotland. We can gauge the impact of changed times on the reach of the armed forces into families and neighbourhoods. Recent figures suggest there are approximately 12,000–13,000 young Scots in the army, 3,000 in the Navy and 4,000 in the RAF.[28] That's one in 129 of the Scottish male population, and one in every hundred Scottish families – a far smaller network than before. Within a few years the figures will be much less, probably closer to 15,000, narrowing further the direct reach the armed forces have into Scottish society.

So today even the traditional British institutions that retain their popularity will struggle to unite Britain in the way the armed services and the monarchy did in wartime.

DEFINING A BRITISH IDENTITY

There have been many suggestions as to how a greater sense of Britishness could be engendered through creating new institutions or supporting old institutions more effectively. I proposed an Institute for British Studies in addition to creating an Armed Forces Day. Others have argued for new requirements placed on applicants for citizenship to understand our country, made proposals for a UK or British patron saint, for hosting British events like the Warriors Games not just in London but in all corners of Britain and for a British day; and, to heighten awareness of our past, there have been proposals I have always supported for more teaching about the history of our country in a comprehensive rather than themed way in our schools.

Part of the problem is that Britain itself is seen to be in decline by many Scots. People used to joke that in the Britain of the 1950s we managed decline, in the 1960s we mismanaged decline and in the 1970s we declined to manage. Harold Wilson's plan that Britain use the 'white heat of the technological revolution' to 'clear the deadwood from the boardrooms' was about reversing decades of decline caused, he said, by the stuffy amateurism of an old private-school elite. Edward Heath's plan to put Britain at the centre of Europe was his antidote to imperial decline and overdependence on America. Mrs Thatcher's strategy of opening the British economy up to global market forces was her attempt to destroy the old collective institutions she blamed for holding Britain back. All were initiatives to redefine Britain for the modern world. And I am drawn to Andrew Gamble's account of post-war history that 'the relative decline of the British economy has been a constant theme in political debate in Britain since the 1880s, and at certain times, particularly in the early 1960s and 1970s, has been a central and obsessive theme', all the more painful because our power was once hegemonic. Gamble argues that 'even if it were concluded that decline was an illusion lacking any objective basis in reality it would still be necessary to explain why such a large part of Britain's political elite interpreted British experience in the twentieth century as one of decline'.[29]

More recently a new dimension has been added to the debate about Britain's status in the world. The rise of China and India, and the accompanying shift of economic power from West to East and from North to South has been unsettling for all the countries of the old 'first world'. We sought to lead not just in the European Union but the UN, the G8 and latterly the G20 but what was not successful was a series of initiatives to present a New Britain to the world. The early idea of a 'Young Britain' and the political embrace of 'Cool Britannia' (which is remembered only for a drunken party of celebrities at Downing Street) simply didn't make sense to people who were used to taking pride in our history, particularly in successful wars in Europe. Perhaps the worst misadventure of all was spending £1 billion on what came to be called the Millennium Dome. All many remember today is a queue of newspaper editors unable to get into the Dome as the clock prepared to strike midnight, but the hangover of the Dome haunted many of our other efforts in government to have a more substantial conversation about who we are as a country.

The reason that Labour's adoption of Cool Britannia, Young Britain and the Millennium Dome did not work, but Danny Boyle's Olympics ceremony did, was that the latter was trying to communicate a substantial argument from history that Britain has a proud and progressive past to build upon – and not pretending that Britain is a blank slate ready to be written upon – as we decide who we want to be in this still young century. Of course there is always a danger that Britain will be characterised only by its past.

Writing from Beijing, Leo Lewis of *The Times* quotes China's *Global Times* tabloid as saying on the eve of the British Prime Minister's visit in 2013 that 'the UK is not a big power in the eyes of the Chinese. It is just an old European country apt for travel and study.' This accords with the popular Chinese view of Britain – enthusiastically played up by public schools and their agents – that it is essentially a large extension of Eton College: traditional, expensive and a producer of leaders. It involves representing Britain as he says 'not with images of high-tech science labs but with faux-sepia snaps of toffs in boating hats. The image (attractive to China's wealthy) is of Britain as an elegantly-quadrangled alma mater that has been peddling elitism for centuries.'[30] That is not my Britain, and it is a Britain to which few Scots can relate.

So neither this elitist version of Britain, nor the faux modern one, really tell the whole truth about a country whose identity changed during the first two centuries of the Union and then changed again on the home front of the Second World War. The material issued by the WWII coalition government's Ministry of Information presented the country as one of shared sacrifice founded on principles of fairness and social justice, and in their official history W. K. Hancock and Margaret Gowing state that 'there existed, so to speak, an implied contract between Government and people; the people refused none of the sacrifices that the Government demanded of them for the winning of the war; in return, they expected that the Government should show imagination and seriousness in preparing for the restoration and improvement of the nation's well-being when the war had been won'.[31]

As McCrone explains: 'The sense of Britishness that came from the war was different from the older imperialist sense to which they had been accustomed. Built on equal social and economic rights for all, the post-war welfare state and National Health

Service confirmed this new more democratic version of Britishness. By mid-century, Scots were if anything confirmed in their Britishness . . . as part of an integrated welfare state.' Change was not complete of course, as deference and hierarchy never died. But instead of Britishness referring to the subjects of an imperial dominion, it was now closer to meaning the shared rights of a common citizenship.[32]

In the next chapter I will talk of the sharing and solidarity that comes from a common welfare state and a National Health Service but one institution that is also part of this common culture is the BBC, created by a Scot with professional ethics favoured by the Scots and a prominent part of what has been called 'the long revolution' that has created a British-wide culture. While now thought of differently in Scotland, with Scots watching BBC Scotland and tuning in to separate Scottish news and current affairs, the post-war BBC is nonetheless something Scots have a great deal of affection for and want to retain. Indeed, a recent survey has shown that 61 per cent of Scots believe that if Scotland became independent the BBC should be available in the same way as it is now, and only 11 per cent would want the BBC to be replaced by a Scottish public TV service.[33] That the Scottish government felt the need to reassure Scots about continuing access to the BBC in its White Paper reflects the underlying truth that across literature, the arts and the media there is both a strong, self-confident Scottish culture and a continuing desire to be part of a wider English language culture represented by the BBC.

So even if all the institutions of the Union are not the great social adhesive they once were, institutions like the BBC continue to foster a British dimension and common culture across the country.

SHARED VALUES

But seventy years on from the refashioning of British identity to respond to shared wartime sacrifices both on the battlefield and on the home front, our British identity is being reappraised yet again under the pressure of profound social and economic changes that often go by the name of 'globalisation', including the global migrations of people that are reshaping our lives. We are, in the words of Matthew d'Ancona, who eloquently edited a book on *Being British*, 'surfing a series of waves coursing around the world, a sociological storm spawned by globalisation, unprecedented population mobility and fluctuating living standards'.[34]

Of course it has always been intrinsic to the Union that we have multiple loyalties – Scots and British, English and British and now today Black and British, and Muslim and British too. Today there is a sense that our identity is multi-layered, containing not just loyalties to family, home town, county, country, nation and continent but personal loyalties that define us, whether membership of a social network, a sports club, a charitable cause, a religious community or a feminist group.

So a British dimension to our identity has to stand alongside the multiple multi-layered identities that are ever more important to our everyday lives. And the concept of 'Unionism' – whose post-1886 form was a defence of the Union with Ireland – does not reflect the modern language of partnership that people seek.

Clearly, too, monarchy, army and parliament are less able to express and shape a modern British identity than they were in the past. Interestingly when we have tried to formulate a citizenship 'test' we have, according to a comparative study of such tests, shied away from history. To me it suggests a lack of confidence about what to root our national identity in. Unable to develop a discourse either in our schools or with 'citizenship tests' about what constitutes British citizenship in the modern world, Britain has 'failed to identify a distinct national notion of belonging', concludes James Hampshire in his study *Citizenship and Belonging*.[35]

And in my view the ties which bind us are strongest when they arise from values we share, which are rooted in our history and culture and expressed through our social and political institutions.

A commitment to shared values may well not be enough in the abstract to hold us together but it is hard to escape from the view that our identity resides in such values, mediated through and brought alive in our institutions like the NHS and in common policies for social justice.

Of course, the values which we hold dear as a nation – such as liberty, equality, fairness, tolerance – are, in the main, shared by most modern democratic nations, and are reflected in the Universal Declaration of Human Rights. But the precise way in which each of those values is expressed and how they interact will reflect the history and culture of each individual country. Here I have been influenced by Miller's and Tamir's work on liberal nationalism, Jurgen Habermas's theory of constitutional patriotism, Taylor's notion of interculturalism, and Calhoun's pioneering studies of social movements. A national identity can be shaped by more than race and ethnicity: by a common story, stretching across generations, by a shared loyalty to common institutions we have built together and by ideas and beliefs held in common that shape these institutions.

Some critics have suggested this sort of civic patriotism is too utopian, that people of different ethnicities cannot develop a shared sense of belonging that transcends their different racial roots; and that, even if they attempted to do so, the basis of consensus will be so abstract or vague that it is meaningless. Of course, anybody who has ever attended an American sporting event or public meeting and watched as people with roots in all the countries of the earth salute the same flag, sing the same anthem and pledge allegiance to the same cause cannot fail to be impressed by what the country has been able to achieve. America is able to unite people because it conceives of itself as more than a destination for 'the huddled masses', as an idea – the land of liberty and opportunity.

In Canada, where 80 per cent of the population of Quebec (which is 24 per cent of Canadians) are French speakers and 80 per cent Catholic, national unity is possible only by balancing the cultural and political autonomy of the Québecois people with a set of shared goals to which all of Canada can subscribe. For Charles Taylor, who has thought more about these issues than any other, the challenge is how the Western liberal can reconcile a preference for liberal democracy with what he calls the 'illiberalism' (at one point he calls it 'propensity to exclusion') necessary for Québecois cultural self-preservation; he concludes that 'a full understanding of the dilemma of democratic exclusion shows that there is no alternative' to what he calls 'sharing identity space'.

First Canada tried to found its unity on the idea of economic interdependence and its mutual benefits. Then under Pierre Trudeau's leadership it tried to reconcile itself to a bicultural identity as a country – French and English – with, in the words of Trudeau, 'no official culture'. 'Nor does any ethnic group take precedence over any other,' he said. 'Cultural pluralism is the very essence of Canadian identity.' But distinguishing between a first-level diversity, which means different people have cultural symbols and practices, and a 'deep diversity', where a whole group – the people of Quebec – now stand apart demanding their distinctiveness be recognised en masse, Professor Taylor says multiculturalism, 'in as much as it emphasises diversity at the expense of continuity' is 'not properly adapted to Quebec's situation'. The rest of Canada has to understand, he has argued, Quebec's 'language-related anxiety', the 'existential anguish of the minority', and their 'concern for the continuity or preservation of an old founding culture'. Pursuing a policy of 'interculturalism' is preferred, he says to 'multi-culturalism' because the Quebec people 'want to accentuate the exchanges between different cultural groups'. But while he sees the basis of unity in a continuing democratic dialogue about what Quebec and Canada have in common, the Quebec minority nationalist administration insisted on publishing their own separate statement including the hardline Quebec Charter of Values, which includes banning the wearing of all religious symbols by public employees. Taylor's contention – that the country can hold together only if respect for the 'deep diversity' of different parts of the country sits beside a commitment to democracy, the rule of law and representative government as defining Canadian ideals – was put to the test – and upheld in the crushing defeat of the Parti Québecois at the 2014 provincial general election.[36]

Canada's experience is of course unique – Britain does not have the extreme cultural, religious or linguistic divides at its core that Canada has – and the people of Quebec have recently turned away from extreme versions of nationalism including the hardline statement of Québecois values, but their experience reminds us of the growing pressures to recognise 'deep diversity' in the modern world. Across Europe, as David Marquand has noted in his study of Europe and its regions, there is an implosion of nationalist breakaway movements: in Spain and Belgium and even in Italy (where Lombardy and Venice are talking of secession). There may be a common strand, that the same juggernaut of globalisation that has brought about a more integrated world economy through the free flow of capital, goods and services has created in its wake popular demands to be protected or sheltered from it and that the best method of resistance people have found to what they see as alien to them is to organise around their traditional identities.

Is it then possible – amid a new world of multiple multi-layered identities and the revival of secessionist tendencies – for a modern British national identity to be forged that recognises the diversity of our home nations but is grounded in shared values that find concrete expression in reformed institutions and ways of sharing the risks and resources of contemporary life? Only it seems if there is enough common ground in a shared culture, shared ideas and shared institutions and, in Britain's case, if the act of sharing our risks and resources across the United Kingdom can cement a sense of belonging and thus a practical and lived solidarity. I referred in an earlier chapter to Ewan McGregor's notion that you can love Scotland but also like the idea of Britain. Indeed I too like the idea of Britain – the notion that I can be Scottish first but also recognise that the people of Merseyside or the Welsh Valleys have a call on my solidarity, and I on theirs, which exceeds that which is owed to all the peoples of the world. In other words I will always be Scottish, and have been a life-long internationalist, but through Britain I can feel part of a moral community bigger than Scotland, and smaller than humankind. I think that suits the moral expansiveness of the Scots and, in fact, allows us to project our values out into the wider world with even more power and reach than we could achieve on our own.

But there is a risk that any statement of the British values we share will be so bland and abstract that it can never be a glue that binds us together or gives us a shared sense of purpose, and in the words of Rogers Smith in *Citizenship, Borders, and Human Needs* is 'too thin to deliver the desiderata of civic solidarity as evidenced by the perennial lurch into nationalism'.[37] So let us try to be precise about what we mean by British values and explain how they are mediated by institutions. I see Britishness defined at its best as a passion for liberty matched by a strong sense of duty and social responsibility and a belief in fair play or fairness. It was Montesquieu who wrote in the eighteenth century that ours was 'the freest country in the world' because of our determination to restrict arbitrary power and both sides in the American War of Independence fought 'in the name of British liberty'.

Of course history is strewn with examples of how we failed to live up to our ideals. But British ideas of liberty did at least mean that for half a century it was Britain that led the worldwide anti-slavery movement and provided a sanctuary for Europe's religious and political radicals. Our tolerance for dissent and the encouragement we gave to free thinking facilitated our creativity and inventiveness and it is no accident that both the agricultural and industrial revolutions began here, or that British pioneers from Charles Babbage and Ada Lovelace right up to Alan Turing and Tim Berners-Lee litter the history of computing. The Scottish contribution to the history of science, engineering and medicine is well documented, but we should celebrate those great inventors alongside a nineteenth-century genius like Isambard Kingdom Brunel and a modern one like Tim Berners-Lee. Today the same dynamism is to be found in some of the most modern and creative British industries – communications, fashion, film, popular music and art, architecture, and many areas of science and the environmental technologies.

At every point this British belief in liberty has been matched by a very British idea of what duty entails. A belief in the duty of one to another is an essential element of nationhood in every country but whether it was influenced more by religious beliefs, or a *noblesse oblige*, or a sense of solidarity, duty in Britain has been, to most people, the foundation of rights rather than their consequence.

I have written earlier about how the modern idea of civic society started in Scotland – but it did not end there. Some of the world's largest NGOs and charities are British institutions and the world continues to come to Britain to marvel at how our ancestors invested in shared green space and magnificent public libraries, galleries and museums. Even as the British state was growing and developing new services to fight Beveridge's 'great evils', the British way continued to recognise local initiative and mutual responsibility in civic affairs and to encourage and enhance the status of voluntary and community organisations – Burke's 'little platoons' – in the service of their neighbourhoods.

In his last speech to parliament in March 1955 – the speech that urged the British people to 'never flinch, never weary, never despair' – Churchill described the essential qualities of the British people and at the forefront was fair play. Fairness is of course a central tenet of most Western democracies – and therefore widely regarded as a universal value. Yet when applied in the context of Britain it means the right but also the responsibility to work and it validates the principle of universal healthcare, free at the point of need rather than a privilege to be paid for. I think the British view of fairness begins with the individual, but is not about individualism. It sees each person as endowed with rights but also recognises that abstract rights are not enough if the community does not offer any guarantees about the ability of each person to exercise them and if the individual does not accept his or her personal responsibility.

There is thus a golden thread that runs through British history of the individual standing firm against tyranny and the arbitrary use of power. It runs from those days in Runnymede in 1215 and Arbroath in 1320 through the debates of the seventeenth and eighteenth centuries to not just one but four great British reform acts within less than a hundred years. But the British story is not one that focuses on political rights and civil liberties alone – for from the Liberal social reforms at the beginning of the last century through the building of the welfare state in its middle, the British people also pioneered new ways of thinking about social and economic rights.

No one should gloss over the dark side of our past or its inequalities. We have had our failures and as we shall see in later chapters there is much to do if we are to end the violation of social and economic rights and thereby right wrongs. But the two dangerous ideologies that have been at the heart of the histories of many other countries have never taken root here. On the one hand an ideology of state power, which choked individual freedom by making the individual a slave to some arbitrarily defined totalitarianism, has found little or no favour in Britain. Indeed as recently as 2009 when the Labour constitutional-affairs minister Michael Wills convened a British-wide discussion on a British Bill of Rights and Responsibilities he found that British people did not feel the British state would trample on their rights.[38] On the other hand, an ideology of crude individualism – which favours the survival of the fittest and every man for himself – has limited resonance for a Britain which has a rich tradition of voluntary organisations, local democracy, civic life and a strong sense of what is fair and unfair.

But British ideas about liberty, duty and fair play would inevitably be dismissed as abstract, eclectic and unable to unite the country if we were not able to show in concrete terms how they influence and shape the way we live our lives as a country. As Samuel Huntington, who has studied the culture of nations suggested, ideology is a 'weak glue' to bind together people otherwise lacking in racial, ethnic or cultural sources of community. But I will show in the next chapter how a modern form of British identity has been coming alive in the way we pool and share risks and resources across the four nations of the United Kingdom to deliver basic rights to pensions and social security, to employment opportunity, to education and – in a unique world-renowned system – to healthcare free at the point of need. In each case the basic social and economic rights that people hold have been established as UK-wide rights, irrespective of whether you are Scots, English, Welsh or Northern Irish. While these rights are grounded in values we share in common, the solidarity they induce is not at a level of abstraction from ordinary life. Instead, the unity that comes, for example, from sharing on a UK-wide basis services for transplants and blood transfusions makes our sharing an everyday, lived reality. The pooling and sharing we engage in is thus more than a set of values we share in common: it is the everyday practice of popular institutions like the NHS and pensions system that brings these values to life. Indeed, no other country in the world has managed to persuade four nations to pool and share their resources in the comprehensive and sophisticated way we do.

I have said that in the absence of a common ethnicity there has got to be something greater than the appeal to a shared heredity that can persuade people to come together.

How far the act of sharing contributes to belonging or vice versa is a debate for the next chapter. But even if belonging to Britain means no more than a reassurance that wherever you live, in Scotland, England, Northern Ireland or Wales, you can count on the same social rights, it is a British achievement that is unique in the modern world. These shared benefits of belonging are founded not on ancient institutions and certainly not on a common ethnicity. They are founded on British values that have shaped and are now instilled in some of our newest British institutions in very practical and specific ways. I believe the development during the twentieth century of these shared rights is one of the proudest parts of Britain's national history, and meets the requirement that a modern British identity must entail a readily accessible common culture, shared values and common institutions that reflect these values. It is to these shared values and common institutions, how they have developed over the last century, and how they might shape our future and become a beacon for an ever-more interdependent world in the next, that I now turn.

CHAPTER 6

The Sharing Union

Just over ninety years ago, in 1921, near where I live in Fife, unemployed miners pushed out of work and facing destitution pressed their Poor Law authority for help. And when in the autumn of 1921 the Wemyss Parish Council finally offered assistance, they not only broke a long-standing Scottish policy to deny help to the unemployed but offered them rates of assistance that were in contravention of the law. Their revolutionary argument – that the costs of unemployment should be met not by local ratepayers but by the United Kingdom as a whole – was to capture public opinion in a wave of fervour for change that started in Wemyss and then spread across Fife and across Scotland and then through the regions of England. Within a few weeks the 300-year-old Scottish Poor Law was all but dead – and one of the building blocks of the British welfare state had been put in place. An agitation for social justice that started in Fife had changed Scotland and Britain for good. And the reformers were Scottish leaders influenced by Scottish values who decided that they should abandon separate Scottish provision, and meet with equal provision – irrespective of nationality or past custom – need right across the United Kingdom. Scots themselves had decided to abandon their separate Scottish institutions and agitate not for their reform but for an all-British system for allocating resources to where needs were greatest.

Over previous chapters we have seen how the Union moved from a war-focused alliance for common security to an economic one, and how Scotland has been able to assert its distinctive interests and secure tangible benefits during the many incarnations of our partnership with England. In this chapter, starting with that 1921 reform, I want to look at what I consider to be one of the crowning Scottish achievements of the last 300 years: the creation of shared social and economic rights across the four home nations.

Indeed today it does not matter which of the four nations you were born into within the UK, or where you currently reside: you have a right to the same basic employment, welfare and general social benefits just by virtue of being a United Kingdom citizen. We take that so much for granted now we can sometimes forget just what a radical idea it is that four nations have agreed to pool and share their resources to give citizens of each nation exactly the same rights. To put it in some sort of context: what we do every day in the UK has no parallel in human history. As I said in the Introduction, there are many examples of 'common markets' and even 'single markets'. There are countries that have agreed to jointly protect civil and political rights. But there is not a single example of a group of countries pooling their resources to provide for the number and magnitude of concrete social and economic rights that every one of us can claim and draw upon without question.

It is an incredible, unlikely, unique and counter-intuitive achievement. It is an all-British system urged by Scots who actually renounced and abandoned their own distinctive institutions to make it happen. Surely before we walk away from it Scotland should take some time to reflect on how we secured this global first?

In an earlier chapter we looked at why Scottish nationalism did not follow the same trajectory as that of other countries in the nineteenth century. In this chapter we are really looking at why the four home nations did something that hasn't been done by any other group of countries in any other century. I think, when we look at it closely, we will see Scottish fingerprints all over Britain's social settlement.

How the change from the Scottish Poor Law to the British welfare system happened is not the only conundrum in our twentieth-century story. We have to ask why we moved not just from a Scottish-run Poor law to a British system of welfare benefit for the uninsured but also from a Scottish-run and – more importantly for this debate – Scottish-funded, local-authority-led healthcare system to, from 1948, a UK-wide healthcare system funded for every citizen of each of the four nations from UK general taxation and UK National Insurance? I want to suggest that it was a Scottish leader in Tom Johnston, the Scottish Secretary of State, who led the way across the UK in rejecting Winston Churchill's proposal to have a locally funded healthcare system in which hospitals charged people for their services. Instead Johnston demanded, and later Aneurin Bevan achieved, a National Health Service throughout the whole of the United Kingdom free at the point of need.

And why did we commit to policies for jobs and pay that see the same rights to dignity at work enjoyed by workers whether they are in Lanarkshire or Lancashire? I want to suggest that from 1919 onwards – starting with the Glasgow marches, through and beyond to the Upper Clyde Shipbuilders' rally in the early 1970s, and then to the Right to Work march we had in the early 1980s – the message was sent loud and clear that economic intervention had to be organised on a UK level so that need should be the deciding factor when resources were allocated to save and create employment.

Scottish Enlightenment ideas about mutual obligation created the drive for a civil society separate from the state. I believe that the twentieth century saw the updating of those ideas for a new era. Where once our values of social responsibility led us to organise separately from the state, in the post-war years they led us to try to shape a new state, one in which all the people of the United Kingdom could have a stake. That's why I say the Union, as currently constituted, is not just to Scotland's benefit – it is nothing less than Scottish values in action.

THE SCOTTISH STAMP ON THE WELFARE STATE

Let me start by showing the significance of the shift from a Scottish Poor Law to a British welfare state. The Poor Law was Scottish in every respect in the seventeenth, eighteenth and nineteenth centuries. Despite the centralisation of economic policy, like the rules for trade and commerce, Scotland retained autonomy right across social policy, much of which was originally run by the Church and then by local civic institutions. Indeed in the twentieth century it would have been perfectly legitimate for us to argue that all social policy should be run by Scots, in Scotland, in a wholly self-contained way, as that is how things had proceeded happily for two centuries after the Union.

After all, the Scottish Poor Law had existed before the Union and had two distinctive aspects. First, communities recognised their duty to help those who were struggling without the need to imprison them in a workhouse. So the system of parish support in Scotland was, in one sense, more compassionate and less stigmatising than that in England. However, as we shall see, it placed a huge burden on the extended family and voluntary organisations before it allowed for the benevolence of the state.

Second, the Scottish Poor Law boards were different because they had never recognised the need or the obligation to support the able-bodied poor who became unemployed. So here Scotland was harsher: if you were sick or disabled you had the right to help, but in general people had a responsibility to work and if none was available locally you should move. That in part explains rates of Scottish emigration in the nineteenth century. So the able-bodied poor in Scotland had a worse deal than in England. Indeed, the influential cleric Thomas Chalmers and the Scottish social reformers of the nineteenth century maintained a harsh approach to the poor, seeing their bad fortune as a sign of moral weakness rather than a failure of the economic system.

So traditionally the Scottish Poor Law was not as generous in its payments. Chalmers wanted both character testing of the poor as a route to moral reformation, and voluntary philanthropy free of state interference. But as urban social conditions deteriorated charity did not come to the rescue. Dr Stana Nenadic has charted how the gentry helped the poor in early Victorian times, but as the century progressed social relationships broke down and more and more wealthy people concluded that poverty was really a result of a deficiency in character. This was the main reason why, 'even in the early twentieth century', she concludes, 'the annual cost of relieving paupers per head of population in Scotland was a full 50 per cent lower than in England'.[1]

So there is a paradox in how Scottish social provision developed. On the one hand, Scotland valued work and was even more obsessed than Victorian England with notions of the deserving and undeserving poor. But a fixation on fair rewards for effort led Scottish social reformers to grasp more quickly than anybody that the mass unemployment of the Inter-war years was not the fault of a feckless few but the result of worldwide economic conditions. Long before the Jarrow March of 1936, Scotland had already formed a consensus that the unemployed should not be left destitute and that the scale of the problem demanded a solution greater than could be provided without UK-wide intervention.

Of course a limited form of national insurance against sickness and unemployment had been created in 1911 but help was available under it only for insured people. As we have seen, the pressure that started in Fife was that relief be given through the Poor Law for the uninsured employed and be a charge paid not by local taxpayers alone, but with help from the national UK budget. It is important to recall how and from where the pressure grew. In the autumn of 1921 the Fife Miners' Union was among many who sent a deputation to the Scottish Board of Health, after they had heard and voted to agree with the parish-council concerns. There followed resolutions from several Scottish local authorities headed by Dundee, who stated in their demands set out on 17 September 1921: 'We are strongly of the opinion that the responsibility for dealing with unemployment must be national.'[2] And there was no doubt what national meant in this context – the United Kingdom government. 'This Conference therefore requests the Government,' they said, 'to take immediate action to deal with this problem by a continuance of unemployed benefit.' And they were clear as to where the money should come from: 'Further, the expense to communities caused by relieving [the unemployed] and their dependents,' they stated, 'should be met by grants in aid from the Treasury.'[3]

At a stroke, they had abandoned centuries of Scottish social-policy traditions. Relief for the poor was no longer to be local. Neither was it to continue to depend just on what local people could afford. And it was not sufficient for the new standard to be just a Scottish one. The clear demand was for an approved UK-wide minimum level of benefits, to be paid for by sharing the cost across the UK.

They showed that only a UK-wide policy could cope with the scale of the unemployment problem. Prompted to take up the

Fife case in the House of Commons, the local Dunfermline MP John Wallace gave the example of Ballingry in Fife saying 'Take a small parish, called Ballingry, in the constituency of my right hon. Friend the Member for West Fife (Mr. Adamson), a parish of very low rateable value, where the poor rate at present is something like 2s. [10p] in the £., this will probably mean an addition of 3s. [15p] or 4s. [20p] in the £ to that poor rate', something that local ratepayers clearly could not pay. So his conclusion was a reversal of a hundred years of orthodox thinking. 'It should be realised by the Government', he said, 'that places of that kind – and there are many of them in Scotland – are carrying not a local but a national burden, and, therefore, that the incidence is most unfair.' And there was no doubt where the responsibility for meeting the need lay: 'The Treasury has seen fit only to grant relief by a system of loans', he continued. 'I think that he [the Chancellor] realises, as we all do, that this burden must be shared as much as possible nationally . . . We ought to realise how very strong all over Scotland at present is the feeling that this burden should be a national one and should not be borne altogether by the local authorities.'[4]

Once the campaign for a UK-wide system of unemployment benefit for the uninsured then spread to other poorer parts of Britain, no one in future would ever dispute the agreement that the costs of benefits would be met by resources not at local or Scottish level but at UK level. Indeed it was already a fait accompli when sixteen years later the Scottish Minister Walter Elliot formally reported to the House of Commons in 1937 that local authorities were now, and for the future, relieved of their liabilities for the unemployed.

These changes, which started in the 1920s, meant that the idea of a separate Scottish welfare state, providing rights for the Scottish unemployed only, was not an issue for Sir William Beveridge when he authored his report on the future of social security. It had already been accepted that neither geography nor ethnicity determined the rights of the unemployed – it was need, irrespective of nationality.

Scottish pressure, therefore, helped establish one of the first and more important building blocks of the emerging British welfare state: everybody pays into the common pool, no matter where in the UK they are from, and everybody can take out of the pot, no matter where in the UK they now live.

The second big shift in policy – to helping not just individuals but areas in distress – was also led by a Scottish demand for change. Depressed areas like Clydeside, the argument went, could not find the resources to rejuvenate themselves, not from within Scotland. Only UK-wide allocation of economic resources based on need could bring economic recovery.

Again we can trace the growth of these new regional and industrial policies to Scottish demands, first from trade-union leaders, and then from Scottish politicians and civil servants. In the 1930s they won their case and 'special areas of assistance' were designated to receive Treasury funds. It is worth noting that this argument – for giving help on the basis of need – was prosecuted so successfully that the help given to Scotland far transcended that of the old 'Goschen formula' that we looked at in a previous chapter: a quarter of the UK funds for special areas were earmarked for Scotland.[5]

The argument under the Goschen formula described in the previous chapter was that Scotland should get out proportionately what she put in, accounting for changes in her population. But now Scotland was getting help on the basis of what she needed, not on the basis of what she was able to give. And there was decentralisation in the administration of this help too: Scotland did not find the money it was receiving administered by a UK department. When funding had been provided to Scotland in 1928–31, it had come through the UK Ministry of Labour. But in 1934, when the designation of Special Areas was first mooted, the Scottish Office moved to ensure that the government grants (to assist public works) were routed through Scottish ministerial control. The Scottish Office was able to argue that it should receive the money and then, within agreed limits, decide how to spend it.

Again, an important principle was being entrenched: to pay for this new needs-based support Scotland did not have to raise all the money itself by redistributing resources from within Scotland: there would be assistance at a British level, determined on the basis of an area's needs. So a principle was established that any area hit by high unemployment across any part of the UK should receive special help not just by a redistribution of local-authority rates money across the UK – one form of pooling and sharing resources that was tried and found wanting – but from the UK exchequer and thus from national taxation, with funds found outside rates from general taxation to pay for meeting these new needs.

If in the 1920s and 1930s new rights were established – the right on a UK basis for individuals to be helped when unemployed and the right on a UK basis for an area to be assisted when in recession – these were rights only to 'first aid' when in trouble. This was, if you like, akin to the UK sending an ambulance when the patient was in trouble – compensating for the current unfairness in the distribution of employment and industry, rather than seeking to rectify and remove it and to build for the future.

So the third shift was from a passive approach to a regional policy of economic intervention – establishing new economic rights for communities and individuals. And this move away from the old, inadequate Band-Aid solutions for people and areas in crisis was also led by Scots. It was a policy implemented by the provision of tax reliefs and cash incentives for incoming and expanding industry, but it often went much wider and included the creation of new towns, the building of advance factories, area growth plans and the direction of industry and people. What is interesting to me is how hard-wired the notion that policy help should be given on the basis of need had become by this point.

The scale and boldness of the ambition cannot be overstated. A plan to bring – or direct – the Ford car company to Glasgow created a huge row. The pressure to bring a steel strip mill to Scotland also created a row, but this time the pressure succeeded. Bringing the Forestry Commission to Scotland – when, contrary to common assumptions, most profits made on forestry came from England – created another backlash in England but it went ahead. Bringing the National Savings Bank to Scotland almost caused a Southern rebellion in parliament.

Of course there were political pressures that could be construed as simply Scottish nationalism on the move. Jim Phillips of Glasgow University has conducted a major study on the Scottish response to deindustrialisation and found in his article 'The Moral Economy of Deindustrialization in post-1945 Scotland' that Scotland would accept the closure of pits and factories if it was by agreement and if there were new jobs to replace old. There was he said 'an assertion by workers of rights to economic security and employment stability, as compensation for the collective and individual hardships of the 1920s and 1930s, and the Second World War. Coalfield deindustrialization in Scotland from the 1950s to the 1990s exemplifies the moral economy framework . . . there was a distinct workers' moral economy framework for understanding and rationalizing this process, with economic assets depicted as social resources, and the move from "old" to "new" accepted not because it offered enhanced commercial profitability but greater social sustainability.'[6] But that depended on British leaders accepting that resources needed to be allocated to Scotland because of our need for new jobs. And if you look at cabinet and cabinet committee minutes, Scottish public opinion was often invoked as the spur to action – but when it came down to making decisions the argument was substantially fought over which area of the country needed help most.[7]

In other words, Scottish MPs may have wanted to argue Scotland's corner irrespective of its needs and rightful claim on resources. But they had to accept that need was the criterion and base their demands on showing that Scotland's needs were greatest. And thus throughout the development of UK polices for economic intervention, a fundamental principle was applied, that allocations could be made across the UK on the basis of need. We would pool and share our resources but the most resources would go where the need was greatest. It was the only public justification that could be given for policy decisions. And as a result, says Jim Tomlinson, 'US firms received substantial incentives from the UK government to locate in central Scotland as well as in northern England and southern Wales, along with Northern Ireland. Such incentives increased "sixteen-fold in real terms" from 1962–3 to 1969–70'.[8]

The decision to locate the new steel strip mill in Ravenscraig was a case in point. Little was going for Scotland in 1958 when the decision was being made: it had little expertise in sheet steel; it had little coking coal; it was far from the main market (the Midlands car industry) and Colville's, the Scottish steel company, had little interest in the project. But with unemployment rising and, in the knowledge that the £160 million on offer would be one of Scotland's biggest-ever investments, successive Conservative Secretaries of State for Scotland made the case for directing help to the area which needed it most – and they won. Likewise when a row arose about relocating the Forestry Commission the choice between Edinburgh and Basingstoke was simple. Edinburgh had an unemployment rate of 4.6 per cent, compared with Basingstoke's 1.7 per cent. Edinburgh won on the basis of need.

And thus while giving priority to Scottish needs started as a Labour demand, it became by the 1960s the dominant view of all parties as we can gauge from a 1962 Conservative government ministerial discussion about the needs of the economy:

The North East and Scotland – the Home Secretary (Henry Brooke) recalled that the Prime Minister [Harold Macmillan] had recently informed the cabinet of the arrangements that he had made to remedy productive and structural weakness in the economy. He had called for immediate action on the short-term problem of the unused margin of productive resources and the recent sharp increase in regional unemployment. He said that the essential feature was the government should concentrate their attack upon the unemployment problem in the North East and Scotland, and would make an immediate start on a long-term plan for the modernisation and rehabilitation of selected areas within them. Thus priority would be given to certain 'growth points' rather than to localities where unemployment happened to be particularly serious. In the long-term plan provision would be needed for a system of road and rail communications suitable for the selected 'growth points', and the right kind of port facilities would have to be provided to give the new local industries direct access to the continent. Provision for air travel would also need to be considered.[9]

At different points in the last seventy-five years, different industrial policies have been in vogue. For a period of time the policy was to attract new industry by directing it, especially the nationalised industries, to Scotland and to areas of need. A further elaboration of this direction of labour came in the form of civil-service relocation – at some key points the public sector was instructed to redirect entire workforces to areas of greatest disadvantage. This was not always popular but the policy of allocating civil-service resources outside London to other areas was justified once more on the basis of greatest need.

There were countervailing pressures. While the public justification for relocation was the different needs of the regions, in the campaign against the relocation of the National Savings Bank other arguments came into play. Professor Ian Levitt records a discussion in 1964 when the Secretary of State for Scotland had to threaten to expose the insularity and selfishness of staff resistance as being the reason why a move to Scotland was being rejected. Ministers however concluded that the transfer of a government office, involving such a substantial amount of clerical employment, would be an important demonstration of the government's determination to deal effectively with the problem of regional disparities.[10]

Of course public pressures mattered but when it came down to justifying a decision the unemployment figures – which were one signal of the degree of need – were decisive: it was fair to transfer civil servants out of London and discriminate positively in favour of the areas of greatest need. This was also the basis on which Scottish Secretary of State William Ross created the Highlands and Islands Development Board in 1965, then the Scottish Development Agency in 1975. Under Labour and William Ross this became the model for development agencies for all of the regions and countries of the entire UK.[11] Regional support has been scaled down by the current coalition government in a number of regions of England but they cannot yet escape the principle that resources have to be distributed according to need.

Economic intervention to meet need is far more extensive and long-standing in British regional and industrial policy than in much of the rest of Europe and elsewhere. An explicit commitment was made to deal with the unfairness caused by unemployment and we sought to narrow if not remove the inequalities between the countries, creating greater convergence between Scotland and England. That is one of the reasons why inequalities between Scotland and England are now much narrower than the inequalities in other parts of Europe.

This could only have happened because of the decision to pool and share resources on the basis of need. One debate in 1953 shows how ingrained the idea of pooling and sharing had become. Speaking in a debate on the Equalisation Grant in 1953 (*Hansard*, 25 November 1953), Tom Fraser, the Scottish Office junior minister in the Labour 1945–51 government, attacked the principle of a rate support grant allocation. He complained that the only transfers were within England, within Scotland and within Wales when there should have been a redistribution within the UK. A territorial allocation, he asserted, remained at variance with meeting need across the whole of the UK.[12] Ian Levitt records how he made his point by comparison with the Highlands of Scotland: 'If we were to accept a Scottish-only equalisation grant we should be accepting the inevitability of that part of Scotland being held to be responsible for aiding the Highland local authorities, instead of making that a responsibility of the nation as a whole.'[13]

The same argument could be made for any part of Scotland where resources fell short of meeting needs. The key factor in deciding twentieth-century social, educational and economic provision was that the standard of provision offered by the state (and local government) should be broadly similar wherever one was located. There may be differences in interpreting how to meet needs, when to alleviate distress and whether to devolve administration, but the basic principle had to be maintained.

BUILDING THE NHS

So we have seen how Scots did not simply acquiesce in the creation of UK-wide rights but were in some of the most important instances the architects of them. I want to consider now whether that is also true of the National Health Service.

Much has been rightly said about the great administrative and political achievement of the Welshman Aneurin Bevan. There is no doubt that what he saw in Wales changed his life – he complained of nurses having to leave the beds of patients to run charity flag days to provide the sick and the dying with basic healthcare. This led him to champion a national healthcare system free of charge.

But before he became Health Minister in 1945, it was Scots Labour leaders, in particular Tom Johnston, who blocked the attempts by the war-time coalition government under Winston Churchill to create a different kind of paying health service, one run by local authorities. If they had not done so it is unlikely the NHS would exist today in the form it does. It was the Scottish leaders who were the first in the detailed bargaining within government to stand out for a free NHS paid for by taxes raised and resources allocated at UK level. In the same way that unemployment benefit and regional policy became a charge of the UK as a whole so too, they said, should healthcare. The principle they argued was that in healthcare above all we should pool and share our risks and resources.

Scottish reformers had been frustrated in the 1920s when a demand to create local-authority general hospitals outside Edinburgh and Aberdeen had been stopped by a familiar alliance of Conservative politicians with the voluntary and charitable hospitals. During the passage of the Local Government Bill the Conservatives had caved in to pressure from the hospitals, thereby stopping an attempt to end the patchwork system. One progressive step, however, was secured: the stipulation that each local authority had to compile an annual report on medical conditions. It led publicly spirited medical officers of health year by year to expose the need for change.

Their campaigning was given a fillip by the outbreak of war, when the UK as a whole was found to be short of nearly 100,000 hospital beds and thus poorly equipped to deal with what were expected to be 300,000 casualties in the first weeks of a world war.[14] In Scotland six new emergency hospitals were created, run not by the local authorities as in England, but by the Department of Health for Scotland.[15] But with far fewer war casualties than expected, the hospitals were quickly put to the general use of the population. It was a testament to the changed view in Scotland, that more had to be done to lessen health inequalities.

The coalition came under increasing pressure to propose a solution, which they eventually did in 1944. But the Secretary of State for Scotland Tom Johnston told local authorities and the medical profession that he did not sign up to the plans of his colleagues. He argued that the model based on local-authority-administered means testing was wholly unacceptable, saying that healthcare had to be universal and free, based on need, not ability to pay. He would not accept the English option – a county-based system of coordination – arguing that Scottish local authorities were ill-equipped to manage a general service. He cleverly marshalled the opposition of GPs to local-authority control. What Johnston wanted was a health service based not on the old Chalmerian principle of stigma and discriminatory care for those with low incomes, but on universalism.

The basic position in 1943 was that the health service was based on a mix of funding: there were those who could pay (essentially those in well-paid middle-class jobs) for GP and hospital care; those who were insured via the statutory health-insurance system for GP care (mainly those working-class workers in steady employment – some of these would also be in an insurance scheme that also covered some hospital care, as well as some dental care); those suffering from infectious diseases who were covered by rate-aided local-authority hospitals; those from the above groups who paid private insurance premiums for hospital care in either voluntary hospitals (if such allowed payment) or local-authority general hospitals (in Scotland these were only the Western General in Edinburgh (previously a poorhouse) and the hospital in Aberdeen (also previously a poorhouse); and finally there were those from the poorest non-insurable groups and dependants of insured workers who could only rely on the Poor Law and the poorhouse/Poor Law hospitals. Thus in Glasgow the Labour city council refused to designate Stobhill Hospital as an open means-tested hospital for any Glasgow resident. It repeatedly stated that the demand from the poorest communities who could not pay anything prevented it opening a hospital like the Western General in Edinburgh.

With Johnston standing out for a nationally coordinated system that was free at the point of need, the 1943 cabinet could not agree. How could you have a national system based on some paying for GP care, and others subject to means tests and others relying on National Assistance to pay? And could the hospital system of the future be organised in this patchwork way ever again?

The Chancellor took the view that the National Insurance scheme should basically cover only the worker concerned, and not their dependants. This was for Johnston an unacceptable continuance of the existing scheme that excluded millions. The Treasury's principal concern was the rise in taxes if the Johnston idea prevailed, so there was no consensus ahead of 1945.

Johnston wanted national control of hospitals to ensure that medical need would be met, wherever it existed. He showed that if we extended NI there were millions without a record of contribution (including many of the elderly). There were also those whose work record was poor (especially in areas of high and persistent unemployment) and in any event he could not justify excluding family members from hospital or for that matter free GP care. The best the Conservatives could offer was an extension of NI to cover the majority of the population (including the middle-class occupations not covered by the 1911 Act) and the use of the means-tested National Assistance for the 20 per cent of the population that would not be covered by NI.[16] As for GP care it would be provided through the local authority medical services, again with a means test applied.

The battle raged on through cabinet committees. The War Cabinet, which met as a committee on reconstruction priorities, heard in August 1943 that Johnston proposed to report soon on 'the establishment of a comprehensive health service in

Scotland'.[17] In September he told them that he was satisfied that a centrally administered service would be acceptable to the medical profession and to the general public, citing the emergency medical services which had been in operation in Scotland during the war and was a centrally administered service that had worked satisfactorily. When in October the English Minister of Health proposed a hospital fee probably at £1 a week, Johnston refused, noting that all the medical witnesses to his reform committee had unanimously opposed demanding such payments from the sick. The Chancellor had to sum up that it was the government's intention to maintain the principle that patients should be called upon 'to make a reasonable contribution to the cost of their maintenance' but accepted he did not speak for the Secretary of State for Scotland.[18] And by digging in the Scotsman paved the way for Labour's 1945 manifesto proposal of a nationalised service free from the means testing Johnston violently opposed. Johnston ensured that nothing had been set in stone that would prevent Nye Bevan and the post-war Labour government from delivering the NHS we love today. Indeed new Prime Minister Clement Attlee took the view that the Scottish plans set out by Johnston were superior to anything he saw for England and Wales.

So why, during all this battle, did Scotland not demand a separate Scottish funding basis for the NHS? After all, we had Scottish voluntary hospitals, Scottish municipal hospitals and the university teaching hospitals in four Scottish cities. They had been independent, so much so that they trained one-third of UK medical graduates in the nineteenth century.[19] You could have put up a strong argument for a wholly different healthcare system based on local autonomy and funding.

But better arguments led by Tom Johnston prevailed: it made sense for an individual to insure in the widest possible pool against the risk that his family might be the unfortunate one hit by illness. And it made sense for each nation to pool resources across the whole country so that if there were a higher incidence of disease and greater health needs in one part of the country their risks could be shared across the whole country and they could be assisted by areas where there was a lower incidence of disease and lesser health needs. The bigger the pool, the more the risks were minimised. The wider the pooling and sharing, the better we can protect ourselves against risks and vulnerabilities.

So again, Scots, who recognised the benefits of a UK health service organised on the basis of need, won through. Having succeeded in stopping the coalition's payment-based healthcare plan, they could now prepare for the Labour government's free NHS. Here again we have the modern Union at work – promoting the pooling and sharing of risks and resources – the policy demands starting with progressive opinion in Scotland which was then reflected back into Whitehall, from where the Scottish Office pressured the government of the day.

SUPPORTING SCOTLAND WITH PENSIONS AND BENEFITS

It is perhaps not that surprising that Scots who remember this fight are among the most supportive of the Union. When I meet pensioners across my constituency they are the first to speak up about what the sharing of resources across the UK meant for how their lives were transformed after the war. But they are acutely aware of the benefits of the Union in another way too, because their dignity in old age is guaranteed by the commitments we make to each other in each corner of these islands.

Before pensions were first introduced in 1908, previous governments had toyed with a pension modelled on the insurance-based scheme introduced in Bismarck's Germany, and the non-means-tested scheme already in operation in New Zealand. Indeed, Arthur Balfour's Conservative government of

1902–5 had discussed using returns from trade tariffs to pay for welfare. Once he became Chancellor in April 1908, Lloyd George went ahead with a non-means-tested scheme, believing that the reform of income tax and the introduction of super tax would provide the necessary funds. This led to the head-on opposition of Conservatives, who controlled the Lords, and who claimed that the scheme could not be funded without a substantial increase in taxation. They viewed the proposal, encompassing a universal state benefit to anyone aged over seventy, as a moral hazard that would discourage savings and private insurance, and a direct attack on the Poor Law, the nineteenth-century principle of self-help and reliance on private insurance to cover 'eventualities'. To win in parliament, Lloyd George agreed to exclude paupers, who were to be left to the mercy of the Poor Law.

That had particular ramifications in Scotland, where the Scottish Poor Law was stricter than in England and demanded that the wider extended family should take care of the elderly if any could be found.

Indeed Scottish provision for the old was so mean that the future King Edward VII, then acting as a member of a Royal Commission into the aged poor, asked if there were cases of people starving on it. That said, both he and his fellow grandees subscribed to the view that it was a moral hazard to provide help to the poor lest they stop trying to help themselves.

Later changes brought Poor Law claimants into the fold, so between 1909 and 1926, the majority of UK pensioners received the old-age pension plus, if they had no other income, a Poor Law allowance – but still based on the family means test. Between 1926 and 1948, the contributory pension took over for the majority who had below-average earnings, but many still required a Poor Law supplement. After 1948, they might still require a National Assistance Board supplement, but the state pension was now set at a higher level under the Ministry of National Insurance Act 1944. Later the Ministry of Pensions and National Insurance was established by the merger of the Ministry of National Insurance and the Ministry of Pensions, in an attempt to provide a more coherent system for paying war pensions and National Insurance benefits.

At every stage, Scots backed the changes. They knew that a system of UK-wide provision would be more generous to them than retaining a Scottish-wide system, but they now also saw a basic unfairness if people who had worked and sacrificed together in British companies and in the British military did not get the same help once they grew old. Once again, Scotland's interests and Scotland's values aligned in backing new UK rights.

The same principles applied to the general system of insurance against sickness and unemployment. Lloyd George introduced the National Insurance Act 1911, which gave British workers the first contributory system of insurance against illness and unemployment. The underlying rationale was that while administration could be done regionally it was cost-effective to pool and share our resources across the UK.

It is worth recognising that not all Scots welcomed National Insurance. Our famed progressive spirit was missing when a farmer by the name of Robert Paterson, of Lendrum near Turriff, became the focus of sheriff's officers' attention when he refused to pay what he called the 'unfair and unjust tax'. A Unionist by nature, he publicly opposed the very idea of National Insurance on selfish grounds: 'because it was a service that farmers and farm labourers would rarely use'. He added that he would not pay the tax imposed by a Welsh-led government (David Lloyd George was Chancellor) and eventually had his only cow seized to pay his accumulated fines.[20]

Concessions had to be made to Scotland: once Lloyd George had conceded a separate Irish National Insurance Commissioner, the Scots and Welsh demanded their own Commissioners too. Iain McLean records how the civil servant in charge, Braithwaite, complained of Scottish pressure – but the pressure was for the devolved administration of a UK scheme not for a separate Scottish National Insurance system. Gradually, however, the National Insurance Acts were extended, as over time people saw the danger if employers were enticed to move around the country to those parts where National Insurance premiums were lowest.

Both the contributory and non-contributory schemes operated under UK legislation and a UK administrative framework. The pooling and sharing worked in practice with no difference in the rates of contribution or benefits north and south of the border. And when in August 1946 family allowances were brought in and later in 1948 when the comprehensive scheme of National Insurance embodying contributory pensions, unemployment benefits, sickness benefits, medical benefits through the NHS and the industrial-injuries scheme was established, no one called for separate Scottish schemes.

None of this was inevitable. After all, Scotland started from a separate social-policy regime – the Scottish Poor Law – and a nationalist argument could have easily won the day. Scots might have demanded that any social-policy changes should respect the distinctiveness of Scottish traditions and conditions and we could have ended up without UK-wide pensions, without UK-wide social insurance, without UK-wide economic intervention, without a UK-wide-funded NHS. That we didn't but instead helped shape the establishment of UK-wide social and economic rights is, in my view, one of the strongest arguments for the Union and one of the things that make me proudest to be a Scot.

Scotland was also both a leading advocate for and a direct beneficiary of a new system of allocating resources across the UK for meeting housing needs. At the end of the First World War, Scotland had a housing crisis. Over 40 per cent of Glaswegians lived in one-roomed slum tenements, and the position in mining communities was little better.[21] In total in 1911 50 per cent of the Scottish population lived in one- or two-room dwellings with only 7 per cent doing so in England.[22] Rents were 10 per cent higher in Scotland than in the northern counties of England, and 25 per cent higher than in the Midlands.

But despite the promise in 1918 of homes fit for heroes, little was achieved in Scotland before the Labour government of 1924, leading to protests by Labour MPs, with James Maxton and John Wheatley out in front. The Housing Acts of 1919–23 covered the whole of the UK and did lead to some houses being built in Scotland. But unfortunately the subsidy in the Conservative government's 1923 scheme was too low to encourage building at the same levels as south of the border, and the comparative construction rate fell below that for England.

There were two additional reasons why half the population was living in slums that had at best two rooms with an outside toilet. First, Scottish building regulations were set at a level designed to meet Scottish weather conditions and thus led to more costly houses. And secondly the local authorities' rateable base was under such severe pressure due to unemployment, the cost of educational provision, the need for road building, and of course the burdens of the Poor Law, that they could not afford the local-authority share of costs of building.

It was John Wheatley, who had pioneered a municipal housing scheme in Glasgow, who stepped in with his 1924 Housing Act, one of the successes of the first Labour government. He offered much higher Treasury subsidies and much better-quality housing in well-laid-out suburbs. While the next Conservative government reduced the subsidy for England, the subsidies that remained were still higher in Scotland because of a UK-wide acceptance that there were higher levels of housing need.

Here again we see UK policy operated on a basis of pooling and sharing resources, allocating most resources to the areas of greatest need. This led to a steady improvement in Scottish housing conditions, reducing the level of overcrowding and enabling slum demolition. Similarly, from 1934 to 1940, the Scottish grant was reset but again at a higher rate than England's, and the government-controlled Scottish Special Housing Association was established to meet needs in areas where the local authority remained too poor to act. Labour leaders had made it clear that without additional support, local authorities would not be able to remove all the slums until well after the turn of the next century. In the inter-war years only one-third of house building in England was led by the public sector but in Scotland it was two-thirds. Of the various measures of the inter-war years, the Wheatley Act 1924 was responsible for the largest number of houses built, but the policy continued in the post-war period, when Macmillan (as UK Minister of Housing) pushed ahead and the Scottish Secretary, James Stuart, followed.

But assertive as Scots have always been of their rights, their leaders always understood that there was not only benefit in pooling and sharing our risks and resources but also benefit in preventing a race to the bottom in standards with a well-performing region undercut by a bad performer and a bad performer undercut by the worst.

This was true most of all when we consider interventions in the wages and conditions of Scottish workers where a Scottish Poor Law system was swept aside for UK-wide laws and protections. There were separate Scottish investigations into social conditions but from 1842 onwards all the laws protecting Scottish children against poor treatment at work – a policy that had been managed in Scotland – became UK laws. And then in 1906 when industry-specific minimum wages were established for the first time, the boards for industry sectors were not Scottish but UK, with the exception of agricultural wages.

Again Scots, proud of their national identity and distinctiveness, could have made the case for separate legislation for Scotland. After all, social policy had been managed in Scotland from the inception of the Union. And yet no one did. And nearly a century later when the Labour government established the national minimum wage in 1998 the same argument applied: we wanted to avoid a race to the bottom between regions and nations. And we believed strongly that no matter what part of the UK you lived in, the right to a basic minimum level of wage and income was sacrosanct.

Today we oppose regionally and nationally varied pay rates. We know that if we didn't have a British national minimum wage, then a race to the bottom would start with separate minimum wages being set in the South West, then in the North East, then in the North West, then in Scotland. The well-paying region would be undercut by the bad, the good nation by the bad, and then the bad by the worst and you would end up with a dog-eat-dog competition in which no employee would win. Even the good employers would lose out, undercut by poor-paying companies moving between regions to find the cheapest labour area.

The national minimum wage, which makes for a national minimum income at a British, rather than a Scottish, level, is indeed one means by which through solidarity and working together we ensure that there are equal social and economic rights for working people.

SCOTLAND'S INTERESTS AND VALUES

So if I am right and Scots have been at the forefront of every campaign to make ours a Union for the pooling and sharing of resources, does that have any implications for the future? I believe that it does – that the achievements of Scots in shaping the Union to reflect both our interests and our values is precisely what should give us the confidence that voting to stay within Britain in September represents a determination to continue to influence policy across the whole country.

Later I will show how the pooling and sharing of risks and resources extends to the BBC, to university research and development, and to defence and security. While the shift from nineteenth- to twentieth-century Britain is shown most acutely in the move from a Scottish Poor Law to a British welfare state, the same principles of pooling and sharing apply to the funding of our licence fee, to the cross-fertilisation of ideas in research and innovation, and to the sharing of costs for the defence and security of the country. By having the largest pool across which to spread risks as widely as possible, everyone benefits from the sharing between nations.

Some would say we cannot hold to these principles now that there are tuition fees in one part of the country and free tuition in another, free prescriptions in one part and prescription charges in another, free personal care in one part and an unmet demand for free care in the rest. But there will always be a need to balance liberty and equality, between the autonomy distinctive administrations seek and the establishment of equity in the country as a whole. Differential charges for tuition, prescriptions and care do not negate the principle that people have basic foundational rights to social security and free hospital and GP care. The differences represent an attempt in some areas of the country to build on these rights, but they do not undermine the basic foundation of rights common to all.

So on the nationalist side there is a fundamental misunderstanding of our history. Not only was the Union not imposed on Scotland back in 1707, its subsequent development owes as much to the projection of Scottish power as it does to English desires.

Today, the distribution of benefits favours any region or nation where there is greater need. If we take pensions, it is not Scotland that is the biggest beneficiary but invariably Wales, the North East and the North West. Indeed, if we look at the distribution of social-security benefits across the United Kingdom we find that the common factor is need not nationality: that Scots have been happy to accept a system where they are now in the bottom half of the table of regions and nations for benefits to pensioners and nearer the bottom than top in housing benefits and tax credits. 'Old-age benefits' are the state pension, pension credit, concessionary TV licences and winter fuel payments. So when we look at the raw figures we see a benefit to Scotland. Old-age benefits spend per person was £1,380 for Scotland, £1,318 for England, £1,465 for Wales and £1,331 for Great Britain in general.[23]

But when we break the figures down by region, Scotland was ranked 7th out of 11 for spending per person on old-age benefits with spending per person higher in the North East, Wales, West Midlands and East Midlands. The reason that, despite this, spending on old-age benefits per person in Scotland is above the average for Great Britain is that spending on these benefits is especially low in London, reflecting the UK capital's more youthful population.[24]

The powerful equalising impact of UK-wide redistribution is also seen in the way the disabled of the different regions and nations benefit. 'Disability benefits' are attendance allowance, carer's allowance, disability living allowance, employment and support allowance, incapacity benefit, industrial injuries disablement benefit and severe disablement allowance. When Scotland was ranked 4th out of 11 for spending per person on disability benefits, below only Wales and the North East and North West of England, it benefited from around £375 million of spending additional to what any allocation based on population would have given us.[25]

Scotland was ranked 5th highest of the 11 regions of Great Britain for overall benefit spending per person, with spending higher in Wales and the North East, North West and West Midlands, and lower elsewhere. But when it comes to housing benefit the biggest recipient is London. When it comes to tax credits and child benefits, the biggest recipients are London and the Midlands.[26] Thus the real beneficiaries of the system are people in need everywhere and Scotland remains to this day part of a system that also benefits other parts of the UK, especially Wales and the northern regions. We all benefit because it is not nationality that decides who benefits, it is need.

How then do Britain's nations fare when we compare their position with that of Europe and America? The table below provides an overview of the inequalities between different countries in Europe, different countries in Asia, different states in America and states which border each other. It demonstrates what can happen when there is no attempt to bridge the differences in social and economic welfare and why the pooling and sharing we have achieved in the United Kingdom is so unique.

Table 4: Inequalities between nations and states

Ratios of GDP per capita, 2012 (current US$)	
UK[1]	
UK: Scotland	**1.01:1**

Source: ONS, Scottish government

EU	
UK: Bulgaria	**5.58:1**
UK: Romania	**4.61:1**
Luxembourg: Bulgaria	**15.00:1**
Luxembourg: Romania	**12.32:1**
Netherlands: Bulgaria	**6.59:1**
Netherlands: Romania	**5.45:1**
Euro Area	
Luxembourg: Estonia	**1.67:1**
Netherlands: Estonia	**2.73:1**
Germany: Estonia	**2.53:1**
Italy: Estonia	**2.01:1**
USA[2]	
DC: Mississippi	**5.03:1**
Delaware: Mississippi	**2.11:1**
New Hampshire: Mississippi	**1.48:1**

Source: US Dept Commerce, Bureau of Economic Analysis

Asia

Singapore: Bangladesh	68.75:1
Singapore: Timor-Leste	48.40:1
Singapore: Afghanistan	75.24:1
Singapore: Cambodia	54.75:1

Bordering nations

USA: Mexico	5.31:1
Singapore: Malaysia	4.96:1
Spain: Morocco	9.75:1
Israel: Palestine (Gaza and West Bank)[3]	15.98:1

Source: World Bank GDP data, unless stated otherwise

Notes:

1. GDP figures are for 2011, without taking into account North Sea Oil

2. Figures are in 2005$

3. GDP figures are from 2005, as this is latest available data for Gaza/West Bank

TOWARDS A NEW BRITAIN

In these great and momentous changes we can see the modern evolution of the Union between Scotland and the three other nations of the UK. You could argue that with the start of UK factory legislation the Union became as early as the mid-nineteenth century a Union of common labour standards. Ours became a Union for pensions early in the twentieth century and then in a succession of steps it became a Union for welfare – first in UK-wide help for the unemployed, then in UK-wide help for distressed areas, and then in UK-wide funding of universal healthcare. Taken together these new social rights, guaranteed at a UK level to citizens of all the home nations, make the Union a Union for social justice. And because much of the pressure for the changes that transformed the Union into one based on a fairness principle came from Scotland, the modern Union, which is in large part a Scottish invention, cannot ever be said to be an English imposition.

Some might argue that the system of social justice between nations that Scots proposed was nothing more than self-interest wrapped up as a principle. Of course in the early years of this sharing union, England paid out to meet the greater needs of Scots pensioners. But we have demonstrated that Scots now pay in to the collective system even though, in the case of pensions, or compared with the north of England, Wales and Northern Ireland, they do not receive the biggest slice in return. A recent poll found that 61 per cent of Scots believed that their taxes should contribute to pensions not just for them but for all citizens of the UK and that only a minority of Scots believed that the revenues from North Sea oil should be only for use in Scotland: what becomes the acceptance by the UK as a whole that resources will be allocated not on the basis of ethnicity or territory but on the basis of need.[27]

Indeed, the first Scottish Labour Secretary of State under the 1945 Labour government risked alienating Labour supporters by saying that while 'it would be possible to build a reputation at the Scottish Office by pretending to be a Scottish St. George fighting the English dragon in the shape of my colleagues in the cabinet', he did not need to do so: he could, he said, take his place as an equal at the table because 'Scotland did not need to beg for favours so long as she had rights'. His comments reflect the obvious truth that even if the case for British welfare provision had started with special pleading for Scotland, Scottish Labour had secured an agreement that need should be met on the basis of rights.

In the next chapter we will look at what might yet be done to further recognise the distinctiveness of Scotland while retaining the bonds of solidarity built up when Scottish activism helped to raise the social floor for everybody in the UK. We know that the early sources of enthusiasm for Britain – anti-French sentiment, sectarian feelings about Catholicism and imperialism – have dried up, and rightly so. We have also seen how the undoubted affection for British institutions like the monarchy and the army is not now strong enough to keep us together when times are tough. What remains is, I believe, not simply the last argument for the Union, but also the best – that there are social and economic rights that the citizens of the four nations have built up and share in common throughout the United Kingdom.

But is the pooling and sharing of resources which has moved the United Kingdom in one century from a minimal state to a welfare state anything more than a mutually convenient and purely instrumental contract between the different parts of the UK that was first conceived in response to the shared sacrifice of war but is now based on nothing more than self-interest? Even if it appears to me like a form of solidarity, is it based on any sentiments that can be described as altruistic, a desire to act for the good of others, or even on close bonds between fellow citizens across four nations, and can it endure?

In her book on liberal nationalism, Yael Tamir suggests that the basis of a welfare union need not be either love for others or sympathy but 'connectedness, the belief that we all belong to a group whose existence we consider valuable'. In other words that the people of Cumbernauld feel they have more ties with the people of Croydon than with the people of Copenhagen. She is demonstrating that we do not need great displays of affection or gestures of self-sacrifice to feel part of a common project.[28] But the ties that bind us seem to me of even greater significance than Tamir suggests. Over time the act of sharing can enhance that sense of belonging, binding people even more closely together. While there is clearly a debate within the United Kingdom about the right of European Union citizens and migrants generally to share the same rights to social security benefits and health care as United Kingdom citizens, there is little questioning in any part of the United Kingdom of the right of the Scots, Welsh or the Northern Irish to share the same social rights of the English majority.

Of course a Britain based on the pooling and sharing of resources would not work if there were discriminatory practices against the minority nations or if some were excluded from rights accessible to others. In many countries – this was true, for example, of the Catholic population of Northern Ireland, too often and for too long denied civil and employment rights – minorities can feel locked out or badly treated. But the unique feature of the development of the UK is that much of the pressure for the sharing of risks and resources came from the minority nations. The minority countries were not swallowed up into a system that they did not want. On the contrary, Scotland – and Wales – played a part in designing a system that suited them, and England showed flexibility in making it work. Behind the pooling and sharing of risks and resources, in my view, is more than mutual interests – also a shared commitment to values that emphasise the important of fairness, creating a Britain based on social justice between the nations and allowing us to define our country as a moral community. There can be no doubt that at the very least, the people of these islands have created a lasting monument to the notion of mutual obligation which Scottish Enlightenment thinkers were wrestling with all those years ago. Britain may not yet conform perfectly to their ideals, and there is much to do to create social justice within the nations, but I still think the Fife miners and Tom Johnston have achievements to their name that would make Adam Smith and David Hume immensely proud.

CHAPTER 7

The New Britain

A good friend of mine was with Donald Dewar and helped him in the hours before he died in 2000. Having collapsed on the steps of Bute House one October morning, he seemed to be recovering by the afternoon but, unknown to anyone, he was suffering from a brain aneurysm that had not been diagnosed. He was taken to hospital in the evening and died the following day.

I was honoured to give the memorial address at his funeral in Glasgow Cathedral and few who were there will forget the single flower on his coffin and then how people stood in the streets of Glasgow to pay tribute to a great Scot.

At the funeral, I told many stories about Donald – reminding people of his staccato speech delivery, of his love of books, of his often very direct but incredibly repeatable comments to constituents, and of everything from his love of food to his hatred of ceremony.

But one story I did not feel it appropriate to tell then, so soon after his death and on the day we remembered all his achievements, was of his comment to my friend when they were talking on the afternoon before he died.

Donald was reflecting on the year he had had. 'You know how difficult the last year has been?' he said, and it was not because of his poor health. It was because he felt besieged by a hostile press and weighed down by what he considered difficult but ultimately transient accusations relating to everything from the cost of the new parliament building to MSP expenses scandals. Donald felt that because the news was dominated by such allegations and exposés, there was little he could do to seize the initiative and set the agenda in Scotland. Building the new Scotland had to take a back seat to dealing with the here and now.

He was right: the minute the Scottish Parliament was achieved, question marks were raised not about its relationship with the UK or its vision for the future but about how MSPs behaved in the Chamber, their presence in the parliament and most of all their salaries, their expenses and their personal lives. There was little warm afterglow following its creation. Members of the Parliament and the Scottish government were not seen as states-men and women trying to enact high ideals but simply politi-cians out for themselves. And none of us were fully prepared for what happened next.

One of my proudest moments was to hear the opening speech of the Scottish Parliament by Donald. Gone were the staid formalities of a British state occasion. Missing were the pomp and ceremony that too often defied common sense. Central to the event was his inauguration address – a memorable speech that talked of a distinctively Scottish commitment to wisdom, compassion, integrity and justice. And when he conjured up memories of Scotland's past, images of Scotland's present, and a vision of Scotland's future, I was one of many who were moved to tears.

But in these early months there was something still missing. It may seem strange – we had, after all, eighteen years to prepare for the Labour government in 1997 – but when we agreed the devo-lution settlement, the Scotland Act 1998, we kept changes out of the Act for fear of damaging our central case. We needed a system for accountability for spending but we did not think through the tax provisions. So for all the greatness of the measure – the first democratic Scottish Parliament – there was and still is more to do. The parliament itself was the unfinished business of the last decade of Scotland's twentieth century. But there is still unfinished business in the unfinished business – we still have to fashion a more coherent, comprehensive and enduring form of government for the twenty-first century ahead.

I tried to square the circle by agreeing in 2008 to Wendy Alexander's bold and innovative proposal to set up a new all-party commission, the Calman Commission. I knew we needed to review the powers of the Scottish Parliament; to scrutinise the constitution anew to ensure Scotland had all the devolution it needed; to make sense of the difficult and often contradictory demands to have proper accountability in Scotland while not damaging equity across the whole of the United Kingdom; and to demonstrate how the UK had to change as well as Scotland. I had a vision of redefining Britishness and Scottishness at the same time. But Calman came at the wrong time for a government then in the midst of a world financial crisis, and the Commission was not given the attention that it needed. While we had a brilliant civil servant running it in Jim Gallagher, with whom I had many discussions, and Jim Murphy MP and the Commissioners did a huge and impressive amount to make it successful, we did not, in the end, create the comprehensive and conclusive results we wanted and needed.

The demand for a 'more perfect' settlement remains. I have seen many interesting proposals – devo max, devo plus, devo more, home rule, the Liberal Democrats' reinvention of federalism – and I have also seen proposals that are wholly unacceptable to me, like fiscal autonomy. But no single set of proposals until the current Labour proposals published in March this year are in line with my desire to show how a stronger Scottish Parliament could work in a stronger UK to fully empower the people of our country to meet and master the challenges of the twenty-first century, and to allow us to talk of 'equality between the nations'.

With time to reflect I have, since 2010, thought long and hard about the best measures to complete the unfinished business of 1998, bringing devolution up to date and showing how Scotland fits into what has to be, in the end, a reformed Britain. It is a vision that I believe even those who want Scotland to play no part in Britain will find of interest and may even welcome. My aim is not just to cement the defence and security union, and to renew the economic union, but also to entrench the best of our modern Union – our agreement to share risks and resources for the common good – while maximizing the decision-making autonomy of the Scottish Parliament.

In the last chapter we looked at the work of Scottish pioneers who, against all the odds and in far more difficult circumstances than we face now, brought the vision of a shared moral community across Britain to life while at the same time seeking to meet the distinctive aspirations of the Scottish people. I think it is time to complete what they started. And so in this chapter, as I explain how I envisage that a risk-sharing and resource-sharing UK can evolve into a power-sharing UK in the future, I want to develop a very traditional Scottish concept for our new world: the idea not of a contract, but of a covenant between the nations of the UK and covenanted rights that we all hold in common irrespective of nationality.

While a contract is best defined as a negotiated agreement between parties for pure self-interest, a covenant starts from a set of principles that people hold in common. I will show that within this covenant – an agreement to guarantee UK-wide rights to defence, security, employment, pensions, healthcare and social security – we can effect maximum devolution to the Scottish Parliament, resolve the challenge of making the Scottish Parliament accountable for tax decisions and codify UK-wide constitutional arrangements that will endure. Under these proposals we will have a Scottish Parliament with the fullest powers consistent with the purpose of the UK, and a UK Parliament that discharges its obligation to pool and share resources across the UK. So in this chapter, I outline proposals for a UK constitution that recognises the unique modern purpose of the Union, to pool and share our resources. I will show how the new partnership could work in practice with power shared across the United Kingdom and with Scottish tax-raising powers in all those areas I define below as 'non-covenanted' rights and services. I will also explain that to address problems for which the different legislatures share responsibility we need to institute common working between the two parliaments.

In making these changes it will also make sense to re-examine what the future UK constitution might look like if we translate into practice our aim of securing equality between the nations. In my conclusions I put the case for moving from the view of the UK as a unitary centralised state founded on Westminster sovereignty to a diverse power-sharing partnership of equals. At the end of the chapter, I try to place my proposals in the context of what is happening in the rest of the UK and beyond, and make suggestions for how the UK constitution could work to meet the distinctive needs of not just Scotland, but also of England, Wales and Northern Ireland. I will explain why the term 'federalism' cannot wholly encapsulate the changes that have occurred in the UK. I am aware that it is almost impossible for federal or confederal models to make sense of a UK where England has 85 per cent of the population and where there will always therefore be an asymmetry in the constitution, but I believe that these are workable and radical reforms the whole of the UK and people who support federalism can embrace.

Perhaps the best way of summing up the powers that I am proposing for the Scottish Parliament is that they come close to the idea of 'home rule within the United Kingdom'. As I conclude the chapter, I will ask whether a second Westminster chamber could provide a brake on policy decisions that do not command full consent from all parts of the United Kingdom – not a vehicle for preventing change, but a means by which we measure the acceptability of reform to every nation and region of the United Kingdom. I suggest that a second chamber to replace the House of Lords might bring the regions and nations of the UK closer together. For twenty-five years of the devolution debate, the rest of Britain has not had to change; the message of this chapter is that, to achieve equality between the nations, Britain must change too.

I am conscious too, in writing this, that it is far from good enough to promise in the abstract that something will be delivered later if you vote No to leaving the Union now. That was the Conservative position in the 1979 referendum, which was utterly discredited by their failure to act in the next eighteen years. Instead voters have a right to see the likely reforms mapped out and to have them on the table before they vote – enabling them to judge the merits of renewing the Union versus the merits of ending it. For years, devolution was talked of as 'a process not an event', echoing Charles Stewart Parnell that there is no end to the march of a nation. But the fact is that when you have a decision-making moment like a Yes/No referendum, you have to be far more explicit and concrete about your future plans. The referendum forces us to set out the purpose of the Scottish Parliament and the purpose of the UK. Indeed it compels the whole of the United Kingdom to set down the principles that will inform Scotland's engagement with the UK in the event of the Scottish people deciding they wish to remain part of it.

So in thinking about the future I have been informed and inspired by two fundamental truths about Scots. First, the Scottish people want to know not only about first principles of reform but also the practical details of what will happen in the real world. Secondly, the Scottish people are hungry for change. They appreciate that we live in one of the greatest countries in the world and want to know how we might fulfil all of the potential in each of our five million people. This is my attempt to answer both of those requirements.

A STATEMENT OF PURPOSE FOR THE UK

As I have shown in the previous chapter, the pooling and sharing of resources through UK-wide pensions, UK-wide provision for social security and UK-wide National Insurance is now a defining feature of the Union. My first proposed constitutional change is to make this explicit by stating formally in a constitutional document the shared purpose of the modern Union. We should make clear and explicit that the benefits we receive from the Union reflect a fundamental moral purpose – that no matter where you reside and what your background is, every citizen enjoys the dignity of not just equal civil and political rights, but the same social and economic rights too.

UK National Insurance is still in substance, if not in its very strict form, social insurance against life's major risks – old age, unemployment, disability and sickness. There is thus an instrumental reason for pooling and spreading those risks across the broadest community and then sourcing the resources to deal with them across the same broad community. The instrumental argument is the actuarial one: first, that risks will even out over the larger risk pool; and second, that at different times, the biggest group of individuals and the widest spread of geographies will be better placed to contribute to the costs.

With National Insurance we make contributions that determine entitlements; the contributions, while not calculated in the form of an insurance premium, are quite different from normal taxation in that they are not simply proportionate to our ability to pay but to some extent include, as it were, a 'fee for membership'. Thus there is a practical argument for the biggest risk pool, which is British rather than Scottish. But there is also a moral normative argument. We choose to share these risks and the relevant resources with the people with whom we have something in common. This gives the Union its ethical purpose, to advance the rights and responsibilities of all, and this should be made explicit: the shared commitment to pool and share our resources equitably to guarantee security and opportunity for all. The belief is that over time people will see that sharing and belonging go together.

So I suggest that we need to draw up and agree a statement of national purpose: a modern British declaration equivalent to the Declaration of Independence and the French Declaration of the Rights of Man. We could link the idea of it to the traditions created by British constitutional declarations including the Magna Carta and the Declaration of Arbroath.

I would like to include a commitment to the eradication of poverty and unemployment across the UK and to universal health care free at the point of need. But at a minimum we should state explicitly that a fundamental purpose of the Union is as follows: 'The Union exists to provide security and opportunity for all, ensuring equality between the nations, by pooling and sharing our resources equitably for our defence, security and the social and economic welfare of every citizen.'

This reflects today's consensus and we should agree that this should be made part of our constitution initially by a declaration of the UK Parliament and, over time, enshrined in UK law. I know that in Britain a statement or declaration as broad and overarching as this is unusual: indeed we have traditionally shied away from the general declarations that are so common in countries like France and America. There is understandable cynicism about high-sounding rhetoric. I remember how strange and un-British many people thought it when the Queen, even in her Queen's Speech, read out a statement that her government was 'for the many not the few'. But I disagree with them.

So it may be that statements to the effect that the United Kingdom exists to provide security and opportunity for all and that we share risks and resources to do so will sit uneasily with traditionalists; but one of the reasons why the UK is under threat is because we have not been explicit about what binds us together and as a result there is little popular understanding of what we stand for and why our four nations continue to be linked together. No one in America questions its purpose – a land of liberty and opportunity for all – and by leaving implicit what should be made explicit we do a disservice to what we as a country have achieved. Thus we should be crystal clear that this is a union with a purpose: securing common dignity for all the citizens for all the home nations of the UK.

In fact there is a case for going beyond a simple statement of the UK's purpose, and seeking agreement for a British Bill of Rights and Responsibilities to which all parts and peoples of Britain could subscribe. An attempt to formulate this was made by the Constitution Minister Michael Wills, when he brought together people from all over Britain in 2009 to discuss whether we could be more explicit about the values that bind us together and the obligations that flowed from this.

While he found people to be nostalgic about a 'golden age' of traditional values, concerned about benefit free riders who might 'game' the system of rights and worried about immigrants who did not share British values, he found people willing to agree on values they shared in common and keen to consider a British Bill of Rights and Responsibilities that encompassed not only civil and political rights but social and economic rights too. Indeed he found that participants described economic and social rights as being more relevant to their daily lives than civil and political rights, and could therefore see the benefits of clarifying entitlements and expectations. While Scots respondents were more aware of their separate legal, educational and constitutional histories, they too saw the benefits of a Bill of Rights and Responsibilities in 'strengthening British culture, values and norms, thereby promoting a shared national identity, bringing people together and increasing cohesion'. But people wanted a Bill of Rights and Responsibilities to emphasise the concrete rather than just the abstract, as the conclusion of the final report states: 'The value of clarifying "fundamental" entitlements, such as access to free health care, benefits and pensions, prompted support from participants for including economic and social rights.'[1]

CONSTITUTIONAL GUARANTEES FOR SCOTLAND

But we should not only clarify the purpose of the United Kingdom – to ensure equality between the nations – we should also clarify the status within our constitution of the Scottish Parliament. Thus the second element of my proposed reforms would be ensuring that the creation of the Scottish Parliament is recognised to have been an irreversible act. Because the UK constitution is unwritten, or more accurately 'uncodified', there is an assumption that promises made in one parliament need not necessarily be honoured by the next or successive parliaments. So, in traditional legal theory at least, the Scottish Parliament could be dissolved or see its powers cut as one UK Parliament becomes another.

Of course Scotland's position within the UK is, as it has always been, ultimately a matter that the Scottish people can decide. We know that in reality the vote of the Scottish people in the 1997 referendum has guaranteed the Scottish Parliament in a political sense. This is reflected in the Sewel Convention, which holds that Westminster does not legislate with regard to devolved matters in

Scotland, or on the breadth of the devolved parliament's powers, without the consent of the Scottish Parliament. The Sewel Convention robustly demonstrated its resilience during the passage of the Scotland Act 2012.

But in my view the parliament has not just to be, but also has to be seen to be, permanent, entrenched in the constitution and indissoluble. We would in effect be building a constitutional pillar that lays to rest the idea that devolution was simply at the discretion of the UK parliament, and replacing that outdated idea with an irreversible and enduring political settlement guaranteed by the constitution. Thus the Scottish institutions of government will be seen to exist in their own right – and not simply for as long as a Westminster parliament desires them. This is the heart of the new Britain: a constitutional relationship that recognises both the permanence of the Scottish Parliament and the purpose of the United Kingdom.

We might state that no law made by the Parliament of the United Kingdom should interfere with the powers of the Scottish Parliament other than at the request or with the consent of that parliament. We could agree that the preamble to the relevant legislation must state explicitly that the legislation has been passed with the consent of the Scottish Parliament. But the clearer and better way to state the reality is to say that the Scottish Parliament is enshrined as a permanent feature of our constitution and we could do the same for Wales and Northern Ireland provided that there is consent from their respective representative bodies. This could take the form of a section of a future Act of Parliament which amends section 28(7) of the Scotland Act 1998 – specifically the statement that 'This section does not affect the power of the Parliament of the UK to make laws for Scotland' – and enshrines the convention that the Scottish Parliament is permanent, entrenched in the constitution and indissoluble as an institution.

Any such constitutional lock is in line with recent decisions of the courts. The judgment in the *Axa* case demonstrated an understanding by the judiciary that both the UK Parliament and Scottish Parliament have democratic legitimacy, and that Holyrood is not just another public body created by Westminster.[2] Already where conflicts about legislative competence exist it is not Westminster but the UK Supreme Court that adjudicates, and it would be wise to affirm this. It would make sense before the referendum vote to announce that the Scottish Parliament will be fully entrenched in the constitution of the United Kingdom, to make its permanence and irreversibility explicit.

Then, consistent with the sharing-resources purpose of the Union, we should seek maximum devolution both within the UK and within Scotland. In other words, the United Kingdom is characterised by the following features: common security and defence; common civil and political rights; a single integrated economy which provides the greatest opportunities for economic growth and stability, and which guarantees economic rights; and a shared fiscal system which supports a single currency, and also provides a proper balance between autonomy and accountability on the one hand, and social solidarity on the other, so that social rights are guaranteed.

Each of these requirements has consequences, but stronger devolution and thus a better division of powers, consistent with the maintenance of this Union, should be considered where it offers opportunities for the Scottish Parliament and government to serve the people of Scotland better. In my view further devolution should be considered in the delivery of employment and skills, ideally devolving power in these areas to a more local level; in the delivery of some social and welfare services; in transport in the running of our railways; in some of the land-related responsibilities of the Crown Estate Commission; and in some areas of health where devolution is incomplete. There is also a case for devolution in the enforcement of health and safety and employment law and the relevant tribunals, and it is right to trust the parliament with the organisation of its elections.

A cornerstone of our social rights is the common UK welfare system, which as I have described transfers resources between individuals, dependent on their circumstances, across the whole Union. So we should not devolve contributory benefits, and there is general acceptance in my view that these should be delivered at a UK level. They are the principal signs of the UK sharing community at work. There are, however, examples where benefit payments are an alternative or complement to services that are devolved, and there may be arguments for altering the boundary here. For instance, the Scottish government provides free personal care, and the UK government provides financial assistance through attendance allowance to enable people to cope with disability. Services to needy elderly citizens could be better coordinated in one integrated service. One could therefore argue that attendance allowance should be devolved to the bodies that are now responsible for providing free personal care. As I show below, this will make it easier for us to address the persistence of poverty. A similar argument is being made for the coordination of UK-managed housing benefit with Scottish-led housing provision.

TRANSFER OF POWERS TO LOCAL COMMUNITIES

The question, however, is not just what powers should be transferred from Westminster to Holyrood, but also what powers should be transferred from Holyrood to local government.

Labour led the way with legislation in its first Scottish Parliament term that established the principle of community well-being – that local government is empowered to act as councils decide. In the Local Government in Scotland Act 2003 a statutory basis was provided for partnerships in the delivery of public services and for community planning. Unfortunately the SNP's centralising agenda has left our local authorities under-funded and increasingly reliant on central funding – indeed councils were forced to follow central diktats in order to access money for 2014–15.

It may be appropriate to establish a constitutional guarantee of powers to local government, and there is a case for Shetland, Orkney and the Western Isles gaining more powers from Edinburgh. Glasgow City Council rightly has new powers from the centre in exchange for greater responsibility to stimulate and support economic growth in the area. And local authorities could also be given more responsibility for this and for the management of employment programmes in their communities.

I agree with the March 2012 House of Commons Scottish Affairs Committee report on the Crown Estate in Scotland, which criticised it as an absentee landlord and tax collector that does not reinvest sufficiently in the communities from which it derives income.[3] There is a case for the land-related work of the Crown Estate to be devolved and then decentralised to local communities.

And just as we have shown the rights of UK citizens should be upheld for pensions, so too should there be Scottish Parliament-legislated rights for local citizens to the essential public services.

IMPROVING ACCOUNTABILITY: TAX POWERS FOR THE SCOTTISH PARLIAMENT

It makes sense for each parliament – Scottish and UK – to be accountable to its electors to the greatest extent possible. So in line with the maximum devolution possible there should be the maximum accountability possible. Many commentators have noted that the Scottish Parliament has very wide spending powers but few tax powers. For example, the Institute for Public Policy

Research (IPPR) report on *Fiscal Options for Strengthening the Union* says: 'The UK is exceptional in conferring limited revenue-raising capacity on its devolved governments, although their spending responsibilities are at least as extensive as those of state or regional-level governments in many federal systems.'[4]

So tax powers should be devolved so that the Scottish Parliament can have the optimum balance between shared UK resources from UK taxes, and its own resources from Scottish taxes, to make it as fully accountable to the Scottish people as possible. In this way we secure the best possible balance between equity and accountability.

But it is important we understand what the guarantees of the UK Parliament to the people of the UK including Scotland are, and what the guarantees of the Scottish Parliament to the people of Scotland are. Our commitment to the pooling and sharing of resources must be sufficiently strong so as to guarantee free healthcare, pensions, a decent family income and universal education as well as defence and security across the UK.

While there is rightly the devolution of the legal and administrative framework for delivering many of these services, the UK government should guarantee that no one in the Union – whether in Scotland or elsewhere in the UK – is prevented from accessing these common social and economic rights, and the services that flow from them, by virtue of a shortage of resources. That is why it is right that all UK taxpayers – Scottish, English, Welsh and Northern Irish citizens together – contribute their taxes at a UK level to fund these common rights and services, thereby guaranteeing that the UK government and where relevant the Scottish Parliament, the Welsh Assembly and the Northern Ireland Assembly have the capacity to deliver them. So we should make provision for the Scottish Parliament, the Welsh Assembly and the Northern Ireland Assembly to have the resources, whatever their own individual decisions on tax, to uphold these rights and deliver these services to the people of Scotland, Wales and Northern Ireland.

I suggest that this should be called covenanted expenditure, because it represents the UK honouring what I would call a covenant: we guarantee that social rights will be upheld by the UK as a whole by pooling our tax revenues from Scotland, England, Wales and Northern Ireland and sharing them based on need. Of course it remains a decision of the separate parliaments and assemblies how they wish to allocate the resources they raise to go further in the provision of the devolved services, but we are committed to financing these ones together.

Broadly speaking the revenue that the UK Parliament should raise should cover non-devolved services and services vital to the maintenance of our welfare state for the young, the sick and the elderly, and the revenue that the Scottish Parliament should raise should cover the other services, like law and order, transport and housing as these are decisions we have agreed should be made by the respective parliaments and assemblies and they should raise taxes to pay for them.

So this would mean, in practice, that there would be scope for devolved taxation to raise something like 40 per cent of the Scottish Parliament's expenditure. As we note above, the tax freedom available to the Scottish Parliament is presently very limited – only 12 per cent of its spending – and under the Scotland Act 2012 that figure will rise to around one-third. There is therefore scope for the Scottish Parliament to hold extra powers to raise around £2–2.5 billion more in devolved taxation beyond the Calman report and the recent Scotland Act, taking us to around 40 per cent of its present spending.

Let me be clear what this means: I reject fiscal autonomy (i.e. Scotland spends only what it itself raises in taxes) because this would end the pooling and sharing of resources that is the reason for the UK's continued existence, and it would undermine a currency union. It is true that the more the Scottish Parliament relies on domestic taxes, the less call it has on UK grants. But I do not accept that this will change the principle that the UK is based on fiscal equalisation and the sharing of resources based on need.

As long as this equalisation element remains, the role of Scottish or, for that matter, Welsh or Northern Irish MPs should not be called into question. If the UK Parliament practises fiscal equity by allocating resources across the UK, and maintains responsibility for welfare, social security, macroeconomic policy, and defence and foreign affairs, it should have a full representation of Scottish members. Indeed if, as we propose, the currency remains a UK currency, then Scottish MPs must have a say in scrutinising the inflation, employment, money supply and macroeconomic objectives of the Treasury and Bank of England. The Union will become less centralised and looser but I do not accept that the price of greater devolution should be less influence at the centre on common issues or a weaker claim on common resources.

The IPPR argues that a package of devolved fiscal powers needs to encompass a range of taxes, to spread risks. It also needs to address practical considerations, including the burden of paying taxes by taxpayers and of collecting and administering taxes by the government.[5]

Applying these considerations, changing the settlement around income tax is the most promising avenue to explore. VAT cannot be devolved for European reasons. The Treasury should adopt a permissive approach to the establishment of any further tax relating to land, but the gains are limited. Corporation tax is not a suitable tax for devolution for administrative and practical reasons but also for fiscal ones: variation in the rate of corporation tax across the UK raises the potential for harmful tax competition. These considerations point to the devolution of income tax as the best option. And yet given the UK-wide provisions for savings, there is no real gain from devolving income-tax reliefs and allowances, and it makes sense to retain a single administrative system for income tax across the UK even if some rates of tax can vary in different jurisdictions.

To raise the money that is equivalent to the cost of non-covenanted services – about 40 per cent of its present budget – the best way forward is to widen the Scottish Parliament's power to vary the income tax, which is currently 10 pence, to 15 pence. Moreover, the Scottish Parliament should be bolder in using the powers it already has to advance social justice. It can adjust council tax and Stamp Duty Land Tax under new powers recommended by the Calman Commission. And much can be achieved by targeting public services to those most in need of help. But the reality, as we will see in a future chapter, is that the Scottish Parliament is failing to secure greater equality in Scotland because of the policies of the SNP, not simply because of the limited powers of the institution.

So under these proposals we can achieve three things. First, the entrenchment of the principle of pooling and sharing resources for what I call covenanted services and under which 100 per cent of the cost of agreed covenanted services will be guaranteed by taxpayers across the UK. Second, the flexibility for the Scottish Parliament to set tax rates to pay for the non-covenanted services. And third, more opportunities to pursue fairness if this is the will of the Scottish Parliament.

POWER-SHARING PARTNERSHIPS

A policy for equality between the nations requires not only a clear division of powers as to which parliament does what but also active partnership arrangements between parliaments and governments in areas where their responsibilities inevitably overlap and where working together makes sense for the common good. If Scotland is to remain part of the UK, the UK and Scottish parliaments should in the future learn from the devolution, quasi-federal and federal arrangements in other countries where governments of different political persuasions have found better ways of working together than we have managed in the first decade and more of devolution. We should draw up cooperation or, more accurately, partnership arrangements and start from the recognition that the different parliaments and assemblies share power in important areas of policy such as employment, skills, science and innovation, and aspects of transport and economic policy. So we should seek to transcend an expectation of perpetual conflict with new rules explicitly agreed for common services and for inter-parliamentary consultation on matters of mutual concern. There would be a case for giving these partnership arrangements a legal grounding, in the form of statutory obligations on both administrations to cooperate in the public interest, or through the creation of a formal council or equivalent bodies with the duty to hold regular meetings between the governments in specified areas of common interest.

Changes might, it has been suggested, include a legal requirement on Westminster to consult the Scottish government and parliament and other devolved governments on new laws in areas of common interest and setting out clearly the period of time these consultations would last. The former Liberal leader Menzies Campbell MP has gone further in recommending that 'some functions of government should constitute a third category – additional to "reserved" and "devolved" powers – namely "partnership powers"' and his proposal should be given consideration.[6]

We should also consider whether the Scottish Parliament should not only consult with the UK authorities and vice versa but also, in areas where it does not have power, have the authority to make proposals that the UK Parliament and government are obliged to consider. Equally, the UK Parliament and government should be able to make proposals on relevant matters within the control of the Scottish Parliament – enabling one part of the UK to make a contribution to new policies in areas where the other part of the UK has lead responsibility.

So before or in the event of a No vote, we should set out how we can improve the mechanisms that help the different parliaments work in partnership for common and shared purposes. Housing is a good example where a joint housing task force that brings both governments together, drawing on local authority and voluntary sector expertise too, might benefit Scotland and Britain. A sensible policy for housing can only be agreed by examining house building and house improvement policy, now under the Scottish Parliament, and housing finance including mortgage finance and housing benefit, currently under the UK Parliament.

Similarly, the wider challenge of tackling poverty cannot be met without using powers over taxes and benefits that come under the UK Parliament – and the powers available for social work, education and urban regeneration under the Scottish Parliament. We should set out plans for a Joint Poverty Commission that contains formal arrangements for working together to address poverty. If eradicating poverty is itself a purpose of the Union – as it should be – then establishing partnerships to deliver this will in itself give even more solid purpose to the Union.

TOWARDS A NEW CONSTITUTION

The United Kingdom was once said to be a union of four nations which worked in practice, but not in theory. Today, after two decades of reform, it does not work either in theory or in practice. A new wave of anti-London sentiment is now a force to be reckoned with: the fear is growing not just in Scotland but across the northern regions of England and Wales that London is becoming a city state, casting itself adrift from the rest of the UK and less willing to share its wealth. We have said that Scotland must change but, to establish equality between the nations, Britain must change too.

Of course English – and sometimes English and Welsh – legislation can be passed only after the whole of the United Kingdom's representatives vote. This is because the UK is a multinational state, but not a federal one, and the UK Parliament and the UK government are also the parliament and government of the English nation. Lord Irvine once said that the best way of dealing with the West Lothian question was not to ask it. Others feel that there is a West Lothian answer as well as a West Lothian question, even when there is little desire on the part of England to have a separate English Parliament.

But if we want to acknowledge English views within the current UK Parliament while preserving an equality of status for all Members of Parliament there are two possible routes, both of which involve an England-only stage for English legislation in the House of Commons. The first innovation was suggested by the last Labour government. On a second reading of an English Bill, English members could be outvoted by the rest of the UK. So it would be standard practice to have a second vote on a second reading, which would allow a period of reflection. The second proposal, which comes from the McKay Committee, is for an English grand committee made up of solely English members – or if it was an English and Welsh Bill, solely English and Welsh MPs – that could amend and return draft legislation before the final vote by all the UK MPs. In both cases English members would have a procedure for their views to be recognised but in each case the final decision would rest with all MPs in Parliament.

THE NATIONALIST POSITION

A brief consideration of the history of Scottish nationalism suggests that their constitutional preferences may be more fluid than the stark Yes/No referendum choice suggests.

Until recently political nationalism had minimal impact on Scotland's development. Of course, nationalist sentiment was a feature of the risings of 1709, 1715, 1719 and 1745. At the outset of the rebellion of 1715, James Francis Edward Stuart, the 'Old Pretender', issued a proclamation declaring that once restored to the Scottish throne he would repeal the Act of Union. A similar promise was made by his son, Bonnie Prince Charlie, in 1745. Indeed 'No Union' was one of the slogans carried on Jacobite banners in both rebellions, although the Stuarts' main objective was to seize power in Britain.

But just as they misjudged the popular mood in the Lowlands, which accounted for most of the population and wealth of Scotland, so too later attempts to create a movement for breaking the Union in Scotland usually petered out. In fact, as we have suggested in previous chapters, British unionism did not appear to be at odds with a strong Scottish national consciousness.

There were nationalist movements that attempted to direct workers' anger towards a solution in Scottish independence: the striking Weavers who marched under the banner of William Wallace in Carlton in 1787; the 1820 insurrection and the attempt at a general strike under the slogan 'Scotland free or a desert'; and John Maclean's Scottish Republican Party after the First World War. But generally Scottish Labour and trade union leaders, from the high points of Scottish Chartism to the present day, have preferred to build collective organisations across the United Kingdom.

What is striking is that the movements for constitutional change, including those that called for self-determination in Scotland, tended to ask for change *within* the United Kingdom, rather than for separation. Thus the National Association for the Vindication of Scottish Rights, founded in 1853 to agitate for increased Scottish representation at Westminster and for limits on the intrusive power of London, made a point of supporting the Union – even to the extent of toasting the British monarchy at its meetings. 'The more Union, the better,' one of the members of this association argued, 'provided . . . the rights of all parties be respected. Union obviates war, encourages commerce, permits of free transit, and abolishes national antipathy. Union – provided it be union and not domination – brings equals together for common benefit.' The association was not a secessionist movement but a call for equal status, a demand to recognise the vital and enduring importance of Scottish institutions, but in doing so to bind us closer into one political union.[7]

By the same token, the Scottish Covenant movement, which flourished in the 1940s and early 1950s, could not be called a separatist movement. It arose from a split in the nationalist movement – from what Neil MacCormick, whose father led the Covenant, called, in *Being Scottish*, a fallout between those who wanted to seek home rule as part of a cross-party initiative and those who favoured a separate party.[8] But when the movement organised their two million strong petition in support of Scottish self-rule, they made it clear, as Colley records, that they did so 'in all loyalty to the Crown and within the framework of the United Kingdom'.[9]

And at its inception even the Scottish National Party seemed more disposed to home rule than independence. The party was formed out of two groups – the Scotland Party, formed in Glasgow Cathcart by Conservatives who left the branch of the Unionist Party because of their worry that Scottish Protestant values were being submerged by the immigrant culture of Catholic Ireland – and the National Party. In their first few relatively unsuccessful decades before 1967 – they had won only one by-election, in wartime Motherwell – the SNP sought what Kidd calls 'a range of different goals', including 'dominion status for Scotland, a co-partnership with England in the running of the British Empire, home rule in a devolved settlement, independence within the European union, independence "lite" within a British social union and outright independence'.[10] Until 2004 the nationalists' objective of 'self-government' reflected the distinctive political grammar of the early and mid-twentieth-century movements for colonial freedom. In the 1970s, for example, the SNP proposed a consultative convention of up to thirty delegates from each part of the UK and an inter-governmental council similar to that of the Nordic states, a new partnership of nations that would still preserve what they called the social harmony of the United Kingdom. Only in 2004 did 'independence' become their formal constitutional objective as their language hardened, ironically at a time when they were embracing the sharing of sovereignty as 'independence within Europe'.[11]

The SNP now define independence as 'the restoration of Scottish national sovereignty by restoration of full powers to the Scottish Parliament, so that its authority is limited only by the sovereign power of the Scottish people to bind it with a written constitution and by such agreements as it may freely enter into with other nations or international organisations for the purpose of furthering international cooperation, world peace and the protection of the environment'.[12] Now of course they seek full membership of the EU and for a time they favoured joining the euro. Today, as Colin Kidd remarks, there remains an ambiguity, part of a tension between gradualists and those who support outright independence – an ambiguity not dispelled by Mr Salmond's remark that the referendum was 'a major step forward in Scotland's home rule journey'.[13] His desire to opt into the UK currency signals his belief that complete separation is inadvisable. Mr Salmond is mistaken, however, to ask to be part of the UK currency without also seeking to maintain Scottish participation in the process of UK economic decision-making.

Some senior nationalists have toyed with federalism, confederalism and quasi-federalism, leaving room for an association with the UK. In fact, James Mitchell has recently argued that a careful reading of the SNP's White Paper 'suggests that what the SNP proposes might be termed confederal'.[14]

Of course the leading proponents of a federal constitution have been the Liberal Party, since the 1880s. In their October 2012 report *Federalism: The Best Future for Scotland*, the Scottish Liberal Democrats argue that: 'The best solution for Scotland is to combine the existing wide-ranging policy and legislative responsibilities of the Scottish Parliament with substantial revenue-raising powers, all set within the structure of a reformed United Kingdom where the home rule powers are respected and entrenched. That solution is a federal United Kingdom.'[15]

Specifically, the report sets out how federalism would work in practice with what they call formalised partnership-working, a model of cooperative governmental action first suggested in an earlier report on a federal UK authored by their former leader, David Steel. This would require statutory consultation; a new 'power of initiation' enabling one government to formally request that another take specific action to facilitate policy objectives; and reform to certain UK-wide institutions such as HM Revenue and Customs in recognition of the fact that they will be expected to serve all parliaments and jurisdictions within the United Kingdom.

Former Prime Minister John Major has also proposed what is, in effect, a federal solution, asking: 'Why not devolve all responsibilities except foreign policy, defence and management of the economy? Why not let Scotland have wider tax-raising powers to pay for their policies and, in return, abolish the present block grant settlement, reduce Scottish representation in the Commons, and cut the legislative burden at Westminster?'[16]

And we should not forget that many of the leading opponents of Union favoured a confederal Britain. James Hodges and George Ridpath advocated a confederal association of England and Scotland in which a Scottish Parliament would guard the privileges of the Scots Presbyterian Kirk, while Andrew Fletcher of Saltoun's proposals ranged from a practical scheme of limitations on the British multiple monarchy to a utopian reordering of Europe into several leagues of modestly sized city states, one of which would comprise the British Isles reorganised into a loose federation of provinces. As Colin Kidd puts it, 'the idea of Britain, or of some British association of states, was not an anathema to the principal critics of Union.'[17]

What would federalism require? Federal systems are typically characterised by a constitution (it is the constitution, not the legislature, which is sovereign), a division of powers, a set of autonomous institutions, a formal division of competence, rules for the resolution of conflict, and the policing of the distribution of competences.

In 1973 the Royal Commission on the Constitution, the Kilbrandon Commission, summarised the case against an English Parliament in the following terms:

> A federation consisting of four units – England, Scotland, Wales and Northern Ireland – would be so unbalanced as to be unworkable. It would be dominated by the overwhelming political importance and wealth of England. The English Parliament would rival the United Kingdom federal Parliament, and in the federal Parliament itself the representation of England could hardly be scaled down in such a way as to enable it to be outvoted by Scotland, Wales and Northern Ireland, together representing less than one-fifth of the population. A UK federation of four countries, with a federal Parliament and provincial Parliaments in the four national capitals, is therefore not a realistic proposition.[18]

The nearest federal equivalent to the UK is Canada, in which 35 per cent of the population lives in one state, Ontario. As for the United Kingdom, the Kilbrandon argument goes, federalism cannot work given that one of the units represents over 80 per cent of the population. This argument is supported by the historic failure of federal systems in which the largest unit dominates

– the USSR by Russia, Yugoslavia by the Serbs, Czechoslovakia by the Czechs.

But do my proposals answer some of the arguments put forward by moderate nationalists and liberal federalists? In rejecting separation but building on previous attempts to fashion home rule within the United Kingdom, my proposals have a core to them that many federalists might support. Indeed, I think it is important to recognise the scale and significance of recent constitutional changes in the United Kingdom.

For the first time the United Kingdom has had come to terms with a divided sovereignty. The 1998 settlement held to the orthodoxy that Westminster is sovereign and that power devolved is power retained. Westminster can, in theory, continue to legislate for Scotland, Wales or Northern Ireland, even on devolved matters; and it can, if it wishes, simply abolish the devolved bodies by a single Act of Parliament, as it did with the Northern Ireland Parliament in 1972. The White Paper 'Scotland's Parliament', which preceded devolution and was published in 1997, declared that 'The United Kingdom Parliament is and will remain sovereign in all matters.' The Scotland Act 1998, section 28(7), repeated this claim, declaring that 'This section', which provided for the Scottish Parliament to make laws, 'does not affect the power of the Parliament of the UK to make laws for Scotland.'

Yet, as we have seen, the reality is that the Scottish Parliament now has decision-making autonomy in its own sphere of responsibilities, and I would suggest that this should be reflected by an amendment to the 1998 Act.

We have moved from the traditional constitutional theory of Westminster sovereignty in another fundamental respect: by instituting a procedure for the adjudication of disputes between the Scottish and Westminster parliaments. This power means that one parliament cannot simply overrule the other and the UK Supreme Court is able to pronounce upon the constitutionality of Scottish legislation, as demonstrated by its decision in *Axa General Insurance Limited v The Lord Advocate* (2011). It is now accepted that where conflicts arise, a resolution will not be imposed by the Westminster Parliament but will be adjudicated by the Supreme Court.

We have progressed from the constitution of the old legal textbooks by developing a mechanism through which constitutional change can happen without a constitutional crisis, without Westminster imposition and without regular referenda. Where there is pressure for change and a consensus on what needs to be done, this can be agreed by Westminster and the Scottish Parliament in the form of an Order in Council under section 30 of the Scotland Act 1998. Of course there will be occasions where agreement cannot be reached and where matters will have to be settled unilaterally by a Westminster statute. But the constitutional will is that agreement by consensus is the best way forward.

And the new understandings on finance also move us from the old idea of the unitary centralised state. While there is no agreement yet between the Westminster parties on the final range of tax-raising powers that the Scottish Parliament will have, there is a sufficiently strong consensus emerging that can form the basis of a tax-sharing agreement. Perhaps more significantly, it looks as if the Barnett formula, the mechanism for the distribution of resources, would not be altered without at least an attempt at a cross-national agreement.

So the changes in and since the 1998 Act have been so extensive that, where conflicts arise, a resolution will not be imposed by Westminster but adjudicated by the Supreme Court and change can now be agreed by Westminster and the Scottish Parliament rather than unilaterally imposed by a Westminster statute.

My proposals do not offer a federal solution because the asymmetry of the constitution remains. But insofar as they entrench a division of powers, a system of adjudication and a method of achieving future constitutional change, many federalists will support our measures. It is not home rule in the strictest sense because not all domestic legislative powers are devolved: indeed not even the nationalists, who want to maintain a currency union, desire this. It is, however, national self-determination in a range of political decisions over which Scotland will have full control.

One further change might help cement the arrangements. While there are vehicles for adjudication of disputes and achieving constitutional change by agreement, there is no forum where consensus between the different parts of the Union is sought. I have suggested joint forums for dealing with issues where powers overlap and coordination would benefit all parts of Britain. There is a potential role in this respect for a reformed House of Lords – to be more representative of the regions and nations, to be more sensitive to their needs and aspirations and to recognise that there are areas so controversial that they may break the Union or create such a polarisation as to jeopardise it.

There is an argument that a reformed House of Lords might help our constitution reflect the diversity of the regions and nations of the United Kingdom. Some argue that the current convention which governs the behaviour of the Lords – that they can hold up legislation for two years where there is no mandate for it in an election manifesto – should be amended to encompass consideration of controversial legislation that has such vehement opposition in one part of the country that it threatens the unity of the whole country. Even if there were a special voice for the regions and nations, this would be a measure that would be very difficult to implement and is the subject for a future constitutional debate. But it is clear that to perform this role, using only the conventions that exist, the House of Lords would need to be elected like a modern Senate. It may even have to subject itself to a super-majority, only exercising this role when it has, for example, two-thirds support in the House.

THE FUTURE

With the entrenchment of the Scottish Parliament, the codification of the purpose of the UK and the power-sharing partnership arrangements I propose, we can enshrine a new set of constitutional rights and indeed a new constitution. Power will be shared between the different parts of the United Kingdom and we will bury for good the idea that Westminster enjoys undivided sovereignty. We will also leave behind the constitutional fiction that Westminster can just overrule or veto the Scottish Parliament in areas where it has formal legal powers, or in matters where there is a conflict or a desire for reform, where in the past Westminster's view would have been supreme.

So we should no longer view the United Kingdom as the all-powerful centralised unitary state of the constitutional textbooks but as a constitutional partnership of equals in what is in essence a voluntary multinational association. At some stage it will make sense to codify the new division of powers and the new power-sharing, tax-sharing rules in a written constitution. My proposals envisage a new Union whose basis is the recognition of difference, whose decision-making mechanism is power-sharing and whose form of government is a constitutional partnership of equals. In adopting these, we would enshrine for our generation a new Britain closer to what people really want: a close association of member nations that have shown and continue to show a unique capacity to come together to share both risks and resources for the common good.

I have written that our future is a global future, revolving around an economics that stresses integration not isolation, a society which emphasises the benefits of interdependence more than independence and whose politics is about the power of people and not just states. By devolving power to where people are most intimately affected by decisions and by creating a constitution that reflects the diversity of nations and peoples, we could lead the response to globalisation throughout the world. Nations need to cooperate but they need not lose their cultural diversity, distinctive values and unique character in doing so.

CHAPTER 8

Building Scotland's Success
in the Global Economy

In a few months' time China will be looking to make big long-term investments to manufacture goods as varied as cars and food on greenfield sites in Europe. They will continue the post-war pattern of rising industrial powers – first America, then Japan and Korea – investing in select locations in Europe and creating a base there from where they sell their products to the large European consumer market. In a few years' time it will be the turn of India, which already owns car and steel works, to step up its investment in Europe and the UK, and then the other emerging-market economies. Without their international investment the world economy will grow far more slowly. So any advanced industrial economy able to combine inward investments from emerging markets with locally generated high-tech entrepreneurship will do well in the future.

I have already asked the Chinese government to look at Scotland when it chooses a European location for its first car plant outside China. Having met the new president and premier when in China, I have followed up my visits by asking them to examine Scotland as a home for new investment and talked to the Chinese sovereign wealth fund and Chinese banks about investing here.

265

Some may think attracting Chinese and then Indian investment to Scotland is a long shot, but there are in my view good
arguments for them – and other emerging-market economies –
directing some of their international investments to Scotland.
The first is our world-renowned engineering expertise, our well-
known craft skills and our record in exporting high-quality products. The second – the advantages of a greenfield site – may seem
counter-intuitive. Scotland had one of the shortest histories of
successful car-making of any advanced industrial country, but the
North East of England had little history of car-making before the
dramatic success of Nissan. And while the Chinese bought old
equipment and shipped a whole Rover plant to China in 2005,
and PetroChina and Lenovo have a share in petrochemicals and
computer companies in Scotland, their revised 2020 strategy is to
make a fresh start with greenfield sites.

A Scottish nationalist, who will give you many reasons why
Scotland is an attractive location for the Chinese and rightly
remind you that Scotland has been receiving almost 10 per cent
of the UK's inward investment, will however forget the one
current advantage that a country like Scotland cannot do without – easy access to British and European markets.[1] And so the
big question: is it realistic to think Chinese investors looking for
a base from which to sell across Europe will come to Scotland if
Scotland is not part of the UK and if Scotland's place in Europe
is not secure?

I ask this question because the debate about Scotland's
economic future needs to start from – and take on board – the
sweeping global changes that will determine our ability to both
attract incoming firms and build new indigenous firms based on
Scottish skills and Scottish innovative technologies.

Innovation is the key to any nation's future. The more inventive
our nation is the more prosperous it will be. While Apple's Chinese
manufacturers earn less than $5 profit on every $400 iPad, their
intellectual property – led by their British design head Jony Ive – is

held in America and yields $70 per iPad. So innovation is where the wealth of the future is to be found and we are fortunate that Scotland has long prided itself on its history as a nation of inventors. Indeed, it is a favourite pastime of Scots to list all the achievements and innovations we have given the world, from the steam engine, tarmacadam and penicillin to the telephone, television and, most recently, Dolly, the world's first cloned sheep.

But as we will see from the evidence cited in this chapter, innovation and independence would not automatically go hand in hand in the future. Today Scotland wins a higher share of R&D funding per head than England, but we do so as part of a network of UK-wide research collaboration. Indeed only a small proportion of the money invested in R&D in Scotland comes from indigenous Scottish sources, and some of it would dry up immediately on independence.

Path-breaking research in medicine is one of our great historic success stories. It recalls a time when Scotland produced one third of the medical graduates of the UK, but the British Medical Association has said that 'in order to ensure that Scotland maintains its existing position it is . . . important to retain current Scottish, UK and European research funding arrangements or ensure similar consistent levels of funding are available'.[2] The Wellcome Trust, which has given £600 million of funding to Scottish research projects in the last ten years, has concluded that 'there is no guarantee that our funding would be maintained at current levels. The majority of the trust's awards are provided by researchers to UK institutions; the funding that we provide overseas is largely focused at low and middle-income countries . . . Introducing new and different sets of approvals could jeopardise Scotland's competitive position for research.'[3]

One sector of medical research dear to the heart of every family in the country is the fight to end cancer. In their last financial year Cancer Research UK spent £34 million on cancer research in Scottish institutions. The National Cancer Research Institute report states that: 'Scotland consistently attracts a higher portion of funding per head of population than the other countries while Wales and Northern Ireland attract less than the average for the UK.' The figure is £12.40 per head in 2011 against a UK average of £8.25.[4] Nobel Laureate Sir Paul Nurse, who spent seven years as a researcher at Edinburgh University, has recently returned from leading the Rockefeller Institute in New York to head Europe's newest and biggest cancer research institute, the London-based but UK-wide Francis Crick Institute – a £650 million investment with an annual budget of over £100 million a year, which will employ 1,400 researchers. It is supported by three UK biomedical research funders, the Medical Research Council, the Wellcome Trust and Cancer Research UK. But he fears that while Scotland has wonderfully innovative biomedical teams and is engaged in path-breaking research projects, our funding sources are, in the main, UK organisations – Cancer Research UK, the Wellcome Trust and the UK Research Councils that between them invest more in biomedical research in Scotland that our main indigenous source, the Scottish Higher Education Funding Council.[5] These three organisations could not easily justify funding research in an independent Scotland from what will be a research budget primarily for the rest of the United Kingdom. Scotland could therefore find itself outside the loop, cut off not just from UK funding of Scottish research but from UK-wide collaborative projects and consequently far less able to play what most Scottish people will want: the fullest part possible in the biggest push Europe has yet seen to find better ways of treating and curing diseases such as cancer.

While our excellence in pure research is at risk from a post-independence reallocation of current UK funding away from Scotland, our record in applied research and especially in in-house company R&D is so poor that it represents only 0.59 per cent of the Scottish economy, compared with 1.09 per cent for the UK economy, which is itself well below our international competitors.[6] It is a poor base from which to increase the number of innovative start-ups and expand the growing 'hi-tech' firms. While we have been doing better in spin-offs out of our universities, we do less well in technology transfer to, within and between firms. And this is the question central to the next stage of Scottish economic development: from where will the new companies with the niche goods and technology-driven custom-built products, and particularly the export-focused firms, come? This question is particularly pertinent given Professor Brian Ashcroft's insight that Scotland's historic weaknesses are 'a low business birth rate, low business research and development spend, low innovation, low quality investment and adoption of managerial best practices', problems which have 'bedeviled Scotland's development and enterprise agencies for years'.[7] Only between 5 and 6 per cent of new UK businesses started in 2013 were in Scotland, with 30,000 Scottish start-ups contributing to the UK total of over half a million.[8] What's more, just at the time investment in start-ups and growing companies should be rising fast, overall gross investment has been falling from a pre-recession 20 per cent of Scottish GDP to just above 15 per cent today.[9]

These examples from manufacturing, R&D and small business showing the practical challenges we face in winning new inward investment, sustaining a leadership position in the advanced sciences, and creating and incentivising new start-ups compel us to think strategically about Scotland's economic future. They force us to ask in an unblinkered and unsentimental way: what are the best policies not just to attract jobs and create new businesses and products, but also to guarantee the best long-term sustainable opportunities for young people? For while most accounts of the Scottish economy start from a static picture – setting out, for example, Scotland's past and present growth rates, fiscal inheritance and debt position – I begin from a more basic set of questions that any country operating in a global economy has to answer: what does Scotland have to do to make the most of its potential in the fast-changing global economy of the first half of the twenty-first century and, more pointedly, what are the opportunities likely to be for our children and our children's children?

My argument will be that Scotland can only succeed as an open trading economy and that to do that it needs both to get things right domestically and cooperate with other countries. What it needs to get right domestically – education, skills and infrastructure – are mostly things it already has the power and competence to achieve at Holyrood but has yet to do.

But of course independence would add a new dimension to the challenge of getting things right internationally. For, like every advanced industrial country, Scotland is being shaped by, and has to respond to, the two big forces that define the most recent wave of globalisation. First, the massive daily global flows of capital mean that most of the investment in Scotland depends on sources of funding that come from outside Scotland. Second, the global sourcing of technology, goods and services means that in a more integrated and complex world economy, every successful country has to be an open trading economy that is both specialist – able to invent and develop niche products that gives it something unique to sell to the world – and diversified – meaning that we should never, in a turbulent world, allow ourselves to become too dependent for our long-term prosperity on one market, or one set of goods or services.

As shown in Chapter 2, our manufacturing sector has fallen significantly, representing only 8 per cent of our economy now. And around 50 per cent were in the traditional export-oriented heavy industries including coal, today the figures are around 8 per cent in manufacturing and 24 per cent in the public sector. So on one count, based on Scotland's employment structure, we are less of a global economy than we were in the past. But, particularly if we were independent, we cannot escape the reality that our prosperity – and indeed our ability to finance public-sector employment levels – will depend, as I will show, on our ability to trade with the rest of the world.

Unable and indeed unwilling to compete on low pay with the emerging-market economies from China to Brazil, Scotland – like the rest of Britain – has been unable to sustain our early leadership as the world's first and biggest manufacturing centre. In fact, today our manufacturing sector, once one of the biggest employers, accounts for a smaller share of employment than it does in most advanced Western industrial nations.[10] And while, according to the Office for National Statistics, we have an estimated £120 billion in proven oil wealth still in the North Sea – and the nationalists make a dubious estimate of £1.5 trillion that denies the cost of extraction – we know that we cannot rely for ever on creating future prosperity from the good fortune of possessing one of the world's scarce resources.[11] So if we are to be a twenty-first-century wealth creator we have no alternative but to become world leaders in mastering new technology.

If the twentieth century was the century of physics and chemistry, the twenty-first century will see physics, chemistry, IT, genetics and a whole range of new general-purpose technologies come together to speed up the pace of technological innovation, with developments accelerating from epigenetics to artificial intelligence, from 3D printing to the newest nano and bio tech, supported by an exponential growth in IT, and surpassing anything we have ever seen before.

And just as no advanced nation will succeed in the next phase of globalisation unless it has a strong enough research base from which to develop new products and processes, so too no advanced economy will flourish unless it has the skills which enable it to exploit new technological advances. Indeed, as I suggest below, there is not one but three major contributions education can make to guarantee economic success – good all-round basic skills, the supply of highly qualified graduate professionals and, perhaps where a nation can deliver most added value today, a supply of research expertise. So the second precondition of success is a high-quality education system.

As we witness an epochal shift of economic activity from the West to Asia and emerging markets like Brazil, Mexico, Turkey and South Africa, Scotland needs, in addition, to be able to sell to the growing markets of the world. This is a basic fact of life for any small nation: no one will deny that, with just over five million people, Scotland's domestic market is too small to support a modern diversified economy selling just to ourselves. America has been able to remain a relatively closed economy but it has a huge domestic market of 300 million consumers.

The UK, on the other hand, with just 60 million people, is more export reliant, which is even true for Scotland. Only 13.5 per cent of American economic output is exports and total trade (imports and exports combined) is 30.5 per cent. The figures are far higher for the UK: 32 per cent for exports and 63.9 per cent for total trade. However, the UK is cushioned by a large domestic market where 60 million people sell on each other. For in every part of the UK we have always recognised that, with a relatively small share of the world's population, our success is built on our ability to trade. Yet Scotland's economy is arguably over-dependent on it, with exports at 54 per cent and total trade at 120 per cent according to the Treasury. It could be much higher, of course, if we include oil: we would be more dependent on what happens outside our borders than the UK as it currently stands.[12]

Later in the chapter I will discuss the theory that small states are more likely to be the economic success stories of the future, but at our peak in 1913 Scotland was 0.26 of the world's population when Britain was just under 3 per cent. Now as Britain falls to 0.91 per cent of the world's population, Scotland's share is 0.08 per cent. At our industrial zenith Scotland was one-twelfth of 1 per cent of the world labour force. In 2010 Scotland had an economically active population of 2.7 million people, 0.08 per cent of the global workforce. Yet, like Britain, Scotland has always punched above its weight. Our share of world output rose from 0.3 per cent in 1700 to 0.9 per cent at the end of the nineteenth century and early twentieth century, and, for a time, Scotland, with only one quarter of 1 per cent of the world's population, accounted for nearly 1 per cent of global economic activity.[13] It was a remarkable achievement: from the mid-nineteenth century to the First World War, you could say that we were an industrial power punching at a level 100 times above our weight in population.

For the foreseeable future our share of world output is likely to be five times smaller than it was in 1914 – around the 0.2 per cent it is today.[14] Even if we assign all oil activity to Scotland, it does not meaningfully alter our share of the world economy. This 0.2 per cent Scottish share of world economic activity – the same now as it was in 1707 – is likely to remain relatively steady up to 2050, and, while we are still punching above our weight, we have, in future, to make our living as a country with a small domestic market by exporting more successfully than now, recognising that we are one of the most trade-dependent economies in the world.

Scotland's level of total trade to economic output is also high in an international context. We outstrip small northern economies such as Switzerland, Denmark, Sweden and Norway (117.1 per cent, 99.2 per cent and 90.4 per cent respectively), and larger countries such as Japan (31.6 per cent), Australia (43.7 per cent), France (60 per cent) and Germany (95 per cent).[15]

But no Western economy, large or small, can ignore the recent shift in economic activity to Asia and new emerging markets. For nearly 200 years the vast majority of the world's production, investment, consumer spending, wealth and income were in the West, shared between America and Europe, with Scotland well positioned on the Atlantic, facing the United States. In 2000, the

West – Europe and North America – had only 10 per cent of the world's population, but still produced more goods and services than the rest of the world combined. Together, large and small countries in the West manufactured more, traded more, invested more, as well as consumed and owned more than the rest of the world. Today for the first time in 150 years only a minority of global economic activity – 40 per cent – is in the West. And within a few years most of the world's consumer spending will be generated outside the West, in Asia. That is also where the new booming global middle class will be found. Already Asia represents one-quarter of the world economy and soon it will be one-third: one estimate suggests that by 2050 Asia will account for half of the world economy.[16]

So Scotland has to think hard about how it can succeed in an increasingly Asia-focused world economy. Less well positioned geographically for the shift in economic power, we are already at a disadvantage – with only 2.2 per cent of our total exports sold to the biggest export market of the future, China. We sell only 0.5 per cent to the country that will overtake China as the most populated in the world, India. We do little better in Africa (4.4 per cent) and other rising economies such as Brazil (1.7 per cent). Yet the significance of these economies cannot be underestimated. In 2012, the BRIC nations (Brazil, Russia, India and China) made up just under half of global GDP growth. America does not do well enough in new markets, sending 13 per cent of exports to the BRIC nations; the UK does even less well, sending only 9.1 per cent to them; but Scotland fares even worse.[17]

SCOTLAND'S TRADE

But does our mix of export markets and products give us a better chance than others of meeting the challenges of trading success-fully in an innovation-led, skill-based future in which wealth depends upon developing new goods and services for new world markets? Scotland is not only more dependent than most coun-tries on trade but also far more dependent than most countries on just one trading partner. Today 70 per cent of our exports go to the rest of the UK, mainly England. In fact, because trade is such a big part of our economy, trade with the rest of the UK accounts for around 40 per cent of GDP when oil and gas are included.[18]

Scottish exports (not counting oil and gas) to the rest of the UK are 4 times bigger than our exports to the EU and over thir-teen times bigger than those to America. Underlining this point is the fact that the value of our trade with the UK grew by £500 million more than our trade with the rest of the world.[19]

Geographically considered, our level of trade with our neigh-bouring nations is significantly high. Sweden sells a tenth of its exports to Norway and Singapore sells 12.3 per cent to Malaysia. Even Hong Kong sells less to China than we do to the rest of the UK, and China sells less to the US and EU combined (33.5 per cent). Even Switzerland, a country with a comparable trade to output ratio, sells the majority of its exports to the twenty-seven nations of the EU, whereas our majority is sold to the three nations of the UK. So it seems obvious that any political movement seeking independence from the rest of the UK should, by now, have attempted to diversify the Scottish economy away from our dependence on trade with England.[20]

A more modern mix of products and services – by diversifying into the new booming sectors from IT to genetics – is important if we are to be confident we will not be left behind. Sadly Scotland's presence in advanced manufacturing, which was once our greatest export to the world, is now small. We have not recovered from the loss a decade ago of half of the electronics industry, with its share falling from 4.6 per cent of GDP in 2000 to just around 1 per cent today, representing a bigger shock to the economy even than the previous loss of Ravenscraig and steel. Today it has halved yet again to just around 1 per cent.[21] The creative media – which includes everything from our film industry to the games industry – sits alongside tourism, life sciences and other enabling technologies to represent growth sectors rightly promoted by the Scottish government. While Scotland is said to have around 25 per cent of Europe's potential offshore wind and tidal energy, and a tenth of Europe's wave power, the development costs are enormous and, because most of the subsidy today comes from the UK as an addition to the Barnett allocations it would have to be refinanced in the event of independence. For the time being, volatile energy markets – with gas prices falling after the shale-oil discoveries – plus the high start-up costs for renewables, have meant the postponement or cancellation of major projects like carbon capture and storage, to say nothing of the increased costs (calculated at £200 on top of the average bill by the UK government) which could face households in an independent Scotland.[22]

Value added from Scotch whisky is reported at around £3 billion – about 2.5 per cent of Scottish GDP – but salaries and purchases of goods and services used in whisky production amount to only about £400 million, suggesting that, because of its largely overseas ownership and the use of transfer pricing, the Scottish economy appears to derive less direct benefit from its most famous product than the official figures suggest.[23] The lesson is clear: from biotech and life sciences to IT and the more sophisticated oil-related products, we need to develop new high-tech products and services for the next stage of our economic development.

Outside oil and gas, finance and insurance are our main exports. But again any study of financial services reveals our dependence on one market, England. The financial sector is one of our biggest employers both directly (85,000 jobs) and indirectly (100,000). It accounts for between 8 and 9 per cent of Scottish GDP, manages over £750 billion of funds and generates around £9 billion for the Scottish economy.[24] In the years before the recession, finance, business services and real estate accounted for more than half of overall growth in Scotland, most of it in finance. And Scotland is well placed in the UK, accounting for 24 per cent of all UK employment in life assurance, and 13 per cent of all banking employment.[25] But Scottish Financial Enterprise (the trade body for the sector) has shown that our market is not international: 90 per cent of their members' customers are to be found in the rest of the UK.[26]

In total, £10 billion of Scotland's exports are financial-services exports to one market, England.[27] With small export markets in computers and electronics and in advanced IT-based manufacturing, Scotland is dependent on too narrow a range of goods and services – financial services, oil-related products, and food and drink – sold to one market (the rest of the UK), which means we are doubly exposed to risk. The risks include companies serving English markets resisting the separate regulatory controls of an independent Scotland and moving to England. As the former civil servant Jim Gallagher states in his Fraser of Allander Institute article: 'Financial services is a highly regulated business, and although cross-border services can in principle under EU law be provided, it is likely that providers would wish to relocate to the regulatory domain which contained the majority of their customers.'[28]

RESEARCH AND DEVELOPMENT

Scottish universities recognise the inescapable truth of the new global era: that our human resources, our inventiveness and our skills, matter more than our physical resources. And Universities Scotland is right to boast that: 'when population is taken into account, Scotland is second only to Switzerland for the highest number of world-class universities per head of population'. Indeed the quality of our graduates and our research are cited as a key 'pull' factor by 45 per cent of major inward investors.[29]

But on close inspection this advantage has been built up within and is best maintained as part of a bigger network. The 217,000 higher-education students in Scotland in 2012 represented 0.1 per cent of the world's tertiary students, compared with 1 per cent a century ago. Using the most reliable data for the number of adults with higher-education qualifications in the industrialised countries of the world – the countries that are members of the OECD – the 700,000 qualified Scots aged 25–64 represent 0.3 per cent of graduates or similarly qualified workers.[30] Scotland is again punching above our weight and yet we still have only a tiny share of the global graduate population. So we have to compete and flourish as a small part of a rapidly growing global higher-education industry and we have to remain globally focused.

The commonly accepted explanation of why America and not Europe has the world's top teaching and research universities is Europe's overly parochial focus on regional and national champions at the expense of world-class institutions. Despite its great history of international research and its worldwide connections, Scotland would have to fight hard to avoid falling into this European trap.

WHAT OF SCOTLAND?

At £700 million of £17.1 billion, Scotland's business R&D spending is just 4 per cent of the UK total. As Brian Ashcroft explains: 'one of these drivers may be the role played by the branches of foreign multinationals located in Scotland. They bring in new products but most of the R&D is done elsewhere. Business in Scotland does relatively little R&D by international standards.'[31]

When we look at the third of UK higher-education research that is funded publicly, particularly from the Higher Education Research and Development (HERD) element, Scotland received £969 million in 2012/13. In the same year, UK Research Council funding to Scottish higher-education institutions totalled £242 million. This money – which is allocated in addition to the Barnett-formula grant – is won in open competition with other UK research institutions and is thus an extra source of income which comes from membership of the UK and is linked to merit. While research money from the Scottish Funding Council would survive after independence, the funding from the UK Research Council grants would have to be foregone or replaced, with huge knock-on effects on Scottish universities, some of which get up to 40 per cent of their funding from this source alone.[32]

So it is clear that most Scottish spending by philanthropic organisations and foundations comes from UK-wide institutions, and most of private-company investment in R&D originates from outside Scotland. Some of this is European Union money, but with the only readily identifiable Scottish source of significance being the Scottish Funding Council – providing only 30 per cent of research funding for Scottish Higher Education Institutions in 2011–12 – the conclusion is that most of Scotland's R&D expenditure is sourced from the rest of the UK and would have to be replaced.[33]

Therefore, at the very time when the clear challenge is to devote more to research, we might be struggling to maintain what we already have. The Scottish government has recently pledged to negotiate to retain the collaborative research network but, once direct national links are severed, possibly in acrimonious circumstances, re-creating the same level of collaboration will be problematic, and especially so if English, Welsh and Northern Irish institutions decide to win for themselves the large research grants that now come to Scotland.

So with invention increasingly collaborative, cross-border and costly, with a critical mass of investment needed to succeed in R&D, there is understandable scepticism about the wisdom of breaking up the tried-and-tested system of collaborative research that spans the UK and from which Scotland has derived so much benefit. The old idea of the lone innovator in the garage – or in Scotland's case the myth of James Watt alone with his kettle of boiling water amid his experiments with steam – does not reflect the wholly new world where there are, as in cancer research, huge cooperative undertakings.

Scotland, through the Chief Scientist Office, has been a member of the Office for Strategic Co-ordination of Health Research (OSCHR) board since 2008. This enables Scotland to contribute to the discussions that determine the overall UK health-research strategy and collaborate on a number of programmes across UK health research. Among just two of the many examples of cross-border collaboration are the eighteen UK-wide experimental cancer medicine centres and the E-Health Informatics Research Centres now enhanced with additional capital from the Medical Research Council (MRC) to create the UK-wide Farr Institute.[34] 'Strength comes from the large, highly integrated, internationally renowned UK research base,' the world-renowned scientist Professor Hugh Pennington has said, 'that means we can invest in the world-leading high-tech – and often high-cost – infrastructure that our researchers demand if we are to remain at the cutting edge. It means those costs are spread over 60 million people, instead of five million. It means we all benefit from the billions of pounds the UK invests in technology, the laboratories, the materials and the space research demands.'[35]

THE SMALL-STATE ARGUMENT

The rise of the nation state – and of political nationalism – was the most important political fallout from the Industrial Revolution of the nineteenth century in the time when Europe, and the West as a whole, came to dominate the world economy. Then, it was argued, sizeable nation states like Germany and Italy – benefiting from economies of scale, and with national communications and transport networks, large domestic markets and an ability to diffuse technological innovation across these large areas – could manage the tensions of industrialisation better than small states.

For a time, nationalists posited an alternative view, the 'arc of prosperity', arguing that the Nordic states, with Ireland and Iceland, offered us a model of small northern states whose island status, long coastlines and ability to innovate, be flexible and access resources led them to perform well beyond expectations. It is an idea that has been fatally undermined by events in Ireland and Iceland. Now, however, an even more ambitious theory – the 'small-state success story' – has emerged. The argument is that when we look at who succeeds and who fails in the modern world, small states are doing much better than large ones. The old question, says Tom Nairn, used to be: 'Are you big enough to survive and develop in an industrialising world?' Today, in a globalising world, the question is: 'Are you small and smart enough to survive, and claim a positive place in the common global culture?'[36]

Writing from Singapore, a small-country success story itself, the writer David Skilling identifies three factors that, he says, are key to the success of small nation states: the benefit they gain from lower tariffs and the removal of barriers to trade (barriers which previously meant small countries were discriminated against by large ones), their greater flexibility and adaptability, and their capacity for innovation. While in the years of the Industrial Revolution larger states were more secure, brought economies of scale and benefited from their bigger domestic markets, Skilling argues that they now seem too slow to adapt, too weighed down by old practices and thus too inflexible to be the leaders in a new wave of technological innovation.[37]

In fact the Scottish government has argued that Scotland's growth rate from 1977 to 2007 is, at 2.3 per cent, weaker than both the UK and small EU countries, who manage 2.8 per cent, although on a 50-year view Scotland was almost certainly growing more strongly than the small EU countries.[38] But does the small-state theory actually hold up when we look at the benefits that come from the trend towards greater integration of economies and particularly when we look at the unique advantages that Scotland gains from its integration with the rest of the UK?

Of course, both large and small states should, at least in theory, benefit from the all-round lowering of trade barriers and the free flow of capital, goods and services which globalisation has brought. But our recent experience is that not all countries benefit equally: the more integrated economies are, the faster they are able to grow. Indeed, while the European single market is a huge advance on the old Common Market, enabling more integrated economies to trade more across old borders, Scotland benefits even more from the far higher level of economic integration within the United Kingdom. While French, Spanish, and German financial institutions, for example, will make it difficult for Scots companies to sell in their markets, there are few barriers to similar sales in England. Thus the Treasury has estimated that, if we lose the benefits from trading in the more integrated UK-wide economy and rely only on the more circumscribed benefits that come from potential membership of the EU single market, then: 'Exports from an independent Scotland to the continuing UK would be 83 per cent lower after 30 years than if Scotland were to remain a part of the UK. Exports from the rest of the UK to Scotland would be 77 per cent lower.'[39]

UK-wide integration may also offer better protection against shocks. The Treasury's analysis suggests that the impact of the recession on small economies was greater and more prolonged than on large ones; this is because of their relative lack of absorptive capacity. The economies of small countries are in general more volatile due to a greater reliance on external trade and the absence of any 'inter-regional insurance' in the form of financial support or fiscal transfers.

Examples include Finland's loss of 11 per cent of its output in the year after the collapse of the Soviet Union, and Ireland's overexposure to the banking crisis.[40] A small open economy like Scotland that is more dependent on external trade than our Scandinavian neighbours is clearly more vulnerable to decisions made elsewhere.

In an independent state, Scotland's banking-sector assets and liabilities would be 12.5 times the size of our economy, compared to a UK banking sector which is seen as too big at around 5 times GDP.[41] Recent experience suggests that no matter where your assets and businesses are located, your liabilities are in your headquarter country and that, as Mervyn King, the former governor of the Bank of England, puts it 'banks live globally but die locally'. The costs associated with bailouts are not just government purchases of shares but also the provision of liquidity made more complex by the currency uncertainties.

The risks cannot be wished away. In a large economy we can specialise and diversify at the same time, while in a small economy the gains from specialisation – as in financial services – are often at the expense of diversification elsewhere and at the cost of a more broadly based economy, more resilient in its capacity to withstand shocks. And we cannot ignore the effects of losing economies of scale, greater volatility caused by shocks in the terms of trade, spillover effects such as the risk to collaborative arrangements, and the heightened challenges in securing technology transfer across the UK.

And of course, while trade flows are significantly lower across international borders than within a country, so too are capital flows and, as we shall see, migration flows. Volatility is an issue. Oil revenues, which exceeded £11 billion in 2011–12, were down to £6.1 billion in 2012–13 and are forecast to be £4.7 billion in 2013–14 and just £3.2 billion in 2016–17.[42] A 2010 paper by the Office for Budget Responsibility estimated that a £10 increase in the oil price per barrel affects UK North Sea oil and gas revenues by £2.4 billion a year.[43] This is why a paper prepared by the Scottish Nationalist Party on the prospects for public expenditure after independence understandably acknowledges the threat from the much greater volatility of revenues, stating that: 'North Sea tax receipts have been more volatile than onshore receipts . . . Given the relative importance of North Sea revenues to Scotland's public finances, these downward revisions have resulted in a deterioration in the outlook for Scotland's public finances.'[44]

Is it not the case that small states are able to adapt more quickly because they are usually more homogenous, more cohesive, have what is called a 'shorter line of communication' and can thereby mobilise their social capital faster? In a major report Professor Michael Keating, Dr Nicola McEwen and Malcolm Harvey find little evidence that, as a small state, Scotland would be better equipped to negotiate its way through the pitfalls of a globalised world. Of course small states can exercise real influence within the EU, he says, but not in the same way as large states. While coalition-building around an expertise in areas like wind power or climate change may give smaller states some advantages, he advises that 'in general, larger states have more influence in the EU than smaller ones. They have greater economic weight. They have more voting power in the Council of the European Union under the majority-voting provisions, which now apply to most areas of policy-making. They can more credibly exercise a veto in those cases where unanimity is required. Big states sometimes make side deals outside the formal decision-making process. Small states cannot do this as easily as they have less to offer in return.'[45]

So we need to be realistic about the nature of Scotland's dependence on economic relationships well beyond our borders. Specifically, the Scotland Office has estimated that 338,000 Scottish jobs are supported by 'businesses operating in Scotland but owned elsewhere in the UK'.[46] By turnover, roughly 70 per cent of manufacturing is owned and controlled outside of Scotland, with only 10 per cent coming from the rest of the UK. As Brian Ashcroft has shown, 22 per cent of manufacturing employment in 1998 came from companies that were foreign-owned and controlled, rising to 31 per cent by 2011. Concurrently, foreign ownership increased, from 41 per cent of manufacturing turnover to 62 per cent.[47]

This level of external control is not of course unique to Scotland and there are advantages such as access to a bigger source of investment capital, but in an era where capital is inescapably mobile, the scope for independent decision-making is more limited, and we are often subject to decisions that are made for other reasons elsewhere.

But of course, whether you are small or large, or have high or low levels of external ownership, it is ultimately the policies that you pursue that decide your levels of productivity and success. We cannot automatically draw any conclusions about a capacity to innovate based purely on size – after all, America is the biggest economy in the world and is also still by far the most innovative in R&D and in creating new products. It comes back to how innovative, skilled and diversified you are and whether you have the capacity, not least through collaboration, to develop new products and services to sell. Not only does Scotland need a higher business birth rate, but also more investment in business R&D, especially in our growing companies, and more overall investment in knowledge equipment and modern infrastructure. Of course with 23 per cent of all Scottish workers (22 per cent if we do not include the nationalised banking sector) working in the public sector, Scotland has a larger public sector than England, where public-sector employees number around 19–20 per cent. But there is little sign that the private sector is 'crowded out' by the public sector and instead it offers a 'cushioning effect' against dramatic falls in economic activity during a recession. This is one of the reasons why from peak to trough the Scottish economy recently lost 5.6 per cent of output while the UK lost 7.3 per cent.[48]

An economy like ours has to link into the knowledge networks through technology transfer, which can come through inward investment, inward migration, and students entering our universities. We need to be able to adopt, adapt and even on occasion imitate technologies from elsewhere as well as innovate in our own right. And nothing we should contemplate should restrict the high degree of openness necessary for that to happen. Indeed, in a world that is globalising and integrating, Scotland has to position itself to benefit from the growth of global hubs and cities, which tend to have lower unit costs and higher productivity because of what has been called agglomeration economies, or economies of scale and scope. Once cities offered access to natural resources and trade flows but today, as Ed Glaeser's work on cities and Richard Florida's work on the 'Creative Class' show us, they are where the most innovative, creative and entrepreneurial people come together. It does not make sense for us to distance ourselves from the global hub of London, which should be seen as a resource from which, as on cancer research, we gain.

As a geographically peripheral location we need good links with the rest of the UK, including the best rail and motorway links to Scotland. So we cannot divorce ourselves from infrastructure decisions within the island we share with England and Wales. The lesson is clear. To be an inventive and innovative nation, as Scotland is, is a matter of great pride. But it may mean little to Scots looking for work and better incomes unless there are companies seeking to turn new ideas into products, finance available to enable them to do that, and a market into which they can sell those products. Scotland, fully integrated into Britain, has all of that – as James Watt discovered.

SCOTLAND'S FINANCES

Any assessment of future prospects comes back to whether Scotland is sufficiently diversified or over-dependent on one partner or one industry, and at least to some extent what happens as the oil runs out.

Already Scotland has seen oil production fall from its peak of 4.5 million barrels per day in 1999 to around 1.4 million barrels per day in 2013. It will continue to fall by an average of around 5 per cent a year.[49] As the Wood report shows, new fields are not being developed at a fast enough rate to stop a halving of oil production by 2030.[50] While the report should be read with all the qualifications necessary when dealing with long-run forecasts, the Institute for Fiscal Studies (IFS) also raises significant questions about Scotland's economy when the share taken by North Sea oil and gas runs down.

The IFS project that debt for an independent Scotland would be 233.3 per cent of GDP in 2062–3, at a time when UK debt is projected to be 77.1 per cent of GDP. To make up the gap in Scottish revenues – i.e. to get back to the IFS projection for the UK's debt position – an independent Scotland would need to grow at 2 per cent per year more than the UK for the next 50 years.[51]

If the IFS are right, Scotland would have to sustain growth of 4.2 per cent per annum to avoid a higher level of fiscal consolidation than would be required by the UK.[52] Given that the most optimistic academic estimates of UK and Scottish growth suggest average growth rates of around 2 per cent, it begs the question of what would be required for Scotland to grow at twice that rate when, as the IFS has pointed out, there are many more risks to an independent Scotland's fiscal position.[53]

Macroeconomic management will not be available as a tool to help Scotland reach these growth rates, given that the Scottish government's plans for an independent Scotland are based on membership of the same macroeconomic framework as Britain – the framework that they have so often criticised for causing low growth in the past. Outpacing English growth cannot come from a difference interest rate or anti-inflation policy. Scotland would be hemmed in by exactly the same pressures to control inflation and money supply that England has to cope with and from a level of currency that is set by the overall performance of Britain.

So how does the Scottish government justify their promise of much higher growth? Unable to point to a better macroeconomic performance than the rest of the UK, they turn to supply-side reforms, specifically to higher levels of employment and thus overall growth, to be achieved both by getting more women into work – through better childcare arrangements – and by immigration.

Enhancing women's employment opportunities so that they can develop and use their talents to the full, and thereby increase the incomes of their families, was one of my objectives in government from 1997 to 2010. It is important for all parents and for the economy that we maximise chances to balance work and family life through generous arrangements for part-time work, the provision of childcare and rights to return to the workplace after children are born. In particular, single parents have suffered because for many years childcare was unaffordable and benefit laws were too restrictive. Through the incentives and tax credits we introduced, and encouragement from great role models like J. K. Rowling, the proportion of single parents in work rose between 1997 and 2010 from 45 per cent to 57 per cent in the UK and from 39 to 59 per cent in Scotland, reversing in Scotland's case the historic discrimination against the employment of mothers.[54]

By 2012, Scotland's rate of female participation had risen to 71.9 per cent and a higher proportion of Scottish women are now in the workforce than in Germany, Austria, Spain, Portugal, Australia and the rest of the United Kingdom. But the gaps in both the availability and affordability of childcare remain big: in the last 6 months, according to one assessment, more than half of Scottish parents have had to rely on grandparent care, compared to just a third across Britain.[55] The Scottish government promises that by the end of the first parliament 'all three and four year olds and vulnerable two year olds will be entitled to 1,140 hours of childcare a year (the same amount of time as children spend in primary school)', and that by the end of the second parliament 'all children from one to school age will be entitled to 1,140 hours of childcare per year'. Phase one – 600 hours to 50 per cent of two-year-olds – is estimated to cost around £80 million. Phase two – doubling to 1,140 hours by 2020 – has been estimated by the Scottish government to cost £700 million. Yet no estimate of capital costs has been provided. The third and final phase – universal provision of 1,140 hours, worth £2,000 per child – is currently un-costed.[56]

Matching Sweden's 78 per cent rate of participation would, they say, put more than 100,000 women into work and output could rise by 1.7 per cent. Matching Norway's rate, they say, could put 68,000 women into work. But in fact their plans for

2020 are simply to match the rates of Finland and the Netherlands, reaching 73.9 per cent, putting an extra 35,000 women into work. The bold unsubstantiated claim is that they would boost the level of output by around 0.6 per cent, but even if this claim could be proven to be reasonable, this would be a one-off, once-and-for-all change that is hardly enough to raise growth to 4 per cent annually, especially when, after cutting women's part-time college training places by 93,000 since 2007, the 35,000 new women workers are unlikely to have the skills we need to move the economy to a far higher and sustainable rate of economic growth.[57]

There is yet another weakness in the SNP's plans. A report from the Scottish Parliament Information Centre has shown that the £700 million in projected revenues from the childcare policy outlined in Scotland's Future will not be produced. While the plan is dependent on 104,000 women returning to the workforce, the Centre has found there are only 64,000 mothers with children aged one-to-five. As such, the policy would actually cost £1.2 billion more than originally thought.[58]

For the purposes of their analysis of the impact of migration on growth and the fiscal position, the Institute for Fiscal Studies assumes that long-term productivity levels in Scotland will be similar to those of the UK, although in the pre-recession years to 2007 labour productivity in Scotland remained broadly in the range 94–6 per cent of the UK figure.[59] But it is doubtful whether a major increase in immigration can give us all the extra growth we need and survey evidence suggests that there is little difference in attitude to immigration between Scotland and the rest of the UK, making it hard to secure public consent for immigration rates at the level Scotland would need.

The Institute for Fiscal Studies has examined the impact of an increase in net inward migration over the next fifty years and calculated the impact of a rise from the current average of 9,000 people a year to 26,000 a year. This trebling of net inward migration would require immigration to exceed emigration by an overall total of more than one million people between now and 2062 and of course, because theirs is a net figure, the absolute number of immigrants would be much higher than that. In fact the UK Treasury has suggested that if the UK market becomes less integrated the first task would be to counteract a slowdown in migration as labour mobility slowed between Scotland and the rest of the UK. The Treasury believes that net migration between Scotland and the rest of the UK, which has been running at 40,000 a year, may fall to 10,000 a year.[60] But even the most optimistic projection – an additional 1.3 million people added over five decades through net migration – would not give us the extra growth we need, according to the Institute for Fiscal Studies, to keep our fiscal position in order. Under its 'high migration' scenario Scottish debt reaches 100 per cent of national income in 2037–8, moving to 154 per cent in 2057–8 and 172 per cent of GDP in 2062–3. This is despite the fact that the IFS projections do not take account of the inevitable fall in productivity from the declining contribution to the economy from North Sea oil and gas.[61]

Levels of debt are managed more or less easily depending on the level of interest rate charged on it. Even if the deficit is small the cost of managing it could be high. The state of California has at times had a rate on its bonds more than 3 per cent above the rate paid on comparable US treasuries even though it is part of the US monetary union, and Angus Armstrong of the National Institute of Economic and Social Research has suggested that an independent Scotland's borrowing costs would be substantially more than those of the UK.[62] And while it is important to put the short-term fiscal and debt issues into their proper perspective as we discuss the long-term opportunities available in the Scottish economy, it is also important not to ignore the impact fiscal policy will have on our prospects.

The recently published Scottish public revenues and spending figures (often called GERS) show conclusively that onshore

Scotland has been in deficit over the period 2008–9 to 2012–13 by between 13 and 17 per cent of our national income. It is a substantially worse position than the UK as a whole simply because, at just 8.2 per cent, Scotland's contribution to onshore UK revenues are below our 8.4 population share while our share of public-sector expenditure at 9.3 per cent of our national income is well above it. Because tax revenues fell between 2008 and 2011 while our share of public spending did not, Scotland's position worsened, giving us an onshore deficit equivalent to at least £1,200 (and overhauls as much as £1,500) per person, a total annual deficit of between £6.3 billion and £7.8 billion.[63]

Today in 2014 Scotland's onshore deficit stands at 12 per cent, twice the UK's 6 per cent, and it is no longer offset by oil revenues irrespective of whether we apportion to Scotland 79 per cent (as the Treasury propose based on HMRC estimates) or 84 per cent as the Scottish government prefer.[64]

So the Scottish government are out of sync with every major forecaster in predicting the oil price, which they say will normally be $9 higher than objective projections, a rate of extraction that they say will be about 15–20 per cent higher and thus North Sea revenues that they make about £4 billion a year greater than the Office for Budget Responsibility and other independent bodies.

But even the most optimistic of oil forecasts leave Scotland in deficit in the years ahead, which is hardly surprising when total North Sea tax revenues have fallen from £11.3 billion in 2011–12 to £6.6 billion in 2012–13 and will fall again from £4.7 billion in 2013–14 to £3.2 billion in 2016–17.[65]

And all this before we have to deal with transition costs incurred in creating a new state, from a new tax-collection and benefits system to embassies and consulates round the world, and address the uncertainty of a policy on the currency and interest rates that would, if the Scottish government have their way, allow monetary policy to be run by England with no formal Scottish input. If they fail to achieve this, it will probably leave Scotland trying to peg our currency to the pound, without the stability that allows Hong Kong to align with the dollar, and Denmark with the euro. But in both scenarios, formally in or out of the UK currency, we would have no control over the exchange rate or interest rate.

The Scottish Yes campaign has launched a major advertising campaign – 'What would you say to living in one of the world's wealthiest nations?' – claiming an independent Scotland would be 14th in the world with an income per head around $39,642 compared to the UK's 18th place.[66] The difference is they calculate absolutely all the revenues from North Sea oil coming straight to the Scottish people, but money paid in profits to the oil majors and other related multinationals headquartered outside Scotland means that in 2011 an estimated £19 billion was sent abroad in profits and post-tax remittances. Not to be outdone, the whisky industry remitted two-thirds of a billion pounds in profits to owners outside Scotland and, because 80 per cent of non-oil private businesses are externally owned, they remit as much as £5.8 billion in profits. Indeed, 20 per cent of Scottish value added is produced by companies head-quartered in the rest of the UK so their profits are sent there from Scotland. The Scottish government has made a partial first estimate of the difference between Scottish Gross National Product and Scottish Gross National Income but the evidence we have is that Scotland is more like Ireland than their estimates suggest.[67]

On the face of it, North Sea oil increases Scottish GDP by 21 per cent before any assignment of relative shares of Scotland and England are made. But while the Scottish government says Scottish GNI is 5 per cent lower, the figure is likely to be higher and more akin to Ireland. And Ireland found that the best estimate of their GNI – which is GDP calculated after income from and to abroad is considered – was between 14 and 15 per cent less than their published GDP. If this were the case it would push Scotland's ranking further down the league.[68]

The young person looking ahead to the future of Scotland will think first of all of what opportunities and job prospects he or she has. Throughout my time as an MP, unemployment, youth unemployment and long-term unemployment have dominated the economic and political conversation. Scotland has 2.6 million men and women in work, but only 1.8 million have full-time work, 435,000 have work paying below a living wage and only 56.6 per cent of Scotland's 16–24-year-olds are in work.[69] As we have seen, independence is not in itself a solution to the question as to where future jobs will come from.

The answer is, and looks set to remain, that jobs are most likely to come at least in part from trade with and being part of the UK. Estimates suggest 360,000 Scottish private-sector jobs are in enterprises with ultimate ownership in the rest of the UK; 13 per cent of employment or 246,830 jobs depend on exports from Scotland to the rest of the UK. Turning to the public sector, many people are, of course, employed directly by the UK government, such as the armed forces and HMRC. Taking the Civil Service as an example, around 29,000 staff out of 45,000 in Scotland are employed by the UK government. Whilst many positions would continue, the ability of an independent Scotland to maintain staffing at current levels is by no means guaranteed.[70] Jobs in research and development would also be at risk if we sever the connections with UK-wide research councils, a group of which provides up to 40 per cent of funding to Glasgow and Edinburgh universities. And with a new border slowing down trade, Scotland would lose the benefits that come from the far deeper integration of our economy with England than is achieved within the European Union.

We also have to consider EU membership, for which Scotland would clearly have to apply and cannot expect automatically. As Chancellor I commissioned the study on whether Britain would benefit from joining the single currency, which concluded that, without a banking union and a fiscal union, any currency union would be unstable and perhaps unsustainable. By contrast, the Scottish government now seeks to opt into the UK currency but by leaving the UK Parliament would opt out of any formal say over the decisions of the UK government, the Treasury and the Bank of England. They have also accepted that they would have to enter into a fiscal pact with the rest of the UK, thus handing over some of the freedom they once sought in taxation and spending to the rest of the UK. For half a century the SNP has called for the levers of power on monetary and fiscal policy to be in Scotland, but now seem prepared to accept that many of these powers would be wielded elsewhere in the UK without any Scottish input. Yet we can only imagine how the Scottish government would react when an interest rate decision was made in the interests of the rest of the United Kingdom that did not suit them. The only logical conclusion that is in the interests of the Scottish people, as opposed to the dogma of independence, is that Scotland should retain the ability to influence decision-making on these matters as part of the UK, with Scottish MPs at Westminster and Scottish representatives in the UK government and Bank of England, to ensure Scottish supervision of the decisions these institutions make.

I started with the question Keynes posed in the 1930s – what are the economic prospects for our grandchildren? Of course if we want independence for other reasons we might be willing to pay the bills, accept the risks, endure the pain of transition and make the necessary sacrifices. But the Scottish National Party's case for independence is the economic gains. Long ago they abandoned their emphasis on the cultural case that independence was about cultural freedom even if we were worse off as a result. Every one of their pronouncements is based on their certainty that we will be richer. Indeed, opinion polls suggest that the main reason why people do support independence is that they believe they will be better off. If they did not think so, they would think twice about supporting change.

Over half of Scots say that they would support independence if they were £500 better off, with only 30 per cent opposing.[71] As the well-known economist Professor John Kay points out, the banner under which independence movements used to march was – in the words of the Virginia rebel in the American War of Independence, Patrick Henry – 'Give me liberty or give me death'. Now it is, he jokes, 'Give me liberty or give me £500'.

The challenge for Scotland is to secure the benefits of global cooperation while at the same time retaining our distinctiveness as a nation. My alternative vision of Scotland's future is of an innovative, skills-led modern economy that is a hub for new technologies and the creative industries – where being part of Britain helps rather than hinders our efforts to grow, innovate, create new businesses and develop new markets.

My agenda for our economic future focuses on the importance of an innovative, skills-based economy that competes not on low pay and low standards but on high levels of skills, innovation and enterprise. This requires a distinctively Scottish focus on skills and education (which I will discuss in the next chapter); an intensification, rather than abandonment, of collaboration on innovation; and a shared effort to win new markets in the high growth economies where Scotland does least well today.

In this chapter I have focused my attention on global trends that will have a significant impact on Scotland's future, far more than on what is happening in the rest of Britain, and to best understand the nationalist argument I have considered Britain unsentimentally as a platform we can use to steer our own path. Yet at every point we are drawn back into unchallengeable facts: the highly intergrated nature of the UK's economy, the benefits of a single currency and market, and the recognition that economic activity within the Union is not a zero-sum game but that we can benefit from our interaction with each other.

So the economic arguments for and against independence are not finely balanced: two-thirds of our exports go to England; businesses enjoy economies of scale and jobs are created as a result of being part of the more integrated UK economy; and we are huge beneficiaries of collaboration in science and technology across the UK in R&D, in a way that, say, the Republic of Ireland is not. And I have no doubt that the benefits of research, collaboration and investment between Scotland and the rest of the UK are greater now than at any time in the history of the Union. At a time when oil is running down, public debt is high and the costs of pensions are rising, the economic arguments for breaking the political connection with the rest of the United Kingdom do not look good.

Nor, as we shall see in the next chapter, does the argument that an independent Scotland under an SNP government will inevitably be a less unequal society add up when confronted with the factual evidence.

CHAPTER 9

The Challenge of Addressing
Poverty and Inequality

It was witnessing at first hand the devastation caused by unemployment in Fife in the 1960s onwards that made me want to do something about it. My first speech in the House of Commons in 1983 was a demand for action on unemployment and poverty in Scotland. During my first year in parliament Robin Cook and I edited a book, *Scotland: The Real Divide*, calling for action on poverty, and when I became Chancellor of the Exchequer in 1997 I implemented a long-planned reform to make the Treasury a department that dealt not only with the national and international economy but with domestic inequality, deprivation and poverty.

The sight of a child missing out on chances because of poverty doesn't just make me sad but angry, because I know we have the power to do something about it. And I know also that my conviction about the evil of poverty is a view widely shared in Scotland, as demonstrated this year in the Church of Scotland's *Imagining Scotland's Future: Our Vision*. It is a report generated from their year-long consultation with the people of Scotland about our priorities for the future, and their conclusion – that Scottish people value respect, honesty, community, opportunity, compassion and tolerance, and want action on equality, fairness, justice and education – is testimony to an enduring belief in fairness.[1]

I remember well how Donald Dewar, John Smith, Robin Cook and I insisted in the pre-1997 debates about the creation of a Scottish Parliament that our attention should not be on what a parliament was but what it would do. That is the same spirit that should inform the debate about the referendum now.

We have already looked in other chapters at questions of national identity and national interest. Now I want to turn to what I consider to be the most important question of all. What kind of country are we trying to build?

Equality, fairness and social justice – and what happens to welfare, childcare, pensions and the bedroom tax – have come to take on a major significance in the broader constitutional argument.

But that debate needs to be rooted in evidence and not just in rhetoric. I want us to make a clear-headed assessment of what is possible with independence, and what is not. Understanding our future starts with an honest account of where we are.

Scotland's Outlook, a joint campaign of important charities from Shelter Scotland and the Poverty Alliance to Macmillan Cancer Support, has highlighted the conditions of the struggling one-sixth of the Scottish population still living in poverty. Indeed, in the six months from September 2013 to March 2014, 23,000 Scots used food banks.[2] Ed Miliband has proposed an energy-price freeze: one good reason to support it is that according to the latest figures over a quarter of Scots live in fuel poverty.[3]

The arithmetic of child poverty presents an even bleaker picture: with 200,000 children in poverty today, the number is close to the total population of Aberdeen.[4] Despite years marked by progress in healthcare, a girl born in one of the poorest areas in Scotland is likely to live for eight years less than a girl born in one of the richest areas, and a boy fourteen years less.[5]

In Scotland, deaths from cancer have fallen by a sixth in the last ten years, but the mortality rate in the poorest areas is 50 per cent higher than the average and it has not shifted over ten years.[6] The Child Poverty Action Group (CPAG) has shown that Scots in the lowest fifth of household incomes are fifteen times more likely to have attempted suicide than Scots in the highest fifth of household incomes.[7]

For the first time in recent memory welfare benefits and tax credits will not rise in line with inflation but between 2013 and 2016 suffer a real-terms cut by rising at just 1 per cent per year.[8] CPAG has estimated that by 2020 there will be 100,000 more children in poverty in Scotland because of cuts both in welfare and in the real value of wages.[9]

THE CHALLENGE

When Labour came to power in 1997, one-third of Scottish children and pensioners were in poverty.[10] The task was immense: according to the Centre for Analysis of Social Exclusion, the UK's level of child poverty was exceeded only by two other OECD nations in the mid 1990s: the US and Italy.[11]

So in 1997 we set a long-term objective: to end child poverty over a twenty-year period. We set staging posts, to reduce child poverty by a quarter by 2004 and by half by 2010, and we committed our government to work to end pensioner poverty.

We wanted to achieve both these objectives using an approach we named 'progressive universalism': good basic universal provision, with rising pensions and rising child benefit, a minimum wage and, even more important, well-funded public services, upon which we built our new progressive measures for an assault on poverty through tax credits – the Pension Credit, the Child Tax Credit, and the Working Tax Credit. Our stance was that tax credits should sit alongside increased benefits to give more to those who needed help most.

Before 1997 one-third of Scottish pensioners were in poverty, but by 2010/11 the figure had fallen to just over one in ten, greater than any achieved by any post-war government.[12] We achieved this by balancing new universal benefits – the Winter Fuel Allowance, free TV licences and a more generous basic pension – with pensioner tax credits that lifted the incomes of thousands of pensioners who had previously been denied any help because of some savings.

In 2010 we had ambitious plans to go much further in reducing pensioner poverty but, disappointingly, that figure is now rising.

In 1997, 360,000 children in Scotland (35 per cent) lived in poverty when we took account of family incomes including their housing costs. By 2003 that figure had fallen to 280,000 (27 per cent) and by 2011 it fell to 220,000 (25 per cent): a substantial reduction in the numbers of Scottish children in poverty.[13]

Overall we lifted more than 320,000 Scots out of poverty over the course of the last Labour government. Tax credits were instrumental in raising people's incomes and, by underpinning our attack on poverty with a minimum wage, we ensured that we would not be subsidising employers who would otherwise have continued to pay the lowest poverty wages they could get away with.[14]

So while some have argued that the minimum wage was too low to be of real benefit, the use of tax credits that went alongside it made an enormous difference to the worst paid, in particular to low-paid women workers. Economists such as Paul Gregg have shown that due to tax credit reforms there were improvements in the 'mental well being' of adults and children.[15] And Richard Dickens has shown that along with benefits, tax credits had four times the impact on poverty reduction than achieved by employment over the same period.[16]

While I wish we could have done more – as indeed we had plans to had we won the 2010 general election – it is important to start with the evidence about what it is possible to achieve in fighting poverty when you have a UK government committed to the task and the strength of the UK's resources behind you.

SNP AMBITIONS

Of course the Scottish National Party argue that independence is the best way to immunise Scotland against UK government cuts, and that an independent Scotland could not do worse than the coalition government when it comes to fighting poverty. That is the sort of rhetorical claim parties make when they are fighting campaigns and I am, of course, sympathetic to the argument that a Conservative government in Westminster is bad for Scotland.

But we need a much more sober examination of the nationalists' unsubstantiated claims about what they will achieve under independence if we really care about fixing poverty, and not just talking about it. They claim that giving Scotland control of the fiscal levers would automatically reduce inequality. But is that true? Deputy First Minister Nicola Sturgeon has claimed that:

> As a devolved government we are seeking to mitigate the damage done by welfare reform . . . we cannot possibly mitigate all of the impacts it will continue to have on children and families in Scotland . . . through our commitments on the social wage and protecting universal benefits we have already demonstrated what we can do with just some of the powers available to us . . . This government wants to eradicate child poverty. I believe Scotland can do better and given the full range of powers that independence will deliver, I believe we will do better.[17]

Their claim is bigger than even a promise to eradicate poverty: they also promise to reduce inequality. The trouble is that achieving big change in people's lives is somewhat harder than simply stating your aspirations. If the SNP would like us to believe that poverty and inequality will be reduced under independence, they need to show us why that is likely to be the case, not simply state that they would like it to be. So let's examine the real state of Scottish inequality in more detail.

TACKLING POVERTY AND INEQUALITY

In his recently published book, *Capital in the Twenty-First Century*, Thomas Piketty has exposed the scale of global income inequality, arguing that there are global forces encouraging convergence in incomes – including the rising demand for educated and skilled workers and expanding public spending and services – which could raise middle-class incomes. But even more powerful global forces, he suggests, are pushing in the other direction, and are likely to see inequality spiral upwards. On that side of the divide he puts the rising salaries and bonuses that financial-sector and business executives are able to command; the increased concentrations of inherited wealth; and the high interest rates paid on capital, which, rising faster than wages or economic growth itself, are widening inequality still further. Welfare systems and public spending which could redistribute resources to lower- and middle-income families through direct spending to the poorest areas and the poorest people are, he suggests, failing to do so in any significant way. And he also highlights the need for international coordination to prevent the avoidance and evasion of tax as increasingly wealthy citizens transfer their money to low-tax or no-tax jurisdictions. On its own neither America, nor Europe – and therefore not Britain – is now powerful enough to stop the drain of money to tax havens.[18]

So, if Piketty is right, many of the forces driving inequality are global in nature. It has proven hard enough for even big states like the UK to resist them entirely, even with a lot of resources at our disposal and under a Labour government completely committed to the task. An independent Scotland would have all these issues to deal with, plus a further challenge of wealthy Scots transferring their income and wealth between Scotland and the rest of the United Kingdom.

So let's start by understanding what an independent Scotland would have to do to reduce inequality. Only seven EU nations have a more unequal distribution of income than Scotland: Latvia, Bulgaria, Portugal, Spain, Greece, Romania and Lithuania.[19] Bear in mind Britain has a tax system that is intended to be redistributive – without it our inequality statistics would be even worse. Measured both before and after tax, Britain has high levels of inequality, and even if we exclude London (which has extreme wage inequality which makes it an outlier in Europe not just in Britain), then Scotland has similar problems with inequality to the rest of the UK.[20]

The biggest worldwide shift during the 1990s and in the first years of this new century has been the growing share of income taken by the top 1–2 per cent. Everywhere, without exception, their share has risen dramatically. In Scotland, as the economists David Eiser and David Comerford have graphically shown, the richest 1 per cent had 6.3 per cent of total pre-tax incomes in 1997, but 9.4 per cent by 2009.[21]

It is easy to blame that, as SNP rhetoric does, on bankers in the City of London. But in fact high-earners in Scotland's own financial services and associated industries have also been taking a greater share of Scotland's pie.

But income inequalities have grown not just because of this increased concentration of income at the top but because of long-term changes in the earning power of low-skilled, semi-skilled and skilled male manual workers. At the same time as the top 1 per cent were moving ahead, the bottom 10 per cent were falling further behind. In other words, both the top and the bottom of the income scale have seen workers pulling away from the average. The hollowing-out of the middle is happening in much of the West, but it is very acute in Scotland, where the detailed work of Eiser and Bell shows that the decline of heavy industry that we charted in Chapter 2 has caused a loss of jobs, a cut in wage levels, a loss of hours and is responsible for 'the major increases in inequality'.[22]

So Scotland and the UK stand out from the rest of the advanced economies of Europe not because overall levels of redistribution through tax have been much lower (Labour's tax reforms were more redistributive than many other nations) but because we start from a far higher level of pre-tax inequality in wages and salaries, due to the combined effect of high salaries and bonuses for top earners and the vastly diminished earning power of the old class of skilled and semi-skilled workers.

And so the real question is, as I found when in the Treasury, what national governments can do without coordinated international support to counteract these two new forces that may hit countries like the UK particularly hard, but are global in origin.

As Bell and Eiser have shown, the liabilities of the top 1 per cent of Scottish taxpayers rose under the policies of the Labour government from 14 per cent in 1997–8 to 20 per cent in 2009–10. Liability for the top 10 per cent rose from 40 per cent to 47 per cent. Likewise transfers through benefits did a lot to raise the take-home incomes of the lowest paid, meaning that the reduction in inequality was faster in the UK than in the industrialised world as a whole. As a result, even countries which have traditionally been thought of as more redistributive – countries like Sweden, Norway, Denmark and Finland – have seen their post-tax inequality rising in recent years, while Bell and Eiser state, 'there has been relatively little increase in inequality in Scotland across most of the distribution', concluding that 'higher taxes and higher benefits reduced the gap between rich and poor households. Accordingly, the inequality of household net income has not increased overall since 1997.'[23]

It is important to stress, though, that this outcome wasn't secured by accident. The Labour government deliberately set out to offset the impact of globalisation on wages with increased government help for families with children, and the elderly. The global forces that drive inequality are enormous – it takes focused government action for equality to even stand a chance.

I go into this history not because I am asking for credit for Labour's record, but simply because I want to explain why it is so hard to tackle the global forces making for greater inequality even when you have levers to pull which are as powerful as those to be found in the Treasury or Number 10.

So if we are serious about reducing inequalities in Scottish pre-tax earnings we have to re-equip the bottom and the middle with new skills to get jobs in areas where Scotland seeks to gain a competitive advantage, as well as address the remuneration of Scotland's owners, executives and managers without pretending top pay is somehow just a London issue.

So a credible pro-equality plan for a post-independence Scotland would focus on education and training, as well as redistribution. I am yet to see robust policies from the SNP on either. For example, altering the rates of Jobseeker's Allowance and Income Support, which would help the lower paid, would according to the Comerford and Eiser study achieve only a 0.15 per cent reduction in inequality even if rates were raised 10 per cent, yet it would be more difficult to achieve if we ended the pooling and sharing of resources inside the UK, and in particular the substantial fiscal transfers that help low-income Scots.[24]

TAXATION OF INCOME AND WEALTH

One of the arguments nationalists use about inequality under independence is that some countries – like Germany – have done a better job of tackling top pay than the UK, so an independent Scotland could simply adopt those policies and get the same benefit. But the countries they cite do not have the same dependence on financial services as Scotland and they do not begin from the same starting point, Scotland like Britain having historically higher levels of pre-tax remuneration at the top.

One of the big drivers of inequality in Scotland is that we have, in Edinburgh, some of the highest-paid financial staff in the Western world. The SNP know that – and it is one of the reasons they've refused to commit an independent Scotland to Labour's proposals for a 50p tax rate. Nor do they support a new top-rate band on council tax (a proposal supported not just by Labour but by the Conservative Mayor of London), or (when stamp duty is transferred to the Scottish Parliament) what is called a Mansion Tax, a higher rate of stamp duty for the most expensive house sales. They don't even support a tax on bankers' bonuses. In fact their main tax pledge is to cut corporation tax by up to 3 per cent, a move that will reduce revenues for public services.

So the SNP do not look to me to be serious about tackling inequality. But we should be clear that that isn't simply a political failing on their part as a party, it is actually a direct result of the notion of independence itself, which focuses on the constitutional status of the whole nation rather than the inequalities within it.

Having looked at the full menu of tax options available to the government of an independent Scotland, Eiser and Comerford found that the use of any of them would lead to minimal reductions in inequality, not least because the disparities between top and bottom in pre-tax income are still the biggest determinant of inequality.[25]

But Eiser and Comerford also remind us that, because we are part of an international economy, these reductions in inequality 'could be problematic because Scotland's high degree of integration with the rest of the UK means such policy change could trigger migration between countries'.[26] In other words, this is not like the old argument from the right that any action to increase UK tax or regulate the City would lead to everyone fleeing London for Geneva. Moving a family from Edinburgh to London, when one earner in the family already spends their working week in the capital, is not at all like uprooting a family from the UK to Switzerland.

So we need to be clear which options are actually available to an independent Scotland, and which are likely to be effective. For much of the last century domestic governments could raise capital-gains tax, inheritance tax and income tax and regulate monopolies in the interests of reducing inequalities in their own country. But today tough action taken in one country to deal with tax abuses is easily undermined by action to attract tax avoiders taken in another. Only heightened international cooperation – to tackle tax shelters, to curtail financial-sector excesses, to clamp down on global monopolies and cartels – can prevent people and companies switching income and wealth round the world.

All open economies, including that of Scotland, are vulnerable to this kind of capital flight, and the UK needs international partners to fight it successfully. So the one thing that is clear is that if we want the sort of global coordination which these issues require, a country with the clout of the UK is much more likely to secure the progressive change we need than Scotland ever could working on our own.

TRANSFERS OF INCOME

When we looked at the sharing union in Chapter 6 we saw how the British state redistributes resources across the United Kingdom to those in most need, especially to pensioners. In Scotland, this is achieved in no small measure due to the high level of spending on benefits and tax credits.

Last year, £3,335 per head of Scotland's population was spent on tax credits and benefits, compared to £3,275 for the UK as a whole. As a result Scotland receives more per head of our population for pensions – £1,805 versus £1,725 – than a population-weighted share would give us.[27] In fact, while 18.7 per cent of the claimant population in the UK are pensioners, the share of pensioners in Scotland is slightly higher, 19.2 per cent.[28] What's true for pensioners is also true for all claimants of disability benefits. We receive £375 million more in disability payments than a population-weighted allocation would give, with £365 spent per capita compared with the UK's £305 figure on all disability benefits.[29]

While we receive less in housing benefit (our rents are lower) and child benefit than a per-capita share would offer, we receive more in jobseeker's allowance, reflecting higher needs among the unemployed in Scotland. So we benefit from a substantial transfer of money, particularly to poor elderly Scots but also to the disabled and the unemployed.

Of course not all benefits help the poorest or relieve poverty. Many are universal benefits paid like the pension to all who are elderly. But when we look specifically at the scale of redistribution achieved through tax and cash benefits it is clear that the British state performs a substantial redistributive role through pooling and sharing our resources.

In both Scotland and the UK, nearly one person in every five is lifted out of poverty because of our taxes and benefit transfers. And while its progressivity has been reduced by the policies of the coalition government, the UK still achieves a greater level of redistribution to those in need than the North American countries and, indeed also, a greater level than some of the northern European and Scandinavian countries.[30]

In fact, without state intervention, 34 per cent of Scots and 35 per cent of UK citizens would be in poverty as a result of low earnings in the marketplace, but as a result of tax and benefits we reduce that figure to 15 per cent and 16 per cent, respectively. The key question is how much of the nearly poor are lifted out of poverty by tax and benefit transfers. America lifts only 26 per cent of its poor out of poverty, Canada 30 per cent and Australia 25 per cent. Germany does better (56 per cent).

France does better than most (62 per cent). But Britain is at the more progressive end of the spectrum and so too is Scotland. Scotland takes 56 per cent of the nearly poor out of poverty. The rest of the UK lifts 55 per cent from poverty. Of course we need to do more, but, at least until recently, the tax and benefit system appears to have a large redistributive effect in favour of the Scottish poor.[31]

The picture looks different, however, when we examine public spending as a whole in Scotland. While tax credits and benefits have a major egalitarian impact, the redistributive influence of public services is much lower. That may surprise no one when the biggest educational expenditure is on university students (about £6,500 per student a year in Scotland), who tend to come from middle- and upper-income groups. But the pattern is repeated in the major spending areas of schooling (£4 billion a year), and health (£10 billion a year), where the redistributive impact of public spending is far smaller than it could be. Universal benefits available only in Scotland account for £500 million of spending by the Scottish government, rising to over £800 million if we include the cost of student support.[32] The question is whether in pursuit of greater fairness governments pursue policies for 'universalism' – all receive the same benefit from services – or progressive universalism – where everyone can get something, but those most in need receive most.

The SNP has favoured the first approach, and while in an ideal world we would want to support everyone, it has meant fewer resources are available to target help where it is really needed. Clearly the SNP's council-tax freeze has been of far greater help to middle- and higher-income Scots than lower-income Scots. While the Scottish government analysis suggests the latter have benefited most, saving 1 per cent of household income, their figure doesn't factor in the effect of council-tax benefit, meaning that many poor households have, in effect, not paid the tax and therefore not made any saving. Indeed, the IFS reported in 2010 that 85 per cent of the poorest households in the UK would not have to meet the costs of a rise in council tax. The greatest benefits of the freeze, therefore, go to those in higher-income households. According to the Scottish government, council-tax payers in Band A properties have saved an average total of £258 since 2008, whereas those in Band H properties have saved £1,535.[33]

What is the overall impact of public spending on the pattern of inequality in Scotland? The ONS study *The Effects of Taxes and Benefits on Household Income, 2011/2012* concludes that in the UK 'the ratio of the richest fifth of households' final income to the poorest fifth's is reduced to less than four-to-one (£57,300 per year and £15,800, respectively)' after taxes and benefits have been factored in. In Scotland too there is a similar levelling effect, as the 'highest income decile has a pre-tax income almost 30 times the lowest income decile, but after tax and benefits the ratio is a little over 6'.[34]

But interestingly a higher proportion of Scots were likely to pay more in taxes than they received in benefits. According to the ONS, in 2010/11 fewer households in Scotland were paid more in benefits than they paid tax than the UK as a whole (52.7 per cent to 53.4 per cent). In total 1.232 million households in Scotland received more in benefits than they paid in tax, a marginally smaller share of households than in the UK as a whole.[35]

So the evidence is that the pooling and sharing that takes place within the social security system of the UK is more redistributive than the pooling and sharing across the public services of Scotland. Indeed when we look at how effective the Scottish government is in pooling and sharing, i.e. redistributing to those most in need, we find that the redistributive impact of public spending on health is limited. The Scottish government could have recognised that tackling the ill health and higher mortality rates of the poorer sections of our community needed additional support but instead they have targeted additional resources on free prescriptions, the main benefit of which goes to middle- and higher-income Scots who do not qualify for the means-tested free-prescription service as well as on free personal care.

Likewise it is clear that by concentrating resources on the universal service for free school meals at the expense of progressive reforms that would offer more to poor school-age children, like educational maintenance allowance to stay on at school, less money is available for areas and people in need. The redistributive effect in education is further limited by concentrating resources on the universal provision of free university tuition at the expense of the progressive element that would offer more to low-income students (a point I will return to later), and by allowing the gap in spending to grow from £4,500 per student in further education, to £6,500 per student per year in higher education.[36]

So whenever the choice was on offer, the Scottish government decided to favour universalism against progressive universalism, preferring to spread resources across everyone rather than target them on those who need help most. That is not, of course, inevitable as the policy consensus of an independent Scotland, but it certainly bodes ill for any Scottish families who are struggling and are assuming that the current Scottish government will be fighting hard for them in independence negotiations, or that it is somehow inevitable that fighting poverty will be top of the list of priorities in an independent Scotland.

Some people believe that the best answer to all this is devo-max, a system that would replace payments made directly from the UK to pensioners, incapacity-benefit claimants and low-income families with allocating money direct to the Scottish government to fund benefits at a level that it chooses. Interpersonal guarantees would be replaced by inter-regional guarantees. This is what is being considered in Belgium, where after being given a fixed annual allocation for services to pensioners, the regional governments will then take responsibility for setting the level of direct payments to individuals. But Bea Cantillon has shown in a study of the advantages of direct interpersonal transfers over inter-regional transfers that they are 'an extremely important instrument to guarantee fundamental social rights, to redistribute income and to combat poverty' because 'expanded "risk pooling" can better resist the consequences of economic and demographic shocks'.[37]

So having pensions and welfare policy organised at a UK-wide level still makes good sense if what you really care about is the widest possible pool from which to give intended beneficiaries the greatest protection against risk. Viewed in this way, independence would reduce the size of the pool across which we share risk and, as I will show, those most vulnerable are Scotland's older people.

Projections over the next twenty-five years suggest that the population of Scotland will rise from 5.22 million in 2010 to just over 5.76 million in 2035. Thereafter, the population is projected to continue rising, passing through the 6 million milestone in 2070 and reaching 6,158,000 in 2080. The number of people of pensionable age will rise from just over one million in 2010 to 1.32 million in 2035, whereas the number of people aged over 75 will increase by 82 per cent in the same period.[38]

The cost of pensions in an independent Scotland will rise from 5 per cent of national income in 2017–18 to nearly 8 per cent as early as 2062–3, according to the IFS.[39] And because the numbers in every other age group will decline, there will be a funding gap as National Insurance contributions from those who are in work will fail to keep pace.[40] But the current plans for independence pose severe risks to the continuity of public and private pensions in Scotland. In their policy paper, *Pensions in an Independent Scotland*, the Scottish government simply promises 'accrued rights will be honoured and protected' but they do not tell us that they will have to start afresh with a wholly new Scottish National

Insurance Fund having to be created in place of the British NI Fund, which would no longer be a fund that Scots are legally entitled to use.[41] What is even more troubling is a legal opinion by Lord Davidson QC that states that, while pensioners and prospective pensioners have paid in contributions to the UK Treasury and NI fund over many years in the expectation that the fund will guarantee their rights, they will have only a political promise, not a legal or constitutional guarantee, that their pensions will be paid.[42]

With higher outlays and large set-up costs the Scottish fund would struggle to register the 16.7 per cent annual surplus recommended for the British NI Fund.[43] And should an independent Scotland become a member of the EU, many UK pension schemes would become cross-border schemes (operating across more than one country). Not only would this incur greater administrative and regulatory costs, but EU regulations which forbid cross-border schemes from having deficits could potentially lead to their closure, which could have a massive impact on savers.[44]

This is especially crucial given that the pension deficit of Scottish private limited companies rose from £3.2 billion in 2012 to £6 billion in 2013, compared to a huge fall in UK private-sector pension deficits from £221.2 billion in 2012 to £27.6 billion in 2013.[45] The private sector shares these concerns: the head of pension research at Hargreaves Lansdown told the *Telegraph* that in an independent Scotland there would be 'poorer returns in the future on ISAs and Pensions due to higher administration costs'.[46]

This raises a vital question to which the people of Scotland are owed a decisive answer: how can the SNP claim independence would reduce poverty and inequality when their plans threaten the value and continuity of our pensions?

WHAT DO WE DO ABOUT IT?

The choice facing Scotland in September is not about whether we care about equality: it is about whether we want to stay in the arrangement that gives us the greatest chance of securing it.

We have seen how current claims about how inequality might be reduced after independence do not stand up to scrutiny, neither for pensioners promised a better deal, nor for workers demanding better-paid jobs, nor for young people demanding further education, nor for the general public promised fiscal policies that are more redistributive than Scandinavia.

But we are now discovering that inequality could be higher than in England if Scotland were to go independent.

EDUCATION

Perhaps the greatest impact a government can make to economic prospects is in the education of its citizens. It has therefore been one of the biggest surprises of all to me that in the independence debate the nationalists want to talk so little about education.

I have written in an earlier chapter of how there has always been a distinctive Scottish approach to education, that the broad-based leaving certificate of the 1960s and 1970s aimed to promote a 'democratic intellectualism'.[47]

Yet following detailed examination Paterson suggests that, since the 1990s, no unifying Scottish curricular philosophy has emerged and our traditional support for a broad curriculum that would teach children how to learn has sadly evaporated. He argues that the Curriculum for Excellence in the Scottish school system is 'not just a reform . . . It's a fundamental philosophical change . . . It will shape the way people think about knowledge, culture, and the role of citizens in a democracy.'[48] For while it marks a significant acceleration in the differentiation between

Scottish and English education, Scotland has, he suggests, chosen to demonstrate its distinctiveness in the wrong way – by rejecting what was always central to Scottish education, the foundational idea that everyone can learn the culture of the country and develop their critical faculties, no matter from what background they came and no matter where they would end up in life.[49]

The move away from traditional hierarchies of knowledge and indeed from respect for traditional knowledge takes many forms, Paterson argues. First, there is a new scepticism about subject boundaries and thus a failure to ground pupils in individual disciplines and to prepare them properly for interdisciplinary study. Second, there is scepticism about the distinction between theoretical and applied knowledge. Third, by undermining the specialisation of knowledge, we are 'marginalising' teachers as sources of knowledge. Fourth, there is a new scepticism about the benefits to children of education that they don't immediately 'enjoy'.[50]

The result is that 'the whole drift of thinking since Curriculum for Excellence has been away from rigour', but more importantly we are undermining what was surely the purpose of democratising education, which 'was to widen access to the most hierarchical structures of knowledge, not to change the structures of knowledge, but to give the people that were excluded from them access to them'.[51]

While Paterson draws out a more general truth that 'Scotland seems to need traditions at this moment in its history as a way of asserting its identity . . . [yet] Scotland has suddenly lost faith in its traditions of liberal universality', he focuses on four elements of the Scottish tradition that he says are all now at risk: the idea of cultivating virtue has gone; training in the use of the intellect rather than instilling character traits has gone also; little is now said of our adaptability as a cornerstone of our objectives for the curriculum; and finally the main aim of the education system – opportunity for all – is also under threat. Only what he considers a rather emaciated version of opportunity remains.[52] Indeed Scotland is allowing educational inequality to widen at precisely the point we should be equipping every child of every background to compete.

The key findings from those studying inequality over the period of university expansion since the 1960s is that general levels of attainment and participation were higher in Scotland; despite starting out facing greater inequalities, working-class Scots outperformed their English peers. Inequalities in participation in higher education (HE) initially rose as HE expanded in the early 1990s but then fell to a level lower than in the 1980s. But these inequalities are deep-seated, as the 'Growing Up in Scotland' study shows. By age three, average vocabulary scores for children from low-income households are already lower than for higher income households. By age five, the scores correspond to a 13-month gap in vocabulary development. And so by age 16 young people from the most advantaged neighbourhoods in Scotland, according to the recent Joseph Rowntree study, are five times more likely to gain a place in an ancient university. Issues of educational inequality are, they say, 'virtually invisible in the key documents that provide advice for schools', with no clear link between deprivation and per pupil spending. Nor do we do enough to cater for non-university 16–18-year-olds. By the late 1990s inequalities at age eighteen were substantially wider in Scotland than in England.

This suggests that while school helps Scottish children from poorer backgrounds more than it does in England, post-school education in Scotland has been deficient and needs to be improved. There has been a slowdown in educational attainment levels, particularly for boys, just at the time there is an increasing worldwide premium on graduate and postgraduate qualifications. So the current trends in Scottish education are exactly the opposite of what we need if we really want to reduce inequality in Scotland.

The SNP's commitment to free university tuition is so entrenched that Alex Salmond has said that 'rocks will melt in the sun' before tuition fees are reintroduced in any shape or form, yet a group of economists led by Sheila Riddell has argued that universal free tuition has 'not been redistributive in its effect' and that spending on programmes that increase access for poorer students to higher education was low compared to England, where three times as much was spent per capita in 2010/11.[53]

As fellow economist Lucy Blackburn has shown, the SNP have stripped the policy of its most progressive element by cutting student grants, which were non-repayable and awarded for each year of study, by around £1,000. The loss of this funding means that every student on a low income will need to borrow up to £2,100 more per year to fund their education, leading to overall debts of up to £26,000 for a four-year undergraduate degree, whereas students from richer families are less likely to require loans, meaning that they will graduate with little or no debt.[54]

And to maintain their universities policy it is now clear that colleges have been subject to cuts. The Scottish college population is now two-thirds that of 2007/08 and as a result there has been a more than 5 per cent reduction in the number of students entering Scottish higher-educational institutions between 2010/11 and 2011/12. While giving greater advantages to the wealthier university student, the shift from targeting support at those most in need has hurt the poorest college students the most.[55]

But just at the very time we need more focus on educational needs we are doing less, and just when investment should be rising it is being cut – with Scottish education sidelined as incidental not integral to the debate. Faced with this wide gulf between the skills young people have today and the skills they need, there is only one way forward in the modern world: we have no choice but to invest in the potential of our children. This means a focus on the strengthening of our schools, on tapping the great talents of our teachers and on reversing the damage done to our colleges. In R&D, it means collaborating across borders to lead the world in renewables, IT including video games, biotechnology and life sciences. Even for employers, corporation tax is of secondary importance to investing in education, training and research.

We have to ask why Scotland has shunned proven reforms from Teach First – bringing newly qualified graduates into schools – to Education Maintenance Allowances that have increased the numbers of teenagers staying on in England. All the powers that we need to improve our education already exist within Scotland, and are held by the Scottish Parliament. An education revolution can happen without a constitutional change. And yet when it comes to fighting inequality, those who most favour independence seem the most reluctant to do what must be done.

In these last two chapters on the economy and society, I have shown that, with or without an independent state, the fundamental policy issues facing Scotland arise from the challenges of responding to globalisation and that the key is to develop strategy for meeting and mastering global change. I have set out the risks of independence and shown that independence is at best a constitutional change in lieu of real change, a political solution that does not in itself answer the economic and social challenges that we must confront. And I have offered an alternative vision of how – through education and social mobility, through investment in trade and innovation, and through a greater attention to reducing poverty and inequality – we might maximise opportunity and minimise insecurity for millions of Scots. It is clear to me that we benefit from our trade links, collaboration in research and the reduction of insecurity through the pooling and sharing of resources in a British-wide system of guaranteed social and economic rights. Just as we led the attempts to mitigate the impact of the Industrial Revolution and to give it a human face, so too we are uniquely placed to show how we can create an equitable and sustainable response to globalisation.

AFTERWORD

THE CAMPAIGN

It was on Sunday, 7 September 2014 that the world woke up to the debate raging in Scotland over its constitutional future. Around the globe, newspaper headlines reported an opinion poll which suggested that a majority of Scots wanted their country to be an independent state. Scotland looked on course to join a list of nations starting with the US and including Ireland, India, Nigeria and many others that had broken with the United Kingdom.

In the days after the vote on 18 September, the Prime Minister David Cameron dismissed the fears of a late surge in support for the Yes campaign as an invention of pollsters. Speaking to Mayor Bloomberg, the Prime Minister said: 'It should never have been that close. It wasn't in the end, but there was a time in the middle of the campaign when it felt . . . I've said I want to find these polling companies and I want to sue them for my stomach ulcers because of what they put me through, you know. It was very nervous.'

We now know, however, that the private polls conducted in secret every day by the government itself were revealing exactly the same trend: a swing towards a majority for independence. Ten days before the referendum, it was time for the No campaign to make its final offer.

On the Monday, as the findings of the poll made waves around the world, I addressed a Labour rally in Midlothian and, after consulting with the main parties in Better Together, set out a timetable for delivering new powers to the Scottish Parliament. The powers included substantial extra responsibilities for the Scottish economy, tax and social policy. On this timetable, the government's White Paper would be published by St Andrew's Day at the end of November, and draft laws would be ready by Burns Night on 25 January 2015. In just over a year, a new Scotland Act would become law.

In the week that followed, I joined colleagues in addressing thousands of people who were now turning out in record numbers to campaign meetings and rallies. But in private, I argued forcibly that while our timetable for additional powers was important, it was not in itself enough to convince people that change was on its way. What really mattered was persuading people that Scotland had secured a wholehearted commitment from all the main United Kingdom parties to deliver these powers quickly. What the Scottish people needed to know was not so much the detail of the individual additional powers but that we were irrevocably committed to – and would deliver – faster, fairer, safer and better change than the nationalists could offer.

So the week culminated in the publication of 'The Vow' in the *Daily Record*, in which the leaders of the three main pro-devolution parties – the Prime Minister, Deputy Prime Minister and leader of the Labour Party – signed up to a promise to deliver change within the UK on the timetable I had previously outlined. And on 17 September, the day before the referendum, I joined the Better Together Chair, Alistair Darling, and the three pro-devolution Scottish Party leaders at the final Better Together rally in Maryhill, Glasgow, where each of us made a direct appeal to the people of Scotland to vote No.

I had never intended to return to frontline politics. I took the view after I left office in 2010 that newer and younger leaders were best equipped to make the strongest arguments about our future. But I could not just opt out of a debate and decision that I knew would have such profound consequences not just for my friends and family, but for my constituents and indeed all of the Scottish people. The referendum was quite unlike an ordinary election: we were making an irreversible decision that would have consequences for generations.

I started in 2013 by helping to organise a series of talks in my home county of Fife, where we tried to explore the history of Scotland and what would best meet the needs and aspirations of Scottish people in the future. Then, over the course of the final months of the campaign, I joined Labour and Better Together leaders in addressing nearly 100 meetings and rallies in cities, towns and villages across Scotland. From my home in Fife, I travelled to make speeches on behalf of both the Labour Party and Better Together in all the major cities – Glasgow, Edinburgh, Dundee and Aberdeen – and in every other part of the country where I was invited, including Perthshire, Lanarkshire, Ayrshire, Midlothian and the Borders. I spoke in schools and at pensioner forums, to the Royal British Legion and Carmelite Nuns, in almost all of Scotland's great universities and at a joint meeting in Glasgow, the largest meeting of all, comprising members of the Hindu, Christian, Sikh, Muslim and Jewish communities.

I listened, and this is what I heard: people wanted change. Whether it was because global economic forces were making their jobs less secure, of inferior status, lower paid, and restricting the opportunities for their children; or whether it was in response to concerns about the bedroom tax, food banks and fears for the future of public services, it became absolutely clear to me that people sought change.

But while in the referendum of 1997, the establishment of the Scottish Parliament was the 'settled will' of the Scottish people, it was evident throughout the referendum of 2014 that the nationalists' proposal for independence was not. Far from uniting the people of Scotland as the proposal for devolution had in 1997, independence divided the country.

For two years, Better Together focused on the economic risks of independence while the Yes campaign spoke of the economic benefits. Indeed, the nationalists sought to be relentlessly positive and constructed their campaign around their judgement that, as long as they appeared wildly optimistic about an independent Scotland's future, people would accept the validity of their case; and they could then attack Better Together for being 'relentlessly negative' and for 'doing Scotland down'.

My own interventions, which arose from the arguments articulated in this book, started from where some people did not: that the vast majority of Scots were not anti-British but felt more Scottish than British. This is the message I gave to the Prime Minister and Chancellor as early as the spring of 2012, when I met them in Budget week. I worried, as I told them, that the nationalists had conspired to make the choice look like one between Scotland and Britain – with the nationalists speaking exclusively for Scotland – when the choice should have been between two visions of Scotland's future: the nationalist vision, which was defined by the desire to break all links with the United Kingdom, against our patriotic vision.

It was because I believed that there was a positive, principled and patriotic case for a No vote that I sought to outline a vision in which sharing with Britain was an integral part of Scotland's future. I constantly reminded my audiences of our recent history, that over the last century Scots had abandoned their own separate Scottish welfare state – which had been called the Scottish

Poor Law – because they were the first to see the value of sharing and cooperating across 60 million people as part of a British welfare state. Sharing across the United Kingdom was, I argued, not an English imposition but a Scottish invention.

I also tried to show that, far from this being a hangover from the twentieth century, sharing and cooperation between nations was the way of the future for our increasingly interdependent world. In the coming years, many more nations will seek the benefits that come from pooling and sharing risks and resources.

The people of Scotland may have seen the benefits of interdependence, but I knew they also wanted change. I firmly believed it was vital to show them that the choice was not between the status quo and independence, but instead between change through further devolution, which carried little risk, and change through independence, which carried enormous risks. In announcing the timetable for a stronger Scottish Parliament, I sought to ensure that the choice being presented to the people of Scotland was a stark one.

The night before my final speech of the campaign in Maryhill, I decided to make my argument even more pointed and direct. This is reflected at one level by the fact that the speech ran to only 13 minutes, in contrast with the 30–45-minute stump speech that I had developed in the campaign! I remember waking up early on the morning of the 17th convinced that, in addition to focusing on the benefits of sharing and on exposing the economic risks of the SNP, we also had to make people feel proud about voting No and demonstrate that it was the patriotic thing to do.

But then, as I listened to the speeches that preceded me – spirited and eloquent testimonies from members of the public drawing on their personal experiences of the NHS, the shipbuilding industry, our education system and pensions – I kept reworking the emphasis of my argument in my head. So the speech I delivered turned out to be different in a number of respects from the formal text I issued to the press.

I began by saying that we were finally hearing from 'the real voices of Scotland' – nurses and patients, the young and the elderly – and that 'the silent majority would be silent no more'. And as I spoke about the benefits of sharing and cooperating across the United Kingdom, I reminded people that we had fought two world wars together. When young men were injured in the trenches they didn't look to each other and ask whether you were Scots or English – they came to each other's aid because we were part of a common cause.

I then sought to counter the claim made by some nationalists that No voters were less than patriotic Scots. I implored the public to 'tell them this is our Scotland'. For Scotland was not owned by the SNP, the Yes campaign or any politician: our country belonged to everyone. I wanted to remind listeners that you could be as proud and patriotic a Scot by voting No as you could by voting Yes.

I hope that what I said accorded with what the majority of Scots felt. While I had seen – and indeed predicted to friends – the dangerous decline in support for the No case as polling day drew closer, I never believed that we would lose. Thus, on the night of the referendum I was nervous only about the scale of the majority for No, which was to be far slimmer than I had originally hoped it would be. Having heard the exit polls and the first result – a clear No in Scotland's smallest local authority area, Clackmannanshire – I felt able to go to bed, and fell soundly asleep at the end of an intensive few days of campaigning around the country. I woke up at around 6 a.m. on Friday, 19 September, just as the nationalist leaders conceded defeat.

THE NEW RISKS TO THE UNITED KINGDOM

Jean Chrétien, Prime Minister of Canada at the time of its divisive referendum on separation with Quebec, wrote that there was six months of ill feeling before wounds started to heal. As someone who fought hard to keep the 300-year-old union between

Scotland and England intact, I have been able to survey at first hand the condition of Britain in the months since the referendum vote and it is best described as fragile. England's and Scotland's relations with each other are in need of being handled with care.

And it may surprise people to know that today I am more worried that the Union may dissolve through neglect and indifference from those outside Scotland than through rising pressure from and support for nationalism within. For if the United Kingdom were to falter now it would not, in my view, be because of Scotland's assertiveness or what may seem like unreasonable demands by the Scottish people to reopen a decision that has already been made, but rather due to the failures and mistaken calculations of the leaders of the United Kingdom – who have to ask themselves whether they are putting the survival of the UK second to other considerations.

Ronan Fanning's book, *The Fatal Path*, on the decisive events between 1910 and 1922 that led to Ireland breaking away from Britain shows how, for British politicians, the Irish question was never the pre-eminent consideration it appeared to be. In fact, even when violence in Ireland was at its height and hundreds of lives were being lost, solving the Irish question invariably came second, third or even fourth to what were seen as more important priorities.

Before the First World War, the greater concern of the then Prime Minister, Herbert Asquith, was keeping his Liberal government, then reliant on Irish nationalist MPs' votes, from falling. His secondary priority was to outmanoeuvre the Conservative opposition, who were themselves attempting to bring down the government by appeasing Ulster.

Between 1914 and 1918, Ireland understandably took second priority to winning the First World War. However, Britain's policy towards Ireland was influenced by the need to get a pro-Irish US on board for the war effort.

And after the war the then Prime Minister, David Lloyd George, calculated that to survive in office the Irish question had to take second place to preventing his Conservative-dominated coalition from walking away from him. Answering the Irish question always came second to other considerations.

So too, it seems, with the Scottish question.

For at seven on the morning after the referendum, in what immediately seemed to me like a kneejerk response to UKIP's English nationalism, the Prime Minister made an announcement in favour of what is commonly called 'English votes for English laws' (EVEL).

When carefully analysed, the Prime Minister's statement was not a proposal for greater English rights, but for fewer Scottish rights. By extending his proposed restriction on the rights of Scottish Members of Parliament to vote at Westminster to decisions as serious as income tax and the budget, he lit a fuse that to this day still threatens the integrity of the United Kingdom.

Almost immediately after the 7 a.m. broadcast, I phoned the Cabinet Secretary, to pass on my view to the government that this was the most ill-judged of interventions. While it may have been calculated to appease English nationalism, I stressed that it did so at the expense of Scotland and would sadly drive a wedge between Scotland and England.

The Prime Minister's speech from the steps of Downing Street meant that there was no happy aftermath in the wake of what was a historic victory. At the very time statesmanship was required to convince people that there was something fundamental about the integrity of the Union, it appeared we had descended into yet another round of political manoeuvring. From my standpoint, it was difficult to see how Britain could easily hold together in the long term if Scots were to be second-class representatives, unable to vote even on income tax decisions within our Union. At the very least, it would have been more appropriate for the Prime Minister to reveal the government's EVEL plans to the Scottish people before they voted in the referendum.

There is, in fact, no democratic country in the world whose main lawmaking body is made up of first and second classes of elected representatives. Yet in the preferred options set out in the government's command paper published on 16 December, 'the mother of parliaments', once lauded across the world as a beacon of fairness and equality, would become home to the first elected body in the world to decree one of its constituent parts – Scotland – half in, half out of its lawmaking process. Second-class status for Welsh and Northern Irish representatives might soon follow as the same principle is applied to the Union's other minority nations. But the issue of Scottish representation is not simply a Westminster insiders' issue, relevant only to the sensitivities of MPs; it is about the status and recognition of Scotland, Wales, Northern Ireland and England in what has hitherto been one United Kingdom. Since 1707, Scotland's representation has always enjoyed an equality of status in the UK. By according a first-class status to England within Westminster and a second-class status to the rest, the constitution would be changed forever.

Yet the proposals do not answer the main constitutional problem. The Conservatives presume that the fundamental issue in the British constitution is that Scottish MPs can vote on England-only laws whereas English MPs cannot vote on Scotland-only laws. But this is only a symptom of the problem. The central issue – and the real asymmetry – is the basic imbalance in the size of the four nations. England represents 84 per cent of the population of the UK, Scotland 8 per cent, Wales 5 per cent and Northern Ireland 3 per cent. When one nation is in the overwhelming majority, fairness of treatment requires sensitivity towards the needs of the minorities who could, at any time and on any issue, be outvoted – hence the devolution of power over time to Northern Ireland, then Scotland and then Wales. Fairness is better secured by rejecting the blanket uniformity of provision represented by 'English votes for English laws', in favour of mechanisms that protect the minority nations.

This is not a problem unique to Britain. The United States, Australia, Spain, Switzerland, South Africa, Mexico, Brazil, Nigeria and many other countries have had to find ways of managing the gross inequalities in the size of their constituent parts. So as the price for keeping their American union together, California accepts that it has just two members of the US Senate to represent 38 million of its citizens, while Wyoming has the same number – two senators – to represent its 500,000 people. Similarly, the price New South Wales pays for Australian unity is one senator for every 580,000 people, in contrast to Tasmania's one senator for every 40,000. And nor is fair treatment for minorities in the Spanish Senate, the Swiss Council of States, the South African National Council of Provinces and the Brazilian, Nigerian and Mexican Senates achieved by the crude uniformity of the EVEL approach, but through special arrangements that recognise minority needs in their states, regions or provinces.

I am, of course, sympathetic to the sensitivities of each nation that comprises the UK and recognise the concerns of Scotland's English neighbours. But Scotland does not seek an unfair advantage within the UK. What Scots want is for their right to join with other nations at the centre of our country's affairs to be upheld. And I believe that a consensual, common-sense solution can be found that meets the needs and aspirations of each nation. The interests of the majority can be safeguarded by practical changes in House of Commons committee proce-dures, rather than through the wholesale constitutional upheaval of creating two classes of MP at Westminster – with all the risk that brings.

This solution may contradict the statements of the Prime Minister in the immediate aftermath of the referendum but is, in fact, in line with the Conservative Party's Strathclyde Commission, which concluded that Scottish MPs, like Welsh and Northern Irish MPs, should continue to vote on all issues that come to the floor of the House of Commons. Its report stated:

In our view, it is important that any sense be resisted that MPs for Scottish, Welsh or Northern Irish constituencies somehow perform any lesser a function than MPs representing seats in England. The establishment of stable constitutional arrangements for the future of the UK must address this. It would be unfortunate if the feeling were to gain ground that there were two classes of MP. Even under a scheme of enhanced devolution, such as we have proposed in this report, MPs for Scottish constituencies will continue to have significant responsibility for safeguarding the interests of those whom they represent.

So it was not the intention of the Conservative Party, as stated by the Strathclyde Commission, to remove the right of Scottish MPs to vote on any issue at Westminster. If, as it seems, this is not now the position of the Conservative Party, it will only serve to fuel the demonstrations, petitions and allegations of betrayal, bad faith and breach of promise that have dominated the debate in Scotland since the vote.

Nationalists have, of course, dined out for centuries on the idea that the Scots were cheated of their freedom in 1707. Scotland's union with England was only possible, they argue, because of a betrayal by a 'parcel of rogues' bribed to sell Scotland out for a few pieces of gold.

Now a new myth of betrayal is emerging: Scots were cheated out of independence in 2014 by a cynical bribe in the form of a last-minute promise of more powers for the Scottish Parliament, a Vow that was then watered down by the Prime Minister's intervention only a few hours after the result. This has led First Minister Nicola Sturgeon to say that the outcome of the Smith Commission, which was set up to deliver the new powers, is 'not so much the home rule promised, in so many respects it's continued Westminster rule'.

Accusations of betrayal are an indispensable part of the nationalists' politics and their view of history. To persuade people to come on a journey with them that will always be about independence to the exclusion of all else, they need to argue that the Scottish people – particularly prospective Yes voters persuaded to vote No because of the Vow – were deceived by London.*

Make no mistake, the sour aftermath of the referendum still lingers. The Yes camps and No camps have yet to move away from the battleground and onto the common ground.

But while the immediate aftermath of the referendum has been difficult, there is hope in the new plans for an enhanced Scottish Parliament that will enjoy a far greater degree of autonomy but will also, in my view, continue to benefit from sharing and cooperating as part of the United Kingdom. By seizing the opportunities this new constitutional settlement presents, Scotland can be a path-breaker for other nations to follow in this interdependent twenty-first-century world.

THE REAL SIGNIFICANCE OF SCOTLAND'S DECISION

Some Scots will always think of themselves as forever deprived as members of a nation without a state. But while never anything other than a small nation, we have always been intelligent in the way we have charted our way in the world and I believe that we have always been ahead of our time.

In the eighteenth century, Scottish Enlightenment philosophers such as Adam Smith led the way in a Scotland that pioneered the very idea of cooperation across borders and a partnership between nations.

---

* In January 2015, Alex Salmond was quoted by *The Courier* as saying: 'I knew The Vow was an issue, it gave them momentum. The Vow was decisive. The fact that someone with credibility was delivering it was an added bonus. It was designed for the 10 per cent of people who were moving to Yes – the swing votes – who could be persuaded that they could still get progress for Scotland without voting Yes.'

From that time onwards, after Smith asked what it meant not just to be a citizen of your local community but also to be a citizen of the world, Scotland has always seemed far more internationalist and at least more outward-looking in its views than can be encapsulated simply in ideas popularised by a narrow nationalism.

Indeed, what inspired the European and Western Enlightenment was not only Adam Smith's idea, in his *Wealth of Nations*, of a world of free trade that transcended state-run mercantilism, but his even more powerful vision, in *The Theory of Moral Sentiments*, of a world linked together by empathy.

Of course, this was an underdeveloped idea in the eighteenth century. Smith said that if we had more information about the outside world and were able to communicate with others directly, then we would begin to see the connection between our interests and the interests of foreigners. In this way, our moral sense would become more highly developed and we would feel greater affinity with people outside our immediate sphere. Smith's 'circle of empathy' would lead to people feeling loyalties beyond their immediate family. He could see how in a connected and informed world, where our moral senses were better educated, we could feel the pain of others and believe in something bigger than ourselves.

This notion of wider interests underpinned the Scots' achievement in partnering England and Wales in the world's first Industrial Revolution. During that momentous and dramatic period of rapid change, Scotland produced some of the world's greatest inventors, starting with James Watt and his invention of the steam engine. But Scotland also gave the world some of its greatest social reformers.

And in the nineteenth and twentieth centuries, we pioneered a new way for citizens, especially for the poorest and most vulnerable, to cope with the traumatic changes wrought by industrialisation.

We abandoned our own distinctive system of Scottish welfare

– the Scottish Poor Law – to champion the idea of a UK-wide welfare state and National Health Service. In doing so, we led the way in demanding that every citizen of the modern world have not just civil and political rights, but social and economic rights too.

No other nations have been able to achieve what Scotland, England, Wales and Northern Ireland managed – to secure equal social and economic rights, as well as civil and political rights, irrespective of nationality. It is the Union that Europe aspires to be and, despite President Obama's nationwide healthcare reforms, a social union still remains beyond the capacity of the US.

And I want to suggest that the cross-border sharing that we pioneered a century ago in our multinational state is even more relevant today. For, in the new interdependent world of the twenty-first century, the path-breakers – the countries that will point the way to the future – will be those far-sighted communities who, while seizing all the advantages of autonomy, also secure all the benefits of cooperation and sharing between and across nations.

The most successful nations will be those who recognise that you are more powerful if at least some of your sovereignty is pooled and shared, and that cross-border cooperation is in fact the best way of securing the benefits of globalisation and ensuring they flow to your people.

And this belief, that there are advantages in greater cooperation across nations, stems from an ever more pressing reality, that all countries must now act together to tackle common causes, from financial instability and trade wars to climate change and terrorism. Whether it is through multinational organisations like the EU, Mercosur, ASEAN or more modest trade associations like NAFTA, which links Canada and Mexico to the US, countries will increasingly share sovereignty not at the expense of their national interest but in pursuit of it. The more open your economy is, the more you will need to – and indeed will have no choice but to – cooperate to maximise your economic potential and to protect yourself against shocks. And nowhere is this more relevant than in a Scottish economy that is far more dependent on trade than most other countries, and thus is far more exposed to the risks of recession and financial instability if the world does not cooperate and coordinate its responses when crises hit.

The idea of cooperating everywhere as the way of managing globalisation is of course difficult for citizens to accept anywhere, given the disruptive and chaotic impact globalisation has had on people's working lives and prospects.

In Scotland, as elsewhere, we have to understand and deal with both the economic and cultural concerns people expressed to me during the referendum about a globalisation that seems uncontrollable. Waves of global change continuously provoke an anger about jobs being lost and prosperity being put at risk as a result of decisions taken in far-off places and lead to understandable demands that decisions be brought closer to home. And while legislators have often been focused only on the political and constitutional reforms that might respond to the rise of nationalism, too often its economic and social roots have been neglected.

For it is a moot question why political nationalism, which has been seen mainly as a feature of Europe's era of industrialisation in the nineteenth century, passed us by. It was an aphorism that 'nineteenth-century nationalism carried off millions but in Scotland it only affected the mind'. But by asking *why* political nationalism moved from the fringes of the political scene – achieving only 0.5 per cent of the Scottish vote in the early 1950s – to centre stage as the majority government in a Scottish Parliament, we might discover what lies behind the disenchantment and anger that characterise much of the debate.

It seems to me that secessionist groups may be on the rise across Europe not in spite of these new global forces that have brought the free movement of capital, goods and people, but *because* of them. For just as in the years of the Industrial Revolution people turned to political nationalism to shelter and insulate their communities against uneven and inequitable patterns of growth, so too more and more people seem to be turning back to – and mobilising around – old loyalties and traditional identities. As we found as recently as the European election results of 2014, they are doing so as they seek to protect themselves against what appears to be an unstoppable juggernaut of economic disruption and social dislocation. To many, this is what globalisation means: a threat that could sweep aside long-established customs, values and ways of life.

You only need to look at the places where the independence vote was highest to see what threatens to shift Scotland from socialist to nationalist: Motherwell, which had lost its all-important Ravenscraig steelworks; Glasgow, which had lost most of its shipbuilding work; Clydebank, which had lost the world-renowned European base for Singer; Dundee, which had first lost its world-beating jute industry and then its replacement, European bases for the American companies Timex and NCR; Kilmarnock, which had lost Massey-Ferguson and then its whisky industry at Johnnie Walker; and Lanarkshire, which lost Gartcosh, Caterpillar and many other household-name companies.

These are permanent symbols of the traumatic collapse of Scotland's worldwide pre-eminence in steel, shipbuilding, engineering and textiles. These are the places where the pain of losing one million heavy-industry jobs has been felt the most. And these were the proud communities, home to some of the greatest skills of the industrial era, that considered the replacement jobs to be lower skilled, lower paid and of lower status in the poorest areas. The feeling has grown that there is little left to lose. It is this sense of loss that has done most to breathe life into a hitherto largely unsupported demand for a separate state.

But strongly felt as these sentiments are, it is important to recognise that to meet and master the challenges of globalisation you need more than a display of anger; you need a clear-headed strategy. Nationalists say that Scotland can be just like other small sovereign states that succeed best by being innovative and flexible. But there can be no comfort in just being innovative, adaptable and fleet of foot – important as these qualities are – if you are exposed and possibly overexposed to every up and every down of the global economy. You also need an answer as to how you best deal with global financial markets and the large international companies that can make decisions from afar that will affect your livelihoods and prospects for the future.

The Scottish people's rejection of separation showed that we are smart and forward-looking in our approach to the future: nations with strong and vibrant identities, even when under pressure to express that identity by going out wholly on their own, can instead choose to share and cooperate with their neighbours. On this view, the result in September can be seen not as 45 per cent of Scots voting to break all links with the United Kingdom, but as 55 per cent voting in favour of a connected world that is coming to recognise and act upon its interdependence. And instead of seeing ourselves as one of the first nations to turn down the chance of independence when we had the opportunity to vote for it, we might see ourselves as one of the first nations to vote for an interdependent future.

Indeed, we might conclude that even when the vast majority of Scots were visibly unhappy with the UK government of the day and were desperate for change, they looked at the realities of the modern age and decided that standing apart from their nearest neighbour made no sense. Of course, commentators will say that the No vote was just a negative vote cast out of fear, and that No voters were persuaded only by the catalogue of risks associated with a dramatic break with their long-term neighbours. But I interpret the vote more positively, as a choice made in favour of a path of cooperation, and one that bodes well for the future of other nation states that also have to decide how to make their future in this more connected world.

So it is important not to fall into a Conservative trap of

characterising a No vote as a validation of the status quo, or uncritically breathing sighs of relief that a potential outbreak of political nationalism was stopped in its tracks, especially when there is now concern that the saving of the Union is a secondary consideration for English nationalists in the rest of the United Kingdom. But might not the rest of the world now congratulate Scots on their self-awareness, their prescience and indeed their visionary outlook in rejecting on 18 September 2014 a proposal to retreat into the nineteenth-century world of independent states?

For I will always consider it a great achievement of the Scottish people that, faced with the chance of voting against an unpopular government, told for years that they would be better off independent because of a windfall of oil revenues coming their way and given the choice between a well-understood idea of independence against what has to be seen as a more futuristic idea – interdependence – we chose the latter.

We did not ignore the reality that we are inescapably part of something bigger. We said No to separation, No to ending solidarity and No to erecting a border between ourselves and the other nations of the UK. And we said Yes to interdependence, Yes to cooperation and Yes to working together for a common cause.

THE NEW SCOTTISH CONSTITUTION

Scots also said Yes to further devolution. In August 2014, two thirds of voters supported more devolution. On the eve of polling three quarters did so. Crucially, this increase reflected an apparent change of heart among many No supporters. Whereas in May a minority of no more than 47 per cent of No voters wanted more devolution, by August a majority of 53 per cent did, which increased to almost two in every three voters by the eve of the poll. In fact, by the time they voted only 28 per cent of No voters backed the status quo.

So it is right to move quickly to lock in the promises of further devolution and honour the timetable agreed by the pro-devolution parties with no new ifs, buts or strings attached. I believe that Scotland's new constitutional settlement can show what a proud nation that wants to play its part in our increasingly interconnected world could look like.

I envisage the parliament as enjoying far greater autonomy in a wide range of areas – from creating the jobs of the future to dealing with endemic poverty – but also sharing and cooperating with England, Wales and Northern Ireland to manage the economy, fund pensions and social security from the widest possible pool of contributors and ensure that we can do best by the poorest areas of the country by a continued willingness to transfer resources from the richest. In this way, Scotland's new constitutional settlement can become a model for how nations can work together to meet shared goals and prosper in the more integrated, interconnected and interdependent world of the future.

Even Yes voters, who may have thought that the only way forward was independence, may find it possible to support the new constitutional settlement arising from the recommendations of the Smith Commission because of the extensive powers that the Scottish Parliament will have. Contrary to the claims of betrayal and deceit following the referendum, the Smith Commission Report shows that the Vow will be delivered in full. And the 2015 Scotland Act will represent the most extensive transfer of power to Scotland in the history of Great Britain.

With the Scotland Act of 2015, Scotland will finally move the United Kingdom away from being one of the most centralised states in the world to one of the most decentralised. From 2016, Scotland will enjoy more autonomous spending power than the states in most federal regimes. It will start with an ability to spend £32 billion a year, which amounts to £6,500 for every Scot.

The Scottish Parliament will not only have more spending power but will also have more taxing power, receiving 62 per cent of its income either from its own decisions to tax its citizens' income or property or from assigned revenues from the UK value added sales tax.

The parliament will be able to devise new policies to help every Scot, from the youngest infant to the oldest pensioner, in employment and employability, in improving our social and economic fabric, in transforming our land use and ownership and in equipping Scotland for the global economic race ahead.

Vitally, the Scottish Parliament will also have the powers to advance social justice. Under the new constitutional settlement, the Scottish Parliament will be able to set the tax rate for the richest person in the country and to determine the level of benefits paid to the poorest. If it wishes, the Scottish Parliament will also be able to introduce new taxes and benefits.

But the new Scottish constitution also recognises the areas where it makes sense for Scotland to continue to share its decision-making with the rest of the UK, when in the interests of the Scottish people to do so. Thus we preserve the basic social and economic rights guaranteed to every citizen of Scotland, England, Wales and Northern Ireland: the right to help when unemployed, sick, elderly or poor; to basic education; and to free universal healthcare.

Foreign affairs also remain a UK responsibility, not least because we benefit from the combined resources of the UK in punching above our weight in international forums. Scotland does not have the population size that would enable us to enter the UN Security Council, G7, G8, G20, the global Financial Stability Board or the senior decision-making committees of the IMF or the World Bank. Defence is similarly a shared responsibility, because despite well-advertised disagreements over the future of nuclear weapons, the majority of Scots recognise a common interest in defending our borders.

And the macro-management of the economy is, as the nationalists themselves acknowledged during the referendum, best conducted on a UK-wide basis, with decisions about interest rates, inflation targets and growth objectives best made in concert with our neighbours, with whom we conduct 70 per cent of our trade. The argument that was eloquently put by Alistair Darling during the referendum campaign convinced a majority of Scots that as part of a common currency we can enjoy greater economic stability, we can better underpin our common trading relationships and we can protect ourselves against financial crises, the kinds of economic shocks that we are now seeing on a more regular basis.

But even with the overall economy and most of social security still managed on a UK-wide basis, the Scotland Act 2015 will bring the United Kingdom as close to federalism as it can be in a country where 85 per cent of its population is in one constituent part, England. And when it is implemented, the challenge will be to demonstrate that the best deal for the people of Scotland is to combine the resources of the Scottish Parliament with the resources of the United Kingdom. This may not enable us to meet the test set by the nationalists, which asks whether Scotland has the most power possible in its own separate parliament. But it does enable us to meet the test that the Scottish people are setting for us, which asks what gives them the most control over their lives.

REFRAMING THE DEBATE

It is clear, therefore, that the new constitutional settlement affords us an opportunity to address some of the most profound challenges facing Scotland in the coming generation. But it will also enable us to challenge the prevailing nationalist narrative that we do not have the powers in Scotland to change people's lives for the better. No longer will anyone be able to say that we cannot act because of London rule, or that it is impossible because

Westminster has dictated otherwise. The old game was blaming London when things went wrong. The brave new world is taking responsibility for our own mistakes.

Take the bedroom tax as an illustration. Scotland quickly concluded that the bedroom tax was an offensive and damaging measure that should not be implemented here. At first, the Scottish government said that it was powerless to act. After two years, it decided it could mitigate the effects of the bedroom tax, while continuing to blame London for its severity. Under the new Scottish constitution, there is no dispute about the power the Scottish Parliament can wield.

Indeed, if the Scottish Parliament disapproves of any measure like the bedroom tax, it can amend it. If it wants to pay the housing benefit that the London Welfare Secretary removed, it can do so. It has the authority to top up any benefit. No longer can we hold London wholly culpable when things are not right.

And so the debates of the future in Scotland will be fundamentally different from the debates of the past. For years, it did indeed have all the elements of a blame game. For years, it was about manufacturing gripes and grievances against London as your means of trying to convince electors that you were standing up for Scotland. For years, it was about cataloguing your complaints against Westminster rule or misrule and claiming your legitimacy to speak for Scotland derived from that. The more vociferous the complaints against London, the more you argued you were speaking for Scotland.

Now the world is different. The person who shouts the loudest against London will never again be seen as the person who is standing up for Scotland most effectively. Standing up for Scotland now means using the extensive powers of the Scottish Parliament to meet the needs and aspirations of the Scottish people.

RENEWING SCOTTISH CIVIC SOCIETY

There is one final concern vital to Scotland's future as a community that I want to address. I have argued throughout this book that Scotland has suffered as a result of the weakening of the authority and status of our civic institutions, from our churches and trade unions to our sports and voluntary clubs and municipal authorities. Once they spoke for Scotland and were listened to. Through them, 'Scottishness' was expressed in an apolitical form of nationalism. You could be Scottish without being a political nationalist and you would identify yourself as a patriotic Scot through your membership of a Scottish church, a Scottish-based trade union and all kinds of Scottish civic associations. But today, as their influence weakens, how do you now express yourself as a Scot?

The Scots of 2015 feel no less Scottish, and any proud Scot will always need a way of expressing his pride beyond support for Scotland at football, rugby, curling or golf and at sporting and cultural events like the Commonwealth Games. All of us need ways and means of expressing our identity. But the decline of our civic institutions has created a void and into it has come a resurgent political nationalism, and a party that claims to be the premier institution standing for Scotland.

Once our Scottish identity was expressed through our civic institutions. Today, the Scottish government would like the voice of Scotland to be the SNP. This is not healthy, even if you are a political nationalist. For when the void created by the decay or disappearance of strong Scottish civic institutions is filled primarily by a political movement linking the individual to the state, Scottish identity becomes something different. The adoption of the Scottish flag, which should be a unifying symbol for the whole nation, as a symbol of political nationalism is just one example. Too often in the referendum, the Saltire seemed more like a weapon to be used by nationalists against their opponents than a flag for the whole country.

We need to think about how we can revive civic society. Social media is of course the new ingredient for contact, communication, debate and community, but we need people from all walks of life to examine how we can breathe new life into existing Scottish civic institutions and create vibrant new ones that can become central to our communal life with a new relevance and authority for the years ahead.

One idea has come from the former head of STV and prominent author Alistair Moffat. The great thing about Scottish people is, he says, that we love to disagree with each other in public. We disagree without being disagreeable. And we love to listen, learn and draw lessons from what we have heard. In fact, Scotland has more book festivals per capita than any other country in the world. I believe that there is merit in what Alistair has called 'Engage' forums to fill the space between the state and the individual, where people can freely discuss ideas about Scotland, the UK and the world.

I sense my fellow Scots are hungry for conversation, participation and debate. In the past two years, Scottish politics has not been confined to parliaments and committees; it has been in our streets, our shops, our workplaces, our community centres, our clubs and our pubs. Now is not the time to stop engaging, but to embark upon a new national conversation with a bigger purpose: to debate and chart our nation's future in the decades ahead.

CONCLUSION

In 1962, President Kennedy called for the US Declaration of Independence of the 1770s to be complemented by a Declaration of Interdependence of the 1960s.

And I have argued that Scotland's rejection of independence in favour of interdependence in September 2014 places Scotland at the very heart of today's progressive movements for change.

I suggest that, with its new constitutional settlement, Scotland does not need the trappings of the old nineteenth-century state to play our full part on the world stage in the twenty-first century. Instead, we can be pacesetters for a new and different path to the future – one that, in time, nation after nation will follow as the better way of responding to the challenges of a more interdependent world.

And we should start by showing that we can bring a divided nation – Scotland – and a divided state – the United Kingdom – back together again.

NOTES

INTRODUCTION

1 Susan Swarbick, 'Actor McGregor backs the Union', *The Herald*, 2 April 2012.
2 Jonathan Freedland, 'As the Ukraine debate rages, both sides are getting it wrong', *Guardian*, 7 March 2014. Online at: http://www.theguardian.com/commentisfree/2014/mar/07/ukraine-debate-both-sides-wrong
3 John Curtice et al. (eds.), *British Social Attitudes: The 30th Report* (NatCen Social Research, 2013), p.145.
4 CBI, 'The Scottish Government's Plans for Independence: An Analysis from Business' (2014), p.3.
5 Scott Macab, 'Scottish Independence poll: Yes losing momentum', *Scotland on Sunday*, 23 February 2014.
6 House of Commons Library (HOCL).
7 Norman Davies, *Vanished Kingdoms: The History of Half-Forgotten Europe* (Allen Lane, 2011); and Ernest Gellner, *Nations and Nationalism* (Cornell University Press, 2nd edition, 2009).
8 Ewen A. Cameron, *Impaled Upon a Thistle: Scotland Since 1880* (Edinburgh University Press, 2010), p.203.
9 A. K. Cairncross (ed.), *The Scottish Economy: A Statistical Account of Scottish Life by Members of the Staff of Glasgow University* (Cambridge University Press, 1954).
10 ibid.
11 ibid.
12 ibid.

13 ibid.
14 ibid.
15 ibid.
16 ibid.
17 ibid.
18 ibid.
19 Scottish Government, *New House Building* (2013). Online at: http://www.scotland.gov.uk/Resource/0043/00439840.xls, author's own calculation; and HOCL.
20 Cairncross (ed.), *The Scottish Economy*.
21 Cairncross (ed.), *The Scottish Economy*; and W. W. Knox, *A History of the Scottish People: Religion in Scotland, 1840–1940*. Online at: http://www.scran.ac.uk/scotland/pdf/SP2_8religion.pdf
22 HOCL.
23 General Register Office for Scotland, Vital Events Reference Tables 2012, Table 7.3a, 'Mean age at marriage, by sex and marital status, Scotland, 1855 to 2012', p.4. Online at: http://www.gro-scotland.gov.uk/statistics/theme/vital-events/general/ref-tables/2012/section-7-marriages-and-civil-partnerships.html
24 HOCL.
25 ibid.
26 David McCrone, 'A New Scotland? Society and Culture' in T. M. Devine and Jenny Wormald, *The Oxford Handbook of Modern Scottish History* (Oxford University Press, 2012), pp.678–9.
27 'Mark Twain', History.com, online at: http://www.history.com/topics/mark-twain
28 Author's own research on the local history of Fife.
29 T. M. Devine, Lecture to the Glasgow Centre for Population Health, 6 December 2005. Online at http://www.gcph.co.uk/assets/0000/0350/Tom_Devine_Transcript.pdf
30 ibid.
31 William McIlvanney, *Surviving the Shipwreck* (Mainstream Publishing Company Ltd, 1991).
32 Cairncross (ed.), *The Scottish Economy*; and Grahame Smith, Address to the 45th Plenary Session of the British-Irish Parliamentary Assembly, 22 October 2012. Online at: http://www.britishirish.org/address-by-grahame-smith-scottish-trade-union-congress-to-45th-plenary-in-glasgow/
33 W. W. Knox, *Industrial Nation: Work, Culture and Society in Scotland, 1800–Present* (Edinburgh University Press, 1999).
34 Michael Rosie, 'Tall Tales: Religion and Scottish Independence', *What Scotland Thinks*, 15 August 2013. Online at: http://blog.whatscotland-thinks.org/2013/08/tall-tales-religion-and-scottish-independence/;

Reeval Alderson, 'The revolution which created the Church of Scotland', *BBC News*, 24 August 2010. Online at: http://www.bbc.co.uk/news/uk-scotland-11065965; and National Records of Scotland, 'Table 7: Religion, Scotland, 2001 and 2011', online at: http://www.scotlandscensus.gov.uk/documents/censusresults/release2a/rel2asbtable7.pdf

35 HOCL.

36 HOCL, author's own calculation.

37 Ian Rankin, 'Worlds Within Worlds' in M. d'Ancona (ed.), *Being British* (Mainstream Publishing Company, 2009), pp.35–6.

38 HOCL.

39 ibid.

40 Gordon Brown, *Courage: Eight Portraits* (Bloomsbury Publishing, 2007), p.35.

41 Craig Calhoun, 'Imagining Solidarity: Cosmopolitanism, Constitutional Patriotism, and the Public Sphere' in *Public Culture*, Vol. 14, No.1 (2002), pp.150–8.

CHAPTER 1

1 T. M. Devine, *To the Ends of the Earth: Scotland's Global Diaspora, 1750–2010* (Penguin, 2012).

2 Christopher Smout, 'Land and Sea: The Environment' in T. M. Devine and Jenny Wormald (eds.), *The Oxford Handbook of Modern Scottish History* (Oxford University Press, 2012), pp.34–8.

3 T. M. Devine, 'Scotland's Global Diaspora', Royal Society of Edinburgh Christmas Lecture, 12 December 2011

4 Alexander Smith, *The Third Statistical Account of Scotland: The County of Fife* (Oliver and Boyd, 1952).

5 Author's own research on the local history of Fife.

6 A. K. Cairncross (ed.), *The Scottish Economy: A Statistical Account of Scottish Life by Members of the Staff of Glasgow University* (Cambridge University Press, 1954); and Jim Tomlinson, 'The Economic basis of Scottish Nationhood since 1870' (2014), p.3.

7 Cairncross (ed.), *The Scottish Economy.*

8 William McIlvanney, *Docherty* (Canongate Books, 2013). First published in 1975.

9 ibid.

10 J. J. Smyth, 'Social change and economic life in Kirkcaldy, 1891–1987: sources and methods, a historical perspective' in David McCrone et al. (eds.), *Interpreting the Past, Understanding the Present* (Macmillan, 1990), pp.83–99.

11 Kenneth Roy, *The Invisible Spirit: A Life of Post-War Scotland 1945–75* (ICS Books, 2013).

12 T. M. Devine and Jenny Wormald, 'Introduction: The Study of Modern Scottish History' in Devine and Wormald (eds.), *The Oxford Handbook of Modern Scottish History*, pp.1, 2, 8.

13 Marc Lambert, 'Grasping the Fizzle: Culture, Identity and Independence' in G. Hassan and J. Mitchell (eds.) *After Independence: The State of the Scottish Nation* (Luath Press, 2013).

14 ibid.

15 Rosemary Goring, 'Was There A Scottish Renaissance?' in *Scottish Review of Books,* Vol. 9, No. 4 (2013).

16 Alex Thomson, '"You can't get there from here": Devolution and Scottish literary history' in *International Journal of Scottish Literature*, Issue 3 (Autumn/Winter 2007), p.10.

17 Robert Crawford, *Scotland's Books: The Penguin History of Scottish Literature* (Penguin Books, 2007), p.653.

18 Hugh MacDiarmid, *A Drunk Man Looks at the Thistle* (Birlin, 2008).

19 Allan Cunningham, *The Works of Robert Burns with His Life: Volume 1* (James Cochrane and Co., 1834), pp.10, 146, 172; and 'Robert Burns and Radicalism', BBC History, online at: http://www.bbc.co.uk/history/ scottishhistory/enlightenment/features_enlightenment_radicals.shtml

20 British Future, *State of the Nation 2014* (2014), p.24.

21 Hugh Keevins, 'I'm riding off into the sunset at a time it's not looking too bright for our national game', *Sunday Mail*, 13 April 2014.

22 Colin Kidd, *Union and Unionisms: Political Thought in Scotland, 1500–2000* (Cambridge University Press, 2008).

23 Kidd, 'The Union and the Constitution', *History and Policy*, September 2012. Online at: http://www.historyandpolicy.org/papers/policy-paper-137.html

24 T. M. Devine, 'In Bed with an Elephant: Almost Three Hundred Years of the Anglo-Scottish Union' in *Scottish Affairs*, no. 57, (Autumn 2006), p.7.

25 Cairncross (ed.), *The Scottish Economy*.

26 ibid.

27 ibid.

28 ibid.

29 David McCrone, *Understanding Scotland: The Sociology of a Nation* (Routledge, 2nd edition, 2001),

30 Kidd, 'The Union and the Constitution'.

31 ibid.

32 W. W. Knox, *A History of the Scottish People: Religion in Scotland, 1840–1940*. Online at: http://www.scran.ac.uk/scotland/pdf/SP2_8religion.pdf

33 C. G. Brown, *The Social History of Religion in Scotland since 1730* (Routledge, 1987), p.187.

34 Brown, *Maxton* (Mainstream Publishing, 1986), pp.9–15; and Ewen A. Cameron, *Impaled Upon a Thistle: Scotland Since 1880* (Edinburgh University Press, 2010), p.156.

35 Kidd, *Union and Unionisms*.

36 Donald M. McFarlan, *First For Boys: The Story of the Boys' Brigade 1883–1983* (Collins, 1982).

37 Anthony D. Smith, *Nationalism: Theory, Ideology, History* (London, 2001), p.18.

38 Lord Sumption, 'The Disunited Kingdom: England, Ireland and Scotland', Lecture to the Denning Society, 5 November 2013, p.23.

39 ibid.

40 Ernest Renan, 'What Is a Nation?' in Geoff Eley and Ronald Grigor Suny, (eds.), *Becoming National: A Reader* (Oxford University Press, 1996), pp.52–4.

41 Yael Tamir, *Liberal Nationalism* (Princeton University Press, 1993), p.84.

42 ibid. p.65.

43 Lambert, 'Grasping the Fizzle'.

44 Alistair Moffat, *The Scots: A Genetic Journey* (Birlinn, 2012); and Moffat, *The British: A Genetic Journey* (Birlinn, 2013); and Daniel Defoe, 'The True Born Englishman', online at: http://www.poetryfoundation.org/poem/173337

45 ibid.

46 Moffat, *The Scots*; and Moffat, *The British*.

47 Devine, 'In Bed with an Elephant', p.8.

48 Laia Balcells, 'Mass Schooling and Catalan Nationalism', *Nationalism and Ethnic Politics*, (19:4), 2013, pp.467–486.

49 Eric Hobsbawm, 'Introduction: Inventing Traditions' in Eric Hobsbawm and Terence Ranger (eds.), *The Invention of Tradition* (Cambridge University Press, 1983), p.1.

50 Devine, 'Carving out a Scottish Identity', *The Scotsman*, 3 October 2013.

51 Devine, *To the Ends of the Earth*.

52 Tom Nairn, 'Globalization and Nationalism: The New Deal', 16th Edinburgh Lecture, 4 March 2008.

CHAPTER 2

1 Peter Kellner et al., *The Sceptered Isle* (British Future, 2012), pp.2, 5, 13–15.

2 House of Commons Library (HOCL).

3 ibid.

4 ibid.

5 HOCL; and Grahame Smith, Address to the 45th Plenary Session of the British-Irish Parliamentary Assembly, 22 October 2012. Online at: http://www.britishirish.org/address-by-grahame-smith-scottish-trade-union-congress-to-45th-plenary-in-glasgow/

6 HOCL.

7 ibid.

8 ibid.

9 ibid.

10 Scotland's Census 2011, 'Release 2A: KS103C, Marital and civil partnership status'.

11 HOCL.

12 ibid.

13 HOCL; and Smith, Address to the 45th Plenary Session.

14 ibid.

15 HOCL.

16 ibid.

17 ibid.

18 Craig Brown, 'Church of Scotland "struggling to stay alive"', *The Scotsman*, 29 April 2014; and Brian Donnelly, 'Census reveals huge rise in number of non-religious Scots', *The Herald*, 27 September 2013.

19 HOCL.

20 National Records of Scotland, '2011 Census: Key Results on Population, Ethnicity, Identity, Language, Religion, Health, Housing and Accommodation in Scotland – Release 2A', 26 September 2013; and Donnelly, 'Census figures reveal huge rise in non-religious Scots'.

21 John Baillie, *Prospects for Spiritual Renewal* (Blackwood, 1943), pp.7–8.

22 Home Office, 'Report of the Committee on Homosexual Offences' (HM Stationery Office, 1957), p.115.

23 'Report of Wolfenden Committee', *The Herald*, 27 May 1958.

24 Kenneth Roy, *The Invisible Spirit: A Life of Post-War Scotland 1945–75* (ICS Books, 2013).

25 Gerry Hassan, 'The Emergence of the "Third Scotland"' in *Scottish Review*, 12 September 2013.

26 Crawford, *Scotland's Books: The Penguin History of Scottish Literature* (Penguin Books, 2007), p.672.

27 Alex Niven, 'Forget Cool Britannia – we need to reclaim the subversive spirit of 1994', *Guardian*, 13 April 2014. Online at: http://www.theguardian.com/commentisfree/2014/apr/13/forget-cool-britannia-reclaim-subversive-spirit-1994

28 Alasdair Gray, *Lanark: A Life in Four Books* (Canongate Press, 1981).

29 Crawford, *Scotland's Books*, p.668.

30 Alex Thomson, '"You can't get there from here": Devolution and Scottish literary history' in *International Journal of Scottish Literature*, Issue 3, Autumn/Winter 2007, p.6.

31 Thomson, '"You can't get there from here"', pp.8–10.

32 James Robertson, *Voyage of Intent: Sonnets and Essays from the Scottish Parliament* (Luath Press, 2005).

33 'The Media in Figures: Scots circulations of national newspapers', *All Media Scotland*, 10 March 2014. Online at: http://www.allmediascotland. com/press/61604/the-media-in-figures-scots-circulations-of-national-newspapers-2/

34 Carol Craig, *The Scots' Crisis of Confidence* (Argyll Publishing, 2nd edition, 2011); and Carol Craig, *The Great Takeover: How materialism, the media and markets now dominate our lives* (Argyll Publishing, 2012).

35 Craig, *The Scots' Crisis of Confidence*; and Craig, *The Great Takeover*.

36 Harry Reid, 'Where are the women to speak for Scotland?', *The Herald*, 24 August 2010.

37 John Curtice, 'Future Identities: Changing identities in the UK – the next 10 years' (HM Government, 2013), p.14.

38 ibid.

39 John Curtice et al. (eds.), *British Social Attitudes: The 30th Report* (NatCon Social Research, 2013), p.145.

40 ibid.

41 Curtice, 'Future Identities'.

42 John Curtice, 'Who supports and opposes independence – and why?' (NatCen Social Research, 2013), p.4.

43 ibid. p.5.

44 ibid. p.8.

45 T. M. Devine, 'Carving Out a Scottish Identity', *The Scotsman*, 3 October 2013.

46 'Douglas Alexander's speech on the Scottish independence referendum: full text', *New Statesman*, 20 September 2013. Online at: http://www. newstatesman.com/politics/2013/09/douglas-alexanders-speech-scottish-independence referendum-full-text

47 Douglas Alexander, 'Scotland's tech-savvy first-time voters will reject independence as they understand the value of being connected', *Daily Record*, 26 January 2014. Online at: http://www.dailyrecord.co.uk/news/ politics/labour-mp-douglas-alexander-scotlands-3062825

48 Devine, 'Carving Out a Scottish Identity'.

49 Fonna Forman-Barzali, *Adam Smith and the Circles of Sympathy: Cosmopolitan and Moral Theory* (Cambridge University Press, 2011).

50 ibid.
51 ibid.

CHAPTER 3

1 Frank Earle, *Reconstruction in the Secondary School* (University of London Press, 1944), p.72.
2 L. Paterson, 'George Davie' in G. Graham (ed.), *Oxford History of Scottish Philosophy* (Oxford University Press, 2015 [forthcoming]).
3 William Storrar, *Scottish Identity: A Christian Vision* (Handsel, 1990), p.3.
4 Lesley Riddoch, *Blossom: What Scotland Needs to Flourish* (Luath, 2013).
5 James Reid, 'Alienation', Rectorial Address delivered in the University of Glasgow on Friday, 28 April 1972. Online at: http://www.gla.ac.uk/media/media_167194_en.pdf
6 R. A. Houston, *Scottish Literacy and the Scottish Identity: Literacy and Society in Scotland and England, 1660–1850* (Cambridge University Press, 1989).
7 R. Anderson, 'The History of Scottish Education, pre-1980' in T. Bryce & W. Humes (eds.), *Scottish Education* (Edinburgh University Press, 3rd edition, 2008), pp.205–14; and Ian Carter, *Farm Life in Northeast Scotland, 1840–1914* (John Donald Publishers Ltd, 1997).
8 George E. Davie, *The Democratic Intellect: Scotland and Her Universities in the Nineteenth Century* (Edinburgh University Press, 1964).
9 L. Paterson, 'Competitive opportunity and liberal culture: the significance of Scottish education in the twentieth century' in *British Educational Research Journal,* Vol. 40, Issue 2 (2014), pp.397–416.
10 House of Commons Library (HOCL).
11 Adam Smith, *The Theory of Moral Sentiments* (1759), I.i.5.
12 Smith, *The Theory of Moral Sentiments*, VI.ii.1.
13 L. Paterson, 'Civil society and democratic renewal' in S. Baron, J. Field and T. Schuller (eds.), *Social Capital: Critical Perspectives* (Oxford University Press, 2000), pp.39–55.
14 Nicholas Phillipson, *Adam Smith: An Enlightened Life* (Penguin, 2011).
15 ScotCen, *Is Scotland more left-wing than England?* (2011). Available online at: http://www.natcen.ac.uk/media/176048/2011-is-scotland-more-left-wing-than-england.pdf
16 ScotCen, *Is it really all just about economics? Issues of nationhood and welfare* (2014). Available online at: http://www.scotcen.org.uk/media/265694/ssa_is-it-really-all-just-about-economics.pdf
17 William McIlvanney, *Surviving the Shipwreck* (Mainstream Publishing, 1991).

CHAPTER 4

1 See, e.g., 'Few Celebrations on 300th anniversary of union with Scotland', *Guardian,* 1 May 2007; '300 years on, and where is the big party to celebrate Union?', *The Scotsman,* 16 January 2007.

2 Alvin Jackson, *The Two Unions: Ireland, Scotland, and the Survival of the United Kingdom, 1707–2007* (Oxford University Press, 2011), pp.340–1.

3 Linda Colley, *Acts of Union and Disunion* (Profile, 2014).

4 *MacCormick v Lord Advocate* (1953) SC 396.

5 James Mitchell, 'The Westminster model and the State of Unions', *Parliamentary Affairs,* Vol. 63, No. 1 (2010), pp.85–8. Available online at: http://pa.oxfordjournals.org/content/early/2009/12/11/pa.gsp052.full

6 Stein Rokkan and Derek W. Urwin (ed.), *The Politics of Territorial Identity: Studies in European Regionalism* (Sage, 1982), p.11.

7 T. M. Devine, *The Scottish Nation: A Modern History* (Penguin, 2012), pp.84–102.

8 Nicholas Phillipson, *Adam Smith: An Enlightened Life* (Penguin, 2011).

9 L. Paterson, *The Autonomy of Modern Scotland,* (Edinburgh University Press, 1994).

10 Tom Nairn, *Faces of Nationalism: Janus Revisited* (Verso, 1998), p.210.

11 C. Whatley, 'Taking Stock: Scotland at the End of the Seventeenth Century' in T. C. Smout (ed.), *Anglo-Scottish Relations from 1603 to 1900* (Oxford University Press, 2004), pp.103–25.

12 Maurice Lee Jr, *The 'Inevitable' Union: And Other Essays on Early Modern Scotland* (Birlinn, 2004).

13 Devine, *The Scottish Nation,* p.7.

14 Ian Levitt, 'Scotland and its financial relationship with the UK in the 19th century', Stenton Symposium, University of Reading, 22 November 2013.

15 Colin Kidd, *Union and Unionism: Political Thought in Scotland, 1500–2000* (Cambridge University Press, 2008).

16 Devine, *The Scottish Nation,* p.213.

17 Daniel Defoe, *A Tour Thro' the Whole Island of Great Britain* (1726), Letter XI.

18 Jackson, *The Two Unions,* p.240.

19 Daron Acemoglu and James Robinson, 'What's the Problem with (Spanish) Catalunya?', Why Nations Fail Blog, March 2014. Available online at: http://whynationsfail.com/blog/2014/3/4/whats-the-problem-with-spanish-catalunya.html

20 Kidd, *Union and Unionism.*

21 Linda Colley, *Britons: Forging the Nation 1707–1837* (Yale University Press, 2009), pp.11–54.

22 ibid. p.19.
23 ibid. p.24.
24 Lord Sumption, 'The Disunited Kingdom: England, Ireland and Scotland', Lecture to the Denning Society, 5 November 2013.
25 Colley, *Britons*, p.25.
26 ibid. p.53.
27 Samuel Johnson, *A Journey to the Western Islands of Scotland,* (1775).
28 T. M. Devine, 'The Transformation of Scotland: 1980–2005', Lecture to the Glasgow Centre for Population Health, 6 December 2005.
29 T. C. Smout, *A History of the Scottish People: 1560–1830* (Collins, 1969).
30 Lord Sumption, 'The Disunited Kingdom'.
31 ibid.
32 Devine, *The Scottish Nation*, p.624.
33 T. M. Devine, *Scotland's Empire: The Origins of the Global Diaspora* (Penguin, 2012).
34 Colley, *Acts of Union and Disunion*, p.92.
35 T. M. Devine, *To the Ends of the Earth: Scotland's Global Diaspora, 1750–2010* (Penguin, 2012).
36 T. M. Devine, 'Three Hundred Years of the Anglo-Scottish Union' in T. M. Devine (ed.), *Scotland and the Union: 1707–2007* (Edinburgh, 2008).
37 Lord Sumption, 'The Disunited Kingdom'.
38 Devine, *The Scottish Nation*, p.185.
39 War Office, *Statistics of the Military Effort of the British Empire During the Great War 1914–1920* (HM Stationery Office, 1922).
40 ibid.
41 Colley, *Britons*, p.383.
42 Colley, *Acts of Union and Disunion*, p.149.
43 Ian Levitt and T. C. Smout, *The State of the Scottish Working Class in 1843* (Edinburgh, 1979); and Rosalind Mitchison, *The Old Poor Law in Scotland, 1574–1845* (Edinburgh, 2000).
44 Ian Levitt, 'The State, 1850–1950' in A. Cooke et al. (eds.), *Modern Scottish History* (Tuckwell Press, 1998), Vol. 2, pp.1–24.
45 ibid.
46 ibid.
47 Michael Lynch, *Scotland: A New History* (Pimlico, 2007).
48 Levitt, 'Scotland and its financial relationship with the UK in the 19th century'.
49 ibid.
50 ibid.
51 ibid.
52 ibid.
53 ibid.

54 Ian Levitt, 'The Scottish Secretary, the Treasury and the Scottish Grant Equivalent, 1888–1970', *Scottish Affairs*, Vol. 28 (1999), pp.93–116.

55 Ian Levitt, *The Scottish Office, 1919–59* (Edinburgh, 1995).

56 I. McLean, 'Financing the Union: Goschen, Barnett and Beyond' in W. L. Miller (ed.), *Anglo-Scottish Relations from 1900 to Devolution and Beyond* (Oxford, 2005).

57 Levitt, 'The Scottish Secretary, the Treasury and the Scottish Grant Equivalent, 1888-1970', pp.93–116.

58 Gavin McCrone, *Scottish Independence: Weighing up the Economics* (Birlinn, 2013).

59 Vernon Bogdanor, *The New British Constitution* (Hart Publishing, 2009), p.113.

CHAPTER 5

1 Scottish Social Attitudes Survey, 2013.

2 Christopher McLean and Douglas Thomson, 'Characterisation of the disadvantaged: explaining differences in levels of support for independence by income levels, economic activity and socio-economic status', *Scottish Affairs*, Vol. 23 (2014), pp.125–47.

3 Joan McAlpine, 'Slaughter of Great War cast a shadow over Scotland that took decades to lift . . . there's nothing to celebrate', *Daily Record*, 5 November 2013.

4 Brian Wilson, 'SNP convert to Olympic supporters', *The Scotsman*, 1 August 2012.

5 Mike Small, 'So, the Olympics has put out the flame of Scottish independence? Hardly', *Guardian*, 14 August 2012.

6 Speech by the author to a Smith Institute conference on Britishness held at the London School of Economics in April 1999.

7 Penny Young, 'A matter of pride', *Sunday Times*, 13 April 2014.

8 Ian Drury, 'British national pride falls to an all-time low as economic downturn and Iraq war fallout hit our morale', *Daily Mail*, 13 April 2014.

9 Alan Massie, 'Waving the flag for Britishness', *Telegraph*, 14 April 2014.

10 Tobias Smollett, *The Adventures of Roderick Random* (1748).

11 Smollett, *The Adventures of Roderick Random*; and Tobias Smollet, *The Expedition of Humphry Clinker* (1771).

12 J. A. Smith, 'Some Eighteenth Century Ideas of Scotland' in N. T. Phillipson and R. Mitchison (eds.), *Scotland in the Age of Improvement* (Edinburgh University Press, 1970), p.109.

13 T. C. Smout, *A History of the Scottish People: 1560–1830* (Collins, 1969).

14 ibid.

15 ibid.

16 R. J. Finlay, 'Scotland and the Monarchy in the Twentieth Century' in W. L. Miller (ed.), *Anglo-Scottish Relations from 1900 to Devolution and Beyond* (Oxford, 2005).

17 Linda Colley, *Britons: Forging the Nation 1707–1837* (Yale University Press, 2009).

18 Krishan Kumar, *The Making of English National Identity* (Cambridge University Press, 2003).

19 ibid.

20 Peter Kellner et al., *This Sceptred Isle* (British Future, 2012), p.12.

21 Scottish Social Attitudes Survey, 2013.

22 Speech by the author to a Smith Institute conference on Britishness held at the LSE in April 1999; Scottish Social Attitudes Survey, 2011.

23 HM Government, *Scotland Analysis: Defence* (October 2013).

24 Scottish Social Attitudes Survey, 2013.

25 Scottish Government, *Scotland's Future: Your Guide to an Independent Scotland* (November 2013), p.251.

26 Scottish Social Attitudes Survey, 2013.

27 ScotCen, *Is it really all just about economics? Issues of nationhood and welfare* (2014). Available online at: http://www.scotcen.org.uk/media/265694/ssa_is-it-really-all-just-about-economics.pdf

28 House of Commons Library (HOCL).

29 A. Gamble, 'Hegemony and Decline: Britain and the United States' in P. K. O'Brien and A. Clesse (eds.), *Two Hegemonies: Britain 1846–1914 and the United States 1941–2001* (Ashgate Publishing, 2002), pp.127–40.

30 Leo Lewis, 'China tells Cameron: Britain is not a big power – but we want more Downton', *The Times,* 4 December 2013.

31 W. K. Hancock and M. M. Gowing, *The British War Economy* (HM Stationery Office 1949), p.541.

32 David McCrone, *Understanding Scotland: The Sociology of a Stateless Nation* (Routledge, 1992).

33 Scottish Social Attitudes Survey, 2013.

34 Matthew d'Ancona, 'Nigel Farage's Big Moment', *New York Times*, 31 March 2014.

35 James Hampshire, *Citizenship and Belonging: Immigration and the Politics of Demographic Governance in Postwar Britain* (Palgrave Macmillan, 2005).

36 See, e.g., Charles Taylor, *The Ethics of Authenticity* (Harvard University Press, 1992); Charles Taylor, *Reconciling the Solitudes: Essays on Canadian Federalism and Nationalism* (McGill-Queen's University Press, 1993); and Charles Taylor, *Multiculturalism: Examining the Politics of Recognition* (Princeton University Press, 1994).

37 Rogers Smith, *Citizenship, Borders and Human Needs* (University of Pennsylvania Press, 2013).

38 Ministry of Justice, *People and power: shaping democracy, rights and responsibilities* (March 2010).

CHAPTER 6

1 S. Nenadic, 'Industrialisation and the Scottish People' in T. M. Devine and Jenny Wormald (eds.), *The Oxford Handbook of Modern Scottish History 1500–2000* (Oxford University Press, 2011), pp.405–22.

2 Ian Levitt, *Poverty and Welfare in Scotland, 1890–1948* (Edinburgh, 1988).

3 TNA CAB 117/118, Cabinet Committee on Unemployment.

4 ibid.

5 Ian Levitt, *The Scottish Office, 1919–59* (Edinburgh, 1995).

6 Jim Phillips, 'The moral economy of deindustrialization in post-1945 Scotland', paper at the Annual Conference of the Economic History Society at Warwick University, 2014.

7 Ian Levitt, 'Scottish papers submitted to the Cabinet, 1945–66: A guide to records held at the Public Record Office and the National Archives of Scotland', *Scottish Economic and Social History*, Vol. 20, Part I (2000); Ian Levitt, 'Scottish papers presented to the British Cabinet, 1917–66: their archival and historical significance', *Scottish Archives*, Vol. 6 (2000); Ian Levitt, 'Scottish papers submitted to the Cabinet, 1966–70: a guide to records held at the Public Record Office', *Scottish Economic and Social History*, Vol. 23, Part I (2001).

8 Jim Tomlinson, 'The Economic basis of Scottish Nationhood since 1870' (2014),

9 TNA CAB134/2396 PE(62)7th, 12 December 1962.

10 TNA CAB/128/38 CM(64) 20th, 24 March 1964.

11 Ian Levitt, 'The Creation of the Highlands and Islands Development Board, 1935–65', *Northern Scotland*, Vol. 19 (1999).

12 Ian Levitt, 'The Scottish Secretary, the Treasury and the Scottish Grant Equivalent, 1888–1970' in *Scottish Affairs*, Vol. 28 (1999), pp.93–116.

13 ibid.

14 Levitt, *The Scottish Office, 1919–59*.

15 Morrice McCrae, *The National Health Service in Scotland: origins and ideas, 1900–50* (Tuckwell Press, 2003).

16 Levitt, *The Scottish Office 1919–59*; and McCrae, *The National Health Service in Scotland*.

17 Levitt, *The Scottish Office 1919–59*; and McCrae, *The National Health Service in Scotland*.

18 Levitt, *The Scottish Office 1919–59*; and McCrae, *The National Health Service in Scotland*.

19 D. Hamilton, 'The Scottish Medical Schools' in G. McLachlan (ed.), *Improving the Common Weal: Aspects of the Scottish Health services, 1900–84* (Edinburgh, 1987).

20 Duncan Harley, 'The Turra Coo', *Scottish Review*, December 2013.

21 Levitt, *The Scottish Office, 1919–59*.

22 ibid.

23 Institute for Fiscal Studies, *Government spending on benefits and state pensions in Scotland: current patterns and future issues* (July 2013). Available online at: http://www.ifs.org.uk/bns/bn139.pdf

24 ibid.

25 ibid.

26 ibid.

27 ScotCen, *Is it really all just about economics? Issues of nationhood and welfare* (2014). Available online at: http://www.scotcen.org.uk/media/265694/ssa_is-it-really-all-just-about-economics.pdf

28 Yael Tamir, *Liberal Nationalism* (Princeton University Press, 1993).

CHAPTER 7

1 Ministry of Justice, *People and power: shaping democracy, rights and responsibilities* (March 2010).

2 *AXA General Insurance Ltd and others v Lord Advocate and others (Scotland)* (2011) UKSC 46.

3 House of Commons Scottish Affairs Committee, *The Crown Estate in Scotland* (Seventh Report of Session 2010–2012, March 2012).

4 Institute for Public Policy Research, *Funding Devo More: Fiscal Options for Strengthening the Union* (January 2013), p.3.

5 Institute for Public Policy Research, *Funding Devo More*, p.3.

6 The Report of the Home Rule and Community Rule Commission of the Scottish Liberal Democrats, *Federalism: the best future for Scotland* (October 2012), p.24.

7 Linda Colley, *Acts of Union and Disunion* (Profile, 2014).

8 N. MacCormick, in Devine and P. Logue (ed.), *Being Scottish: Personal Reflections on Scottish Identity Today* (Edinburgh University Press, 2002), p.150.

9 Colley, *Acts of Union and Disunion*, pp.92–3.

10 Colin Kidd, 'The Defence of the Union: Ironies and Ambiguities' in G. Hassan and J. Mitchell (eds.), *After Independence: An Informed Guide to*

Scotland's Possible Futures for Anyone Who is Pro or Anti Independence, Unsure or Just Generally Curious (Luath, 2013).

11 J. Mitchell, 'SNP Conference Reflections', *The Future of the UK and Scotland*, 11 April 2014. Available online at: http://www.futureukandscotland.ac.uk/blog/snp-conference-reflections

12 Constitution of the Scottish National Party, clause 2. Available online at: https://www.snp.org/sites/default/files/assets/documents/constitution-ofthescottishnationalparty.pdf

13 Kidd, 'The Defence of the Union: Ironies and Ambiguities'.

14 J. Mitchell, 'SNP Conference Reflections'.

15 The Report of the Home Rule and Community Rule Commission of the Scottish Liberal Democrats, *Federalism: the best future for Scotland*, p.17.

16 Nick Robinson, 'Sir John Major dresses in tartan for devolution argument', BBC News, 9 July 2011.

17 Colin Kidd, *Union and Unionism: Political Thought in Scotland, 1500–2000* (Cambridge University Press, 2008), p.69.

18 Royal Commission on the Constitution, HMSO 1973, Cmnd 5460, para 531.

CHAPTER 8

1 HM Government, *Scotland Analysis: Business and microeconomic framework* (2013), p.6.

2 BMA Scotland, 'Independence Referendum 2014: Implications for Health, a discussion paper' (2013), p.8.

3 Steven Swinford, 'Scottish independence risks medical funding, charities warn', *Telegraph*, 21 December 2013.

4 National Cancer Research Institute, 'Cancer Research spend in the UK 2002–2011' (2013), p.4.

5 The Francis Crick Institute, 'About Us'. Online at: http://www.crick.ac.uk/about-us/

6 'Scottish Business Enterprise R&D (BERD) expenditure was £707 million in 2012. This represented 0.59 per cent of Scottish GDP; the comparable figure was 1.09 per cent for the UK.' High Level Summary of Statistics Trend Last update: Wednesday, 18 December 2013 R&D Business Expenditure, online at: http://www.scotland.gov.uk/Topics/Statistics/Browse/Business/TrendRandDBusiness

7 J. Cuthbert and M. Cuthbert, 'It's the economy stupid . . . but who's making the best case?', *Sunday Herald*, 26 May 2013.

8 'More Scots starting up their own businesses', BBC News, 14 February

2014. Online at: http://www.bbc.co.uk/news/uk-scotland-scotland-business-26171214; and 'New figures reveal regional entrepreneurial hotspots', StartUp Britain, 26 January 2014. Online at: http://www.start-upbritain.co/news/2014-01-26/new-figures-reveal-regional-entrepreneurial-hotspots

9 Brian Ashcroft, 'Nicola! Don't Forget the Day Job!', Scottish Economy Watch, 26 September 2012. Online at: http://www.scottisheconomy-watch.com/brian-ashcrofts-scottish/scottish-economy/page/3/

10 House of Commons Library (HOCL).

11 Office for National Statistics, 'Monetary Valuation of UK Continental Shelf Oil & Gas Reserves' (2013), p.1; and Severin Carrell, 'Alex Salmond's £1.5tn oil wealth figure is targeted by Treasury', *Guardian*, 4 September 2013.

12 World Trade Organization (WTO), *Trade Profiles 2013* (2013), pp.192–3; Brad McDearman et al., 'Export Nation 2013: U.S. Growth Post-Recession' (Brookings, 2013), p.3; and World Bank, 'Exports of goods and services (% of GDP)', online at: http://data.worldbank.org/indicator/NE.EXP.GNFS.ZS

13 ibid.

14 HOCL.

15 WTO, *Trade Profiles 2013*, respective country profiles.

16 Gordon Brown, *Beyond the Crash: Overcoming the First Crisis of Globalisation* (Simon & Schuster, 2010), p.6; HOCL; and Asian Development Bank, *Asia 2050: Realizing the Asian Century* (2011), p.32.

17 Scottish Government, *A National Statistics Publication for Scotland: Scotland's Global Connections Survey 2012 – Estimating Exports from Scotland* (2014), online data; 'When giants slow down', *Economist*, 27 July 2013; Michelle Jamrisko and Ilan Kolet, 'BRICs Demand for U.S. Exports Set to Beat E.U', Bloomberg, 19 February 2013; and ONS, 'Economic Review, September 2013' (2013), p.14.

18 Brian Ashcroft, 'Independence Fact No.4', Scottish Economy Watch, 25 November 2013. Online at: http://www.scottisheconomywatch.com/brian-ashcrofts-scottish/2013/11/independence-fact-no-4.html

19 Shawn Donnan, 'Scots exports would be worth almost £100bn after independence', *Financial Times,* 29 January 2014; and Collette Smith, 'Scottish Independence: Is Scotland the 14th richest in the world?' BBC News, 18 March 2014. Online at: http://www.bbc.co.uk/news/uk-scotland-scotland-politics-26614122. NB *Financial Times* figures for trade including oil and gas do not include petroleum.

20 WTO, *Trade Profiles 2013*, respective country profiles.

21 Ashcroft, 'Losing Grangemouth', Scottish Economy Watch, 24 October 2013. Online at: http://www.scottisheconomywatch.com/brian-ashcrofts-scottish/2013/10/losing-grangemouth.html

22 Scottish Government, 'Energy in Scotland: Get the facts', http://www.scotland.gov.uk/Topics/Business-Industry/Energy/Fact; 'Big Six UK Energy firms see supply profit margins grow', BBC News, 25 November 2013. Online at: http://www.bbc.co.uk/news/business-25092169

23 John Kay, 'Is recent economic history a help?' in Sir Donald McKay (ed.) *Scotland's Economic Future* (Reform Scotland, 2011), p.19.

24 HM Government, *Scotland analysis: Financial services and banking* (2013), pp.17–18.

25 Scottish Financial Enterprise, 'Financial Services in Scotland: Facts', online at: http://www.sfe.org.uk/facts.aspx

26 HM Government, *Scotland analysis: Financial services and banking*, p.59.

27 Scottish Government, *Estimating Exports from Scotland*, p.10.

28 J. D. Gallagher, 'The Economic Case for Union' in *Fraser of Allander Institute Economic Commentary*, Vol. 37, No. 3 (March 2014).

29 Universities Scotland, *Grow, Export, Attract, Support: Universities' Contribution to Scotland's economic growth* (2013), pp.1,13.

30 HOCL.

31 Mark Williamson, 'Scottish business bucks UK trend to boost R&D spend', *The Herald*, 19 December 2013; and Brian Ashcroft, 'Scotland's R&D Problem Or Opportunity', Scottish Economy Watch, 12 May 2012. Online at: http://www.scottisheconomywatch.com/brian-ashcrofts-scottish/2012/05/scotlands-rd-problem-or-opportunity.html

32 Scottish Government, *Scotland's Future: Higher Education Research in an Independent 2014* (2014), p.23; and Chris Marshall, 'Universities link will be broken after Yes vote – MP', *The Scotsman*, 27 March 2014.

33 ibid.

34 HOCL.

35 Hugh Pennington, 'Scotland's research and development sector thrives as part of the UK. Why put it at risk?', Better Together, 4 November 2013. Online at: http://bettertogether.net/blog/entry/scotlands-research-and-science-industries-thrive-as-part-of-the-uk.-why-put

36 Tom Nairn, 'Globalization and Nationalism: The New Deal', 16th Edinburgh Lecture, 4 March 2008.

37 David Skilling, 'In Praise of Small States', Global Brief, 17 June 2013. Online at: http://globalbrief.ca/blog/2013/06/17/in-praise-of-the-small-states/

38 Brian Ashcroft, 'Scottish Independence: Assessing the Case For and Against', Scottish Economy Watch, 26 May 2013. Online at: http://www.scottisheconomywatch.com/brian-ashcrofts-scottish/independence/

39 HM Government, *Scotland Analysis: Macroeconomic and fiscal performance*, (2013), p.63.

40 Yuriy Gorodnichenko et al., 'The Finnish Great Depression: From Russia with Love' in *American Economic Review*, 102 (2012), pp.1619–44.

41 HM Government, *Scotland analysis: Financial services and banking*, p.18.

42 HM Treasury, *Budget 2014* (2014), p.108.

43 Office for Budget Responsibility, *Assessment of the Effect of Oil Price Fluctuation on the Public Finance* (2010), p.3.

44 'One thing in public, another in private', Better Together, 7 March 2014. Onlineat:http://bettertogether.net/blog/entry/one-thing-in-public-another-in-private

45 Michael Keating et al., 'The Role of Small States in the European Union: lessons for Scotland'(ESRC Scottish Centre on Constitutional Change, 2014), p.1.

46 Scotland Office, 'Scottish referendum information pack: overview', 20 January 2014. Online at: https://www.gov.uk/government/publications/scottish-independence-referendum-factsheets/scottish-referendum-information-pack

47 Brian Ashcroft, 'Losing Control', Scottish Economy Watch, 2 February 2012. Online at: http://www.scottisheconomywatch.com/brian-ashcrofts-scottish/2012/02/losing-control.html

48 HOCL; and 'Outlook and Appraisal' in *Fraser of Allander Economic Commentary*, Vol. 37, No. 2 (October 2013), p.6.

49 'North Sea oil: Facts and figures', BBC News, 24 February 2014, online at: http://www.bbc.co.uk/news/uk-scotland-scotland-politics-26326117

50 Sir Ian Wood, *UKCS Maximising Recovery Review: Final Report* (2014), p.32.

51 Michael Amior et al., *Fiscal Sustainability of an Independent Scotland* (IFS, 2013).

52 ibid.

53 ibid, pp.3, 14.

54 HOCL.

55 Scottish Childcare Costs Survey 2013. Online at: http://www.familyand-parenting.org/news/Press-releases/2013+Press+Releases/Scottish+Childcare+Costs+Survey

56 Scottish Government, *Scotland's Future*, pp.192–6.

57 Scottish Government, *Scotland's Future*, pp.192–6; 'Scottish independence: Scottish government childcare plan questioned', BBC News, 3 April 2014. Online at : http://www.bbc.co.uk/news/uk-scotland-scotland-politics-26877767; and Jim Hood, 'Divisions weaken and togetherness will strengthen us', *Daily Record*, 26 April 2014.

58 Tom Peterkin, 'Report reveals tax blow to SNP's Childcare policy', *The Scotsman*, 4 April 2014.

59 Amior et al., *Fiscal Sustainability*, p.14.

60 Amior et al., *Fiscal Sustainability*, pp.26–28; and HM Government, *Scotland analysis: Macroeconomic and fiscal performance*, p.33.

61 In 2010, California's 30 Year Build America Bonds had a yield set at 325 basis points above the comparable US Treasuries. See John Kay, 'American lessons in how to run a single currency', *Financial Times*, 20 July 2011.

62 Scottish Government, *Government Expenditure & Revenue Scotland 2012* (2014), pp.4, 5, 27.

63 Scottish Government, *Government Expenditure & Revenue Scotland 2012*, p.5.

64 HM Government, 'Summary of forecasts of the Scottish deficit in the proposed year of independence' (2013), p.2.

65 Scottish Government, 'Scotland's International GDP Per Capita Ranking' (March 2014), online at: http://www.scotland.gov.uk/Resource/0044/00446013.pdf

66 Brian Ashcroft, 'Sterling and Scottish Independence', Scottish Economy Watch, 26 April 2013. Online at: http://www.scottisheconomywatch.com/brian-ashcrofts-scottish/2013/04/sterling-and-scottish-independence.html

67 Brian Ashcroft, 'The Economist and Scotland's Seven Strengths', Scottish Economy Watch, 17 April 2013. Online at: http://www.scottisheconomywatch.com/brian-ashcrofts-scottish/2012/04/the-economist-and-scotlands-seven-strengths.html

68 HOCL.

69 'Employment continues to rise in Scotland as number of people in work jumps for 10th month in a row', *Daily Record*, 13 November 2013. Online at: http://www.dailyrecord.co.uk/news/scottish-news/employment-figures-number-people-work-2786753

70 HOCL.

71 John Curtice, 'The Score at Half Time: Trends in Support for Independence' (ScotCen Social Research, 2013), p.10.

CHAPTER 9

1 The Church of Scotland, 'Our Vision: Imagining Scotland's Future' (2014), p.9.

2 'Charities claim Scotland faces "humanitarian crisis" caused by poverty', BBC News, 4 March 2014. Online at: http://www.bbc.co.uk/news/uk-scotland-26424477

3 'Fuel Poverty in more than a quarter of Scottish homes in 2012', BBC News, 10 December 2013. Online at: http://www.bbc.co.uk/news/uk-scotland-25319365

4 Gerry Mooney, 'Poverty, "austerity" and Scotland's constitutional future',

in Child Poverty Action Group (CPAG), *Poverty in Scotland 2014: The independence referendum and beyond* (2014), p.4; Population figure from 2011 census.

5 Joseph Rowntree Foundation (JRF), 'Monitoring Poverty and Social Exclusion in Scotland 2013' (2013), p.5.

6 JRF, 'Monitoring Poverty and Social Exclusion', p.1.

7 CPAG et al., 'Poverty in Scotland: Summary Briefing', August 2013. Online at http://www.cpag.org.uk/sites/default/files/CPAG-scot-briefing-poverty-in-scotland-update-August-2013.pdf

8 Mooney, 'Poverty, "austerity" and Scotland's constitutional future', p.7.

9 Russell Leadbetter, 'UK austerity measures will push 100,000 more Scottish children into poverty by 2020, according to a new report', *Sunday Herald*, 9 March 2014.

10 Scottish Government, 'Statistical Publication: Poverty and income inequality in Scotland', 13 June 2013, p.24.

11 Ruth Lupton et al., 'Labour's Social Policy Record: Policy, Spending and Outcomes 199–2010', Centre for Analysis of Social Exclusion (June 2013), p.9.

12 Scottish Government, 'Statistical Publication', p.24.

13 ibid.

14 ibid.

15 Richard Dickens, 'Child Poverty in Britain: Did Work Work?' in Paul Gregg and Jonathan Wadsworth (eds.), *The Labour Market in Winter: The State of Britain* (Oxford, 2011), p.241.

16 Vidhya Alakeson, 'Employment and child poverty' in Lindsay Judge (ed.) *Ending Child Poverty by 2020: Progress Made and Lessons Learned* (CPAG, 2012), p.33.

17 Jim McCormick, 'A Review of Devolved Approaches to Child Poverty' (JRF, October 2013), p.19.

18 Thomas Piketty, *Capital in the Twenty-First Century* (Havard University Press, 2014).

19 OECD Statistics database, and Department of Work and Pensions, Households Below Average Income (HBAI).

20 ibid.

21 David Comerford and David Eiser, 'Constitutional change and inequality in Scotland', *The Future of Scotland and the UK*, January 2014, p.6.

22 David Bell and David Eiser, 'Inequality in Scotland: trends, drivers, and implications for the independence debate', *The Future of Scotland and the UK*, November 2013, p.3.

23 ibid. pp.2, 4, 17, 23.

24 Comerford and Eiser, 'Constitutional change and inequality in Scotland', p.24.

25 ibid.
26 'Tackling income inequality presents challenges for Scotland', University of Stirling website, 20 January 2014. Online at: http://www. stir.ac.uk/news/news-archive/2014/01/tacklingincomeinequalitypresentschallengesforscotland/name-64806-en.html
27 Department of Work and Pensions figures.
28 ibid.
29 ibid.
30 OECD Statistics database, and DWP's Households Below Average Income (HBAI).
31 ibid.
32 House of Commons Library (HOCL).
33 ibid.
34 Office for National Statistics (ONS), *Statistical Bulletin: The Effects of Taxes and Benefits on Household Income, 2011/12* (July 2013), p.1.
35 ONS, 'Scotland – Household Taxes and Benefits: update', October 2012. Online at: http://www.ons.gov.uk/ons/media-centre/statements/ household-taxes-and-benefits--update/index.html
36 HOCL.
37 Bea Cantillion, 'Belgian social federalism: Quo Vadis?' (The David Hume Institute, 2013), p.1.
38 National Records of Scotland, 'Projected Population of Scotland (2010-based)', (National Statistics, 2011), p.5.
39 IFS, 'Fiscal sustainability of an independent Scotland', p.20.
40 IFS, pp.2, 16.
41 Scottish Government, 'Pensions in an Independent Scotland', p.ii.
42 Letter to the author from Lord Davidson QC.
43 HOCL.
44 National Association of Pension Funds, 'Scottish independence: the implications for pensions', November 2013, pp.10–12.
45 'Scottish Pensions Index – Putting Scotland plc pensions in context' Hymans Robertson Report (November 2013), p.1; and 'UK pension deficit falls in Dec, raising hopes for investment', *Financial Times*, 14 January 2014.
46 Steve Hawkes, 'Scottish independence will hit "savings and pensions of millions" across the British Isles', *Telegraph*, 28 November 2013.
47 W. Elliot, 'The Scottish heritage in politics', in Atholl et al., *A Scotsman's Heritage* (Maclehose, 1932).
48 Paris Gourtsoyannis, 'Break it down', *Holyrood*, 18 June 2013. Online at: http://www.holyrood.com/2013/06/breaking-it-down/
49 ibid.
50 ibid.

51 ibid.

52 L. Paterson, 'Does Scottish education need traditions?', *Discourse: Studies in the Cultural Politics of Education*, 30 (2009), pp.253–68.

53 Sheila Riddell et al., 'Widening Access to Higher Education: Scotland in UK Comparative Context', October 2013, p.3. Online at: http://www.esrc.ac.uk/_images/Briefing_TT2_widening%20access_tcm8-28589.pdf [marker should be at the end of 1st para, p.319]

54 Lucy Hunter Blackburn, 'Who pays for free higher education? The case of Scotland', *Economics of Higher Education*, 9 December 2013. Online at: http://economicsofhe.org/2013/12/09/who-pays-for-free-higher-education-the-case-of-scotland/

55 HOCL.